FOOD&WINE
MAGAZINE'S

O F F I C I A L

WINE
GUIDE
1 9 9 9

ON-LINE

Send us your comments and wine ratings;
log on to FOOD & WINE On-line:
www.foodwinemag.com

We are interested in what you have to say. Join
FOOD & WINE magazine on-line throughout the year
for wine information, tips, and surveys. We would like
to know your ratings of the wines in this guide and of
your other favorite wines.

SPECIAL SALES

Bulk purchases of FOOD & WINE Magazine's Official
Wine Guide are available to corporations, organiza-
tions, wineries, and retailers at special discounts.
For more information, write to Retail Sales, Consumer
Marketing, FOOD & WINE, 1120 Avenue of the Ameri-
cas, New York, NY 10036.

————

FOOD & WINE BOOKS

Editor in Chief: Judith Hill

Art Director: Nina Scerbo

Project Director: Barbara A. Mateer

Senior Designer: Rachael McBrearty

Designer: Leslie Andersen

Copy and Production Editor: Amy Schuler

Editorial Assistant: Evette Manners

————

Cover photograph: Brian Fraunfelter/Marge Casey Associates
Wine glasses courtesy of 67 Wine & Spirits Inc.

Copyright © 1998
American Express Publishing Corporation
1120 Avenue of the Americas
New York, NY 10036

ISBN: 0-916103-46-3   ISSN: Pending

FOOD&WINE

MAGAZINE'S

OFFICIAL
WINE
GUIDE
1999

BY STEPHEN TANZER

FOOD
&
WINE
BOOKS

A Division of American Express Publishing

Contents

4

▣ CONTENTS ▣

How to
Use this Guide

Food & Wine Magazine's Official Wine Guide 1999 is as
timely a guide as you can find: Unlike most wine books,
it lists the bottles that are being released for *this year*.
Besides rating wines that will be on the shelves in 1999,
the recommendations emphasize inexpensive and moderately priced wines that offer exceptional value.

Overall Organization

This guide is organized geographically because that is how
wines are usually arranged in wine shops and on restaurant
wine lists. As a rule, information on European countries is
presented by region (for example Bordeaux) and for other
countries by grape variety (such as Pinot Noir) since this is
how their respective wines are typically labeled.

For a handful of wine-growing areas—Alsace and
Burgundy, Barolo and Barbaresco, and all of Germany—
producers are listed rather than particular bottles. Wineries
in these places tend to release many different wines each
year, most of them in limited quantities. Your chance of
coming across a good wine from one of these fine producers
is much higher than that of finding a specific bottle.

Special Features

AT THE TABLE Throughout the guide, after the introduction to
each category of wine, you'll find advice on pairing the wines
with food. For an index to these discussions arranged by the ingredients and dishes covered, see pages 207 through 211.

THE BOTTOM LINE In each section directly after At the Table,
you'll see The Bottom Line, which will tell you how much the
wines of that group should cost and whether or not they are a
good value in general (all the listed wines are excellent value).

"WHAT TO BUY" VINTAGE RATINGS Vintage ratings appear just above the lists of recommended wines for that category. The ratings grade the current and recent vintages you're most likely to see in wine stores right now–from A+ to F.

"READY, SET, DRINK" VINTAGE GRAPHS Whenever the best bottles of a particular type of wine (for instance California Cabernet) benefit from aging, a graph will show you whether your cellared wines need more time, are ready to drink, or are past their peak.

SHORTCUT TO YOUR FAVORITE VARIETALS If you know you especially like Chardonnay or Merlot or any of a dozen other popular varietals, turn to page 203 for a listing of every wine-growing area discussed in this book that makes your favorite, along with the pages to consult for recommendations of specific bottles.

WINE-STYLE FINDER Often you may know the style of wine you want–say, a full-bodied, dry white or a light, fresh red. Look to pages 204 through 206 for a complete rundown on all the wines in the guide that fall within the category you seek and the pages on which they're listed.

Key to Symbols

The top line of the description for each recommended wine includes symbols that represent a quality rating, the price range, and an indication of availability.

QUALITY		
	★★★★	Outstanding: worth a search
	★★★	Excellent: true to its variety and region
	★★	Very good: noteworthy intensity of flavor
	★	Good: soundly made, everyday wine

PRICE		
	$$$$	More than $40
	$$$	$26 to $40
	$$	$13 to $25
	$	$12 or less

AVAILABILITY		
	♉♉♉	Widely available
	♉♉	Moderately available
	♉	May require a search

Wines in each section are presented in descending order of quality, and within each quality level, in descending order of price. When wines are the same in quality and price, they are arranged in descending order of availability; when they are the same by all measures, they're arranged alphabetically.

FRANCE

FRANCE IS INDISPUTABLY THE WORLD'S WINE LEADER. Not only does it offer a wider range of outstanding bottles than any other country, it produces more wine than any nation except Italy.

Grapes & Styles

Whereas New World wines are normally labeled by grape variety, the French usually name their wines after places and often blend two or more varieties of grapes. The wines tend to express the soil, climate, and sun exposure that produced the grapes (what the French call *terroir*) rather than simply varietal character. That said, France also sets the standard for virtually every varietal style popular in today's international market, including Chardonnay and Pinot Noir (at their finest from Burgundy), Cabernet and Merlot (Bordeaux), Sauvignon Blanc (the Loire Valley), and Syrah (the northern Rhône Valley). Among more general types, clearly Champagne is the benchmark for sparkling wines and Sauternes for dessert wines.

The best French wines tend to be more complex than New World wines, suaver in texture, less aggressively fruity, less abrasively tannic, and less obviously alcoholic. In short, they're more harmonious.

On the Label

•Most of France's finest wines, and nearly all that are exported to America, are entitled to the designation **Appellation d'Origine Contrôlée** (AOC), or controlled name of origin. For each appellation,

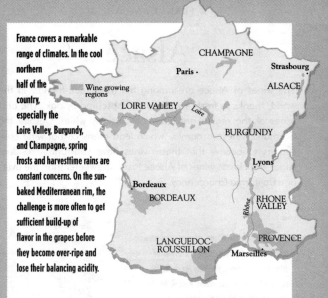

France covers a remarkable range of climates. In the cool northern half of the country, especially the Loire Valley, Burgundy, and Champagne, spring frosts and harvesttime rains are constant concerns. On the sun-baked Mediterranean rim, the challenge is more often to get sufficient build-up of flavor in the grapes before they become over-ripe and lose their balancing acidity.

strict regulations control numerous variables, including when each year's harvest may begin, the grape varieties used and their minimum ripeness, the alcoholic strength of the wine, and vinification techniques. This system of signifying and control-ling wine quality protects producers from imitators and guarantees authenticity to consumers.

The best appellations are excellent spots within broader areas. An AOC can be the name of a major region, a district or subdistrict within the region, a village, or a single vineyard. In general, the more specific the designation, the better the wine.

• After AOC, the next rank of French wines, of which there are relatively few, is **Vins Délimités de Qualité Supérieure** (VDQS), defined wines of superior quality.

• Next come **vins de pays,** or country wines, a des-ignation that is always followed by a place name.

• Finally, there are simple **vins de table,** everyday drinking wines that carry no geographic indication other than *France* or *français.*

Alsace

The wines of Alsace are among the most food-friendly in the world, thanks to fresh fruit flavors unobscured by oak. The best wines of the region are almost exclusively white. Despite the Germanic vineyard names, which lead many casual wine consumers to believe that these wines have substantial residual sugar, the classic wines of Alsace taste no sweeter than the average California Chardonnay.

Although Alsace has a long, relatively cool growing season and northerly location, it is one of the driest areas of France, thanks to the sheltering effect of the Vosges mountains. Most of the vineyards are strung out along the lower hills of that chain.

On the Label

Unlike most French wines, those from Alsace are labeled by grape variety. Labels often include other terms, including proprietary names and the villages or even specific vineyards from which the grapes came.

The heady, powerful wines designated Vendange Tardive (vawn-dawnj tahr-deev) come from late-picked, very ripe grapes; these higher-alcohol wines range from completely dry to moderately sweet. The very expensive and rare Sélection de Grains Nobles (SGN), supersweet if not downright nectarlike, comes from even riper grapes, usually heavily affected by the noble rot *Botrytis cinerea* (see the box on page 135).

VARIETALS

GEWURZTRAMINER

The highly perfumed aromas of rose petal, smoked meat, litchi, spice, and grapefruit in Gewürztraminer (geh-VAIRTZ-tra-MEE-ner) are immediate and captivating. Some examples can seem a bit coarse owing to low acidity and high alcohol. Most bottlings are dry to slightly sweet.

At the Table

These exotic, spicy wines can easily overwhelm food that is not equally flamboyant. Gewürztraminer is therefore good with spicy cuisines such as East Indian, Thai, Malaysian, and Moroccan. Try it with curried shrimp, *pad thai*, or sweet-and-sour spareribs. Ripe, pungent cheeses such as Alsace Munster also taste fabulous with Gewürz. As it's often low in acidity, it works where a brisker wine would seem too tart, for instance with preparations that incorporate vinegar. In Alsace, Gewürztraminer is routinely paired with rich pâtés and foie gras.

The Bottom Line

Expect to pay at least $15 to $20 for better wines, and single-vineyard and *grand cru* bottlings can be considerably pricier.

What to Buy: Gewürztraminer

1994	1995	1996	1997
A-	B	B	A-

PINOT BLANC

This supple, generously flavored white wine, with peach, apple, and butter notes, is often called the poor man's Chardonnay.

At the Table

Crisper, more minerally versions of Pinot Blanc are good with fish mousses and terrines or crudités; they also go well with finfish and mildly seasoned poultry. The richer versions can stand in for Chardonnay, thanks to their substantial body, lower acidity, and tropical fruit. These pair well with poultry and pork and are aromatic enough to work with spicy crab or Southwestern dishes that incorporate exotic fruits, chiles, or cilantro.

11

The Bottom Line

Bottles costing less than $15 from well-placed, low-yielding vines may well be Alsace's most striking values.

What to Buy: Pinot Blanc

1994	1995	1996	1997
B-	B	B+	B+

PINOT GRIS

One of Alsace's trinity of top grapes, along with Gewürztraminer and Riesling, Pinot Gris is characterized by fruit tones of peach, apricot, and orange and deeper notes of smoke, butter, spice, and honey. Pinot Gris is traditionally dry to just off-dry, with an alcohol content of 13 percent or more giving it substantial body and impact on the palate. Most of these wines are still labeled Tokay–Pinot Gris after the old name Tokay d'Alsace, despite a ban on this designation by the European Union to prevent confusion with the very different Hungarian Tokay.

At the Table

The full-bodied nature of these wines, combined with their smoky complexity, begs for foods like grilled pork tenderloin or fish (particularly richer fish such as tuna, salmon, and bluefish). Exotic cuisines can bring out the spicy character of Pinot Gris, especially slightly sweet Thai coconut curries and Indian dishes served with fruit chutneys. In Alsace, Pinot Gris is served with a wide range of dishes not usually thought of with whites, including sausages and all red meats, even venison, not to mention the regional specialties onion tart and foie gras.

The Bottom Line

Prices for Pinot Gris begin at about $15 to $20; the best bottles represent good value.

What to Buy: Pinot Gris

1994	1995	1996	1997
C+	B	B+	B+

RIESLING

The finest expression of Alsace winemaking and its most ageworthy variety is Riesling. Classic Alsace Riesling is dry and crisp, with aromas and flavors of citrus fruits, apple, pear, flowers, and minerals.

At the Table

Riesling, particularly from Alsace, is one of the most versatile of wines. Crisp, minerally versions go with delicate freshwater fish and with shellfish (try them with poached oysters). Larger-scaled or slightly sweet renditions are perfect with fleshier fish, such as salmon and striped bass, as well as with chicken in butter-based sauces. Riesling has the acidity to take on butter and cream sauces, especially if the dish incorporates a citrus element. Try seared scallops in a lightly curried beurre blanc; the sweet but delicate scallops and exotic spices will marry perfectly with a spicy, off-dry Riesling. Riesling is traditionally served with onion tart and with choucroute garni in Alsace.

The Bottom Line

Expect to pay $12 to $15 for decent Riesling, but $25 to $30, and sometimes much more, for the best bottlings from *grand cru* vineyards. Wines costing between $15 and $20 offer good value.

What to Buy: Riesling

1993	1994	1995	1996	1997
B+	B	B+	A	A-

Ready, Set, Drink: Alsace Riesling

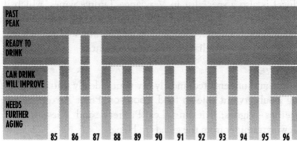

13

OTHER ALSACE WINES

Other Alsace varietals frequently seen on retail shelves include Sylvaners and Muscats. The former are often thin and neutral but, at their best, are spicy and penetrating. The finest Muscats offer a distinctly floral perfume.

PRODUCERS and THEIR WINES

JEAN-MICHEL DEISS ★★★★ **$$-$$$$** ♟♟

Rather intellectual wines that emphasize the *terroir* character of Deiss's many sites rather than the particular grape variety. Serious, very concentrated wines that reward aging. **LOOK FOR:** Pinot Blanc Bergheim; Muscat Bergheim; all Rieslings (especially the *grands crus* Altenberg and Schoenenbourg); Tokay–Pinot Gris Bergheim; and the Gewürztraminers St-Hippolyte, Bergheim, and Altenberg.

WEINBACH ★★★★ **$$-$$$$** ♟♟

Powerful, stylish wines, often from late-picked grapes. Drier and less exotic than wines made here as recently as the early 1990s. Expensive. **LOOK FOR:** Muscat; Pinot Réserve; Riesling Cuvée Théo, Ste-Cathérine, and Schlossberg Ste-Cathérine; and Gewürztraminer Cuvée Théo and Cuvée Laurence.

ZIND-HUMBRECHT ★★★★ **$$-$$$$** ♟♟

One of the world's great white-wine producers, with correspondingly high prices. Remarkably opulent, concentrated wines from low-yielding, late-picked vines, often with significant residual sugar. Vendange Tardive and Sélection de Grains Nobles wines are legendary. **LOOK FOR:** Anything you can find and afford, from basic bottlings to the supernal late-harvest wines from *grand cru* vineyards.

HUGEL ET FILS ★★★ **$$-$$$$** ♟♟♟

Firm but supple wines with relatively low residual sugar and considerable aging potential, from Alsace's most famous producer. Hugel is also a specialist in Vendange Tardive wines, which it occasionally bottles in significant quantities. **LOOK FOR:** Tradition and Jubilee bottlings, especially from Riesling and Pinot Gris; also a consistently reliable, inexpensive Gentil.

JOSMEYER ★★★ **$$-$$$** ♟♟

Subtle and understated, mostly dry wines ideally suited to playing a subservient role to food. **LOOK FOR:** Pinot Auxerrois "H" Vieilles Vignes; Riesling Les Pierrets; and Riesling and Gewürztraminer from the *grand cru* Hengst.

KUENTZ-BAS ★★★ $$-$$$ ♥♥

Refined, slow-to-open wines with dense textures but modest levels of residual sugar. A very good source of late-harvest wines. **LOOK FOR:** the very reasonably priced Réserve Personnelle series (including the Muscat); the *grand cru* Gewürztraminers Pfersigberg and Eichberg.

TRIMBACH ★★★ $$-$$$ ♥♥

Focused, powerful, ageworthy wines with crisp citric and mineral character and very low levels of residual sugar. **LOOK FOR:** The Réserve series of bottlings (the basic bottlings offer reasonable value but lack excitement); this producer's Riesling Frédéric Emile, Riesling Clos Ste-Hune, and Gewürztraminer Seigneurs de Ribeaupierre are three of Alsace's most famous wines.

The Concept of Terroir

A notion bordering on the mystical, *terroir* (tair-wah'r) incorporates everything unique about a particular vineyard site: its soil and subsoil, drainage, slope and elevation, and microclimate (including temperature, rainfall, and exposure to the sun). The French have long believed that the site, not the varieties planted, is of greatest significance in determining the wine. *Terroir* is important where wines are made from a single variety that is grown in highly specific vineyard sites and also in regions where vintages vary widely. The concept of *terroir* is crucial in Burgundy to a variety like Pinot Noir, because the grape is hypersensitive to its environment, reflecting the slightest nuances of soil and climate in its tastes and textures. Examples of other *terroir*-influenced wines include Riesling in Germany and Alsace and Barolo and Barbaresco in Italy.

LEON BEYER ★★★ $-$$$ ♥♥

Uncompromising, ageworthy wines, typically with high alcohol (often approaching 14 percent) and very little residual sugar—meant to be consumed with food. Best known for full-bodied but dry Gewürztraminers. **LOOK FOR:** Pinot Blanc de Blanc, Riesling Cuvée des Ecaillers, Riesling Comte d'Eguisheim, Gewürztraminer, and Gewürztraminer Comte d'Eguisheim.

LUCIEN ALBRECHT   ★★ $-$$$ ♥♥♥
Round, supple wines that offer satisfying early drinkability
thanks to rather low acidity. Relatively inexpensive for Alsace
wine. **LOOK FOR:** Pinot Blanc and Tokay–Pinot Gris (reliable and
cheap); also Riesling and Tokay–Pinot Gris Pfingstberg, especially when bottled as Vendange Tardive.

PIERRE SPARR   ★★ $-$$$ ♥♥
Full-bodied, soft, rather glycerol wines, packed with fruit and
perfect for early drinking. Ideal introductory-level Alsace wine
at low prices. **LOOK FOR:** Pinot Gris and Gewürztraminer Réserve;
Riesling and Gewürztraminer Mambourg.

ADDITIONAL TOP-NOTCH POSSIBILITIES
Bott-Geyl, Albert Boxler, Ernest Burn, Jean-Pierre Dirler, André
Kientzler, Marc Kreydenweiss, Albert Mann, Mittnacht-Klack,
André Ostertag, Rolly-Gassmann, Charles Schleret, Bernard Schoffit

Bordeaux

The top châteaux of Bordeaux—the classified growths named
back in 1855—are considered by many to produce the world's
greatest red wines. The region remains the model around the
globe for wines based on Cabernet Sauvignon and on Merlot.
Bordeaux also makes excellent dry whites, and Sauternes are
among the most prized of sweet wines.

The general appellation of Bordeaux contains
a number of smaller appellations. In the case of
Médoc, there are further appellations within its
borders, such as St-Estèphe, Pauillac, St-Julien,
and Margaux. The best white Bordeaux
comes from Graves in the south.

RED WINES

Over three quarters of Bordeaux's wine is red (traditionally called
claret by the English). The "big seven" appellations (St-Estèphe,
Pauillac, St-Julien, and Margaux in the Médoc [meh-doc]

region; Graves to the south of the city of Bordeaux; and Pomerol and St-Emilion on the right bank of the Dordogne) are familiar to wine lovers. Lesser-known districts such as Côtes de Bourg also produce very good wines. All the best bottles of Bordeaux carry the name of the specific château (for example Lafite-Rothschild) on the label.

• In general, Médoc producers base their wines on Cabernet Sauvignon, with some Merlot and Cabernet Franc (and, in some instances, a touch of Petit Verdot and Malbec) in the blend. These tannic reds, frequently austere when young, are among the world's longest-lived wines. They display aromas and flavors of black currant, black cherry, licorice, and herbs, plus the cedar, cigar box, vanilla, and spice notes that are the result of aging in small oak barrels.

• Reds from the Graves appellation can often show aromas of smoke and tobacco. They become enjoyable to drink earlier than the Médocs.

• Wines from St-Emilion and Pomerol are usually blends based on the Merlot grape, which is characteristically softer than Cabernet Sauvignon. The best of these wines are capable of improving in the bottle for decades.

At the Table

Bordeaux with lamb is the local favorite; the touch of sweetness of the wine complements the savory sweetness of the meat, and the wine's acids and tannins cut through the fat. Although the trend is toward wines with softer tannins and riper acidity, young clarets need fatty or full-flavored foods to smooth out their rough edges: Beef and lamb, game (such as venison), and game birds are all ideal partners. Fruit-based sauces will bring out the cherry and dark-berry notes, while buttery sauces will sweeten and soften the dry tannins of young wines. Bordeaux also pairs well with hard, sharp cheeses such as cheddar or aged dry Jack. But note that maturing, aromatically complex, and less tannic clarets are shown to best advantage alongside lightly seasoned, simply prepared meat dishes that will not overwhelm the more delicate of their flavors.

The Bottom Line

Prices for wines from Bordeaux's top châteaux in famed appellations have soared in recent years, and wines once widely available at retail are now hard to find. The price explosion is due to several factors, including the high quality of the 1995 and 1996 vintages, which followed a string of less exciting years, and the burgeoning demand from countries new to the fine-wine market. Today, prices for Bordeaux's big names have as little to do with underlying quality as those for any other limited commodity targeted by speculators. Look for wines of lesser pedigree: *crus bourgeois*, *petits châteaux*, and wines from outlying appellations. Wines simply labeled Médoc or Bordeaux Supérieur can be especially good values, particularly in the ripest vintages, like those of 1995 and 1996. Bottles from less known districts like Côtes de Bourg tend to be lower in price.

What to Buy: Médoc

1988	1989	1990	1991	1992
B-	A-	A+	D+	C

1993	1994	1995	1996	1997
B-	B	B+	A-	B

What to Buy: Graves

1988	1989	1990	1991	1992
A-	A	A-	C	C

1993	1994	1995	1996	1997
B	B+	B	B	B-

What to Buy: Pomerol & St-Emilion

1988	1989	1990	1991	1992
B-	A-	A+	D+	C

1993	1994	1995	1996	1997
B-	B	B+	A-	B

CLASSIFIED GROWTHS and THEIR EQUIVALENTS

Château Lafon-Rochet 1995, St-Estèphe   ★★★ $$$$ ♈♈♈
Smoke and currants on the nose. Medium-bodied and velvety,

with lovely sweetness and good grip. Flavors of black raspberry, minerals, and graphite. The tannins are substantial but even.

Château Pichon-Longueville-Baron 1995, ★★★ $$$$ ♥♥
Pauillac Black-cherry, beefsteak tomato, and licorice scents, plus nutty, cedary oak. Sweet entry, then very good flavor intensity, with cassis and grilled-nut flavors. Substantial tannins are in balance with the wine's fruit.

Château Latour Haut-Brion 1995, Graves ★★★ $$$$ ♥♥
Shy nose hints at cherry, red currant, tobacco, leather, and smoke. Stylish and ripe but in a drier style, with penetrating essence-of-claret flavor. Long on the aftertaste. A shapely wine with moderate acidity.

Château Pape-Clément 1995, Graves ★★★ $$$$ ♥♥
Inviting nose combines raspberry, hot stones, tobacco, and smoky oak. Rich, sweet, and mouth-filling. Complicating notes of smoke, leather, and tar. Builds slowly on the sweet finish, which features fine, dusty tannins.

Château Haut-Bailly 1996, Graves ★★★ $$$ ♥♥
Expressive aromas of plum, raspberry, minerals, and spices. Sweet, rich, and, atypically powerful for this wine, with a velvety texture, lovely ripe acidity, and terrific ripeness. Finishes firm and long, with thoroughly buffered tannins.

Château La Lagune 1995, Haut-Médoc ★★★ $$$ ♥♥
Red currant, tobacco, smoked nuts, and oak spice on the nose. Gives an initial impression of brisk acidity, but grows suppler and sweeter in the glass. Finishes with substantial tannins and notes of black cherry and herbs.

Château Smith-Haut-Lafitte 1995, Graves ★★★ $$$ ♥♥
Warm, enticing aromas of plums, hot bricks, leather, and spice. Lush and expansive in the mouth, with smoke and plum flavors. Subtle flavor really expands on the finish. Tannins are quite suave. A lovely drink.

Château Gruaud-Larose 1995, St-Julien ★★ $$$ ♥♥♥
Expressive aromas of red currant, roasted coffee, and smoked meat. Silky and lush in the mouth, with black-cherry, currant, and licorice flavors. Good underlying structure. Slightly dry tannins call for patience.

Château d'Armailhac 1995, Pauillac ★★ $$$ ♥♥

Sappy red-currant and spice nose. Bright, fruity, and juicy in the mouth; firmly built and fairly intensely flavored, but shows slightly drying tannins.

Château Branaire 1995, St-Julien ★★ $$$ ♥♥

Lively blue-fruit and brown-spice aromas and a jammy note. Intense dark-berry and licorice flavors, currently tightly wrapped. Finishes with substantial dusty tannins. Needs some bottle aging.

Château La Grave à Pomerol 1995, Pomerol ★★ $$$ ♥♥

Raspberry, brown spices, and smoky oak on the nose. Silky-sweet, rich, and smoky; low acidity gives the wine a texture of liquid velvet. Not especially complex, but satisfying for early drinking.

Ready, Set, Drink: St-Estèphe, Pauillac, St-Julien & Margaux

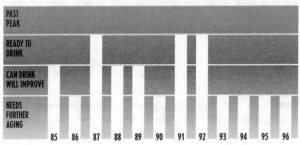

Ready, Set, Drink: Pomerol & St-Emilion

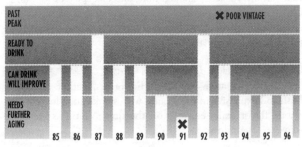

RED BORDEAUX of LESSER PEDIGREE

Clos du Marquis 1995, St-Julien ★★★ $$$$ ♥♥

Expressive aromas of blueberry, raspberry, game, and roasted nuts. Sweet and velvety but very young. Lively acidity gives it a penetrating quality. Stylish and impeccably balanced. The second wine of Château Léoville-Las Cases.

Château de Chantegrive 1995, Graves ★★ $$ ♥♥♥
Quintessential Graves aromas of smoked meat, tobacco, and leather. Complex bitter-cherry, red-currant, mineral, and iron flavors in the mouth, along with slightly vegetal, earthy nuances. Supple and sweet aftertaste.

Château Loudenne 1995, Médoc ★★ $$ ♥♥♥
Sweet, ripe nose dominated by dark berries. Very round, velvety, and sweet; flavor of baked cherry. All fruit, little oak. Attractive and pliant, finishing with good persistence and gentle tannins.

Château Potensac 1996, Médoc ★★ $$ ♥♥♥
Cassis, blueberry, smoke, shoe polish, and tobacco leaf on the nose, plus a faint jammy quality. Good sweetness and density; tastes like a Pauillac. Finishes with dusty, even tannins. Youthful and strong for this wine.

Château Poujeaux 1996, Moulis ★★ $$ ♥♥♥
Attractive, slightly candied aromas of boysenberry, cassis, and violet. Ripe, sweet, and dense, but with good clarity of flavor. Solidly structured for aging. Finishes fresh, with very good length and ripe tannins.

Château Charmail 1996, Haut-Médoc ★★ $$ ♥♥
Highly aromatic nose of black cherry, raspberry, caramel, tobacco, and sweet butter. Rich in the mouth, though still a bit withdrawn; flavors of currant and tobacco. Substantial and serious.

Château de Cruzeau 1996, Pessac-Léognan ★★ $$ ♥♥
Deep purple. Brooding aromas of tobacco, iron, and cherry. Rich and plump in the mouth, with fruit-driven flavors of blackberry jam, mint, sage, and licorice. Juicy acidity and melting tannins.

Château Fourcas Loubaney 1995, Listrac ★★ $$ ♥♥
Deep ruby with purple highlights. Rich, sweet, black-cherry aroma. Round and supple in the mouth, with fresh, pure blackberry and cassis flavors. Not particularly large-scaled but rather elegantly styled, with smooth tannins.

Château Franc-Maillet 1995, Pomerol ★★ $$ ♥♥
Deep ruby in color. Aromas of cherry, spice, and mint. Tangy, generous flavors of cassis and blackberry framed by ripe acidity.

The wine finishes with soft tannins and repeating notes of cassis and blackberry.

Château Reignac 1996 Cuvée Spéciale, ★★ $$ ♟♟
Bordeaux Supérieur Sweetly oaky, floral nose. Fat, supple, and sweet, with enough plummy fruit to support the flamboyant oak tones. Finishes with substantial but ripe tannins. Should give early pleasure.

Château Bonnet 1996, Bordeaux ★★ $ ♟♟♟
Sappy sweet cherry aroma shows a tarry nuance. Supple and fairly dense, with black-cherry and blueberry flavors. Rich and nicely focused, with firm acidity. Finishes with good ripeness and supple tannins.

Château Les Moiselles 1996, Côtes de Bourg ★★ $ ♟♟♟
Aromas of bitter cherry and berry skin. Fresh and crisp, thanks to juicy but ripe acidity. Nice balance of berry fruit and soft tannins. Finishes with good length and a tarry nuance.

Château de Parenchère 1996, ★★ $ ♟♟♟
Bordeaux Supérieur Fruity aromas of black raspberry and cassis. Rich and creamy, with blackberry and cassis flavors enlivened by juicy acidity. Slight Cabernet greenness adds to the wine's interest. Finishes with good length and supple tannins.

Château Pitray 1996, Côtes de Castillon ★★ $ ♟♟
Ripe, roasted Cabernet-dominated nose. Sweet and juicy, with sound acidity framing the cherry/berry fruit. Hint of licorice. Medium-bodied and rather stylish. Finishes with light, harmonious tannins.

DRY WHITE WINES

A number of châteaux in the Graves region and elsewhere in Bordeaux produce dry white wine from the same grape varieties used to make the sweet Sauternes. Sémillon provides a subtly honeyed richness, while Sauvignon Blanc contributes acidity and freshness. Many wines previously made mostly from Sauvignon Blanc in stainless steel now contain more Sémillon. They are also vinified and aged in oak and spend many months being enriched by contact with their spent yeasts. White Bordeaux has vastly improved in the past 15 years.

At the Table

Lean, citric white Graves make excellent aperitifs. They're also good with raw shellfish, delicate fish preparations, and salads (*salade niçoise*, greens with chèvre). The much fuller, oakier, new-wave versions will take on richer, spicier fare: broiled or grilled salmon or tuna steaks, lobster or scallops with butter- or cream-based sauces, or even boldly flavored dishes featuring curries, chiles, or pungent herbs. With their assertive and sometimes exotic personalities, these wines can overwhelm subtle flavors.

The Bottom Line

High-end white Graves are scarce and exorbitantly priced, and even the midrange wines are now quite expensive ($30 to $50). Dry white wines from the more generic Bordeaux or Entre-Deux-Mers appellations, as well as lesser Graves, are considerably cheaper and can offer good value.

What to Buy: Dry White Bordeaux

1995	1996	1997
B	B	B-

Château Carbonnieux 1996, Graves ★★★ $$$ 🍷🍷🍷
Rich, buttery aroma, with a subtle oak overlay. Thick but dry; pineapple and peach fruitiness complicated by toasted nut, malt, and mineral nuances. Finishes with good grip and freshness.

Château Olivier 1996, Graves ★★ $$ 🍷🍷🍷
Focused, bright citric aromas of orange peel and lemon cream. Crisp despite noticeable oakiness; opens nicely to show baking spices and honey. Fairly light on its feet. Finishes with firm acidity.

Château Reignac 1997 Cuvée Spéciale, ★★ $$ 🍷🍷
Bordeaux Supérieur Pure, complex aromas of lemon, grapefruit, oak spice, honey, and mint. Fat, silky, and impressively concentrated; floral fruit boasts noteworthy depth for the price. Oak tones sweeten the strong, very long finish.

Château Boisset 1996 La Chapelle, ★★ $ 🍷🍷
Entre-Deux-Mers Aromas of honeydew melon and pear. Juicy

pear and apple flavors. Medium-bodied, clean, emphasizing fruit over oak. Fairly rich but not at all heavy. Acidity holds it together.

Les Comtes de Jonqueyres 1996 Cuvée Alpha,   ★★ $ ♟♟
Bordeaux Intriguing nose suggests hay, plum, dried peach, and roasted pear. Peach and pear flavors repeat in the mouth, joined by a vanilla note. Supple and fat; could use a bit more brightness.

Château Bonnet 1997, Entre-Deux-Mers   ★ $ ♟♟♟
Aromas of fig, pear, and apple. Supple and pliant in the mouth, with rather low acidity. Grassy in a Loire-like way. A soft, easy-going wine that could use a bit more verve.

Château Menaut 1995, Graves   ★ $ ♟♟♟
Restrained mineral and lime aroma. Round, citric fruit buttressed by ripe acidity. Rather stylish, youthful, understated. Good palate presence. Complex finish hints at honey, orange, and lemon.

Jean-Michel Arcaute 1997 Sauvignon, Bordeaux   ★ $ ♟♟♟
Restrained nose suggests orange, pineapple, and grass. Rich, supple, and soft, with modest acidity, good palate presence, and a flavor of fresh pineapple. Pleasantly tart aftertaste.

SAUTERNES and SAUTERNES-STYLE WINES

Sauternes (saw-tairn) is the name for the complex, unctuous, ageworthy white wine made in five villages southeast of the town of Bordeaux: Sauternes itself, Fargues, Preignac, Bommes, and Barsac. Making great Sauternes is a risky business: The grapes must be left on the vines well into autumn in the hope that the beneficent fungus known as *Botrytis cinerea* (see the box on page 135) will develop. It does so about half the time. We had good botrytis years in 1988, 1989, and 1990, an incredible windfall to producers, but then not again for six years until the 1996 vintage. Of all the world's sweet wines, the Sauternes Château d'Yquem (dee-kem) is probably the best known.

Sauternes and the similar wines produced in the region are typically about 80 percent Sémillon, the balance being mostly Sauvignon Blanc. They're quite sweet (5 to 8 percent residual sugar) and high in alcohol (14+ percent). Nearly all of today's top Sauternes are at least partially aged in new-oak barrels, which add notes of spice, vanilla, and crème brûlée to their fruit flavors.

At the Table

Although Sauternes is best reserved for dessert, these luscious wines figure in some of the most dramatic wine and food matches imaginable. Sauternes with foie gras is a decadent combination of textures; the wine's acidity cuts the richness of the meat. Sauternes and Roquefort play on the contrast between the sweetness of the wine and the saltiness of the blue cheese. For dessert, choose fresh fruits or tarts that will echo the fruit tones that characterize Sauternes: peach, apricot, pear, banana. Desserts based on toffee, caramel, almonds, and vanilla also pair well with Sauternes.

The Bottom Line

Sauternes are expensive and rare, due to high production costs and a succession of poor vintages in the early 1990s. The better wines from satellite appellations such as Sainte-Croix-du-Mont can offer much better value, but only in the best years. Distribution of sweet Bordeaux in the U.S. is currently spotty, and there is very little truly interesting wine available for less than $25. Sharp-eyed shoppers may still be able to find top-notch examples from 1988, 1989, and 1990 in the $40 to $60 range.

What to Buy: Sauternes

1988	1989	1990	1991	1992
A-	A-	A+	C-	F

1993	1994	1995	1996	1997
F	C+	B-	B+	B+

Château de Malle 1996, Sauternes ★★★ $$$$ ♥♥
Very ripe aromas of peach, apricot, and honey. Spicy, sweet, and intensely flavored; lush but shapely. The noble rot shows more in tangy flavor than thick texture. Lovely ripe acidity.

Château Lafaurie-Peyraguey 1996, ★★★ $$$$ ♥♥
Sauternes Honey and spice on the rather inexpressive nose. Fat and honeyed in the mouth, with lovely freshness of fruit. Concentrated and very rich. Finish is spicy and slightly aggressive, but quite persistent. Developing very slowly.

Château La Tour Blanche 1996, Sauternes ★★★ $$$$ ♆♆
Aromatic pineapple and grapefruit nose, plus pungent oak and notes of licorice, mint, and other fresh herbs. Rich, moderately viscous, and intensely spicy. A green herbal note adds complexity.

Ready, Set, Drink: Sauternes

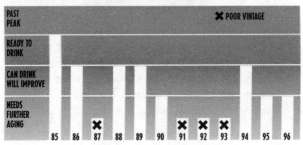

Château Rayne-Vigneau 1996, Sauternes ★★★ $$$$ ♆♆
Exotic, super-ripe aromas of peach, apricot, marmalade, marzipan, and honey. Very rich but high-pitched, with intense spiciness and mouth-filling texture. Finishes sweet but quite firm, with good acidity and a note of almond extract.

Château Sigalas-Rabaud 1996, Sauternes ★★★ $$$$ ♆♆
Classic aromas of apricot, honey, and spicy oak. Very sweet and sappy; really stuffed with fruit. Lovely combination of power and elegance. Finishes strong, with notes of spice and barley sugar.

Château Doisy-Daëne 1996, Barsac ★★★ $$$ ♆♆
Expressive aromas of apricot, honey, lime, and toasty oak. Intensely flavored and pure but tightly wound. Juicy and almost painfully spicy, with bright acids and deep fruit. Finishes very long, with notes of charred oak and nutmeg.

Château Tirecul La Gravière 1996, ★★★ $$$ ♆♆
Monbazillac (750-ml bottle) Intensely spicy aromas of apricot, honey, mace, and toasted hazelnut. Concentrated and thick, with spicy sweetness, bright balancing acidity, and flavors of fresh and dried apricot. Long, spicy finish.

Château La Rame 1995, Sainte-Croix-du-Mont ★★ $$ ♆♆
Fruit-driven aromas of apricot, pineapple, licorice, marzipan, and toast. Rich and concentrated, with a note of fennel seed giving the sweet fruit a refreshingly bitter edge. Excellent value.

Burgundy

The famous labels of Burgundy—*Bourgogne* in French—appear
on bottles of some of the world's rarest and most expensive dry
wines. But while the best Burgundies, whites as well as reds, are
among the most aromatically complex and sensuous wines
made anywhere, it is all too easy to spend $60 for a bottle of
shockingly ordinary stuff. When buying a Burgundy not listed in
this book, it would pay to ask your wine merchant for advice.

Pinot Noir, at once the most elegant and temperamental of
red-wine grapes, reaches its apotheosis in the Côte d'Or, the
heart of Burgundy. The same area is the source of the world's
finest Chardonnays. At the other end of the price scale, simple,
gulpable Beaujolais, from the Gamay grape, also comes from
Burgundy. And in between are areas like the Côte Chalonnaise
and the Mâconnais, which produce good, less expensive wines,
such as Pinot Noirs and Chardonnays.

CHABLIS

COTE D'OR

Burgundy encompasses a broad range
of wines. The roughly 35-mile-long strip
of vineyards called the Côte d'Or, for
instance, produces some of the world's
most long-lived wines, whereas
Beaujolais, from the south, is meant to
be drunk young.

Rully
Mercurey   COTE
Givry   CHALONNAISE
Montagny

MACONNAIS
Saint-Véran   Pouilly-Fuissé

BEAUJOLAIS

On the Label

The wines of the Côte d'Or are classified into four basic categories based upon the quality of the vineyard site. In ascending
order, they are:

•**Generic Burgundy** may come from anywhere in Burgundy. The
label simply reads Bourgogne.

•A special category of generic wines called **village wines** is entitled to use a regional designation on the label (for example,

Côte de Nuits-Villages). These come from vineyards located entirely within the boundaries of one of a group of favored villages. The label normally lists only the name of the village, for example, Chambolle-Musigny.

• **Premiers crus,** or first growths, are specially designated vineyards with particularly good soil and exposure to the sun. The name of the *premier cru* vineyard is added to the village name on the label (such as Vosne-Romanée Les Suchots), and the label always specifies *premier cru*.

• **Grands crus** are at the top of the pyramid. These are world-famous, ideally situated vineyards like Chambertin and La Tâche. Long ago, several villages capitalized on the reputations of these famous vineyards by appending the name of the local *grand cru* to their own village name, which can cloud the important distinction between a great vineyard (Musigny) and the village in which it is located (Chambolle-Musigny).

At the Table

Regional favorites are red Burgundy with boeuf bourguignon and game birds, but more mature Burgundies also go well with lamb and full-flavored cheeses. Since you've shelled out serious money for these wines, serve them with simple, direct foods that will not overwhelm their delicate fruit and specific soil flavors. Grilled meats will probably be too pronounced in flavor, as will spices like chiles, cumin, and coriander; stick to mellow herbs like thyme and bay. With their combination of richness and acidity, white Burgundies from the Côte d'Or are ideal with roasted chicken, broiled fish steaks, and butter-based sauces. Since oak can be a prominent flavor component in younger white Burgundies, avoid delicate preparations (such as freshwater fish or crabmeat) that might be overshadowed by the vanilla and butterscotch notes in these wines.

The Bottom Line

Worldwide demand for Burgundy far surpasses supply, and fans of these wines are usually not only avid but price insensitive. The least expensive generic Bourgognes start at around $15, *premiers crus* are typically $35 to $70, and *grands crus*, both reds and whites, generally begin at about $60 and can easily climb to three digits. The name of a top producer on the label is usually a more reliable indicator of Burgundy quality than the vintage or the vineyard. Thus, the recommendations here focus on producers whose wines can actually be found in the U.S. retail market. The list singles out their most reliably interesting wines at a variety of price levels.

COTE d'OR

The Côte d'Or—literally golden slope—is the wine world's most expensive strip of real estate, yielding the finest examples of Pinot Noir and Chardonnay. Winemakers on almost every continent have tried to duplicate red Burgundy's perfumed fruit flavors, silky texture, and subtle hints of flowers, spices, minerals, and earth. At the same time, the region's whites, along with those of Chablis on Burgundy's northern outskirts, are the reason Chardonnay is universally prized by wine drinkers.

Red-Wine Producers and Their Wines

What to Buy: Pinot Noir

1993	1994	1995	1996	1997
B+	C+	A-	B+	B

DOMAINE ROUMIER ★★★★ $$$–$$$$ ♟♟
Aromatically complex, slow-developing wines from very low-yielding old vines. Their spicy red-fruit character gives them an uncanny succulence. LOOK FOR: Chambolle-Musigny, Morey St-Denis Clos de la Bussière, and Bonnes-Mares.

DOMAINE ALBERT MOROT ★★★ $$$$ ♟♟
Solidly built, consistent wines from several of Beaune's best *premiers crus*. Real bargains for their quality. LOOK FOR: Beaune Cent-Vignes, Grèves, Marconnets, and Teurons.

DOMAINE DUJAC ★★★ $$$$ ♟♟
Flamboyantly aromatic, stylish wines that showcase pure Pinot red fruit and spice rather than power. Silky and deceptively accessible when young, but capable of aging. LOOK FOR: Morey St-Denis, Charmes-Chambertin, Clos St-Denis, Clos de la Roche, Echezeaux, and Bonnes-Mares.

DOMAINE BRUNO CLAIR ★★★ $$$ – $$$$ ♟♟

Vibrantly fruity, minerally wines that make few concessions to current tastes for sweet new oak and early drinkability but have a history of developing well in the bottle. **LOOK FOR:** Marsannay Grasses-Têtes and Longerois; Savigny lès Beaune Dominode; Gevrey-Chambertin Cazetiers and Clos St-Jacques.

DOMAINE JEAN GRIVOT ★★★ $$$ – $$$$ ♟♟

Harmonious, intensely flavored wines with tangy aromas and flavors of black fruits, minerals, and spices. Solidly structured, thanks to firm acidity and substantial but pliant tannins. **LOOK FOR:** Vosne-Romanée Beaumonts, Nuits-St-Georges Boudots, and Echezeaux.

MAISON LOUIS JADOT ★★★ $$$ – $$$$ ♟♟

Traditionally made, uncompromising Burgundies that are true to the soil. The wines come from an astonishing array of sites spanning virtually the entire Côte d'Or. **LOOK FOR:** Beaune Clos des Ursules; Corton Pougets; Clos Vougeot; Bonnes-Mares; Gevrey-Chambertin Lavaux St-Jacques and Clos St-Jacques; and Chambertin-Clos de Bèze.

DOMAINE MARQUIS D'ANGERVILLE ★★★ $$$ – $$$$ ♟♟

Ageworthy wines of finesse, with sweet cherry and raspberry fruit and graceful but substantial structure. A distinctly understated style that does not rely on the sweetening influence of new barrels. **LOOK FOR:** Volnay Champans, Taillepieds, and Clos des Ducs.

Ready, Set, Drink: Red Burgundy

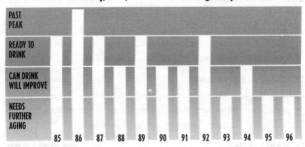

ADDITIONAL TOP-NOTCH POSSIBILITIES—OFTEN EXPENSIVE
Domaine Ghislaine Barthod, Domaine Claude Dugat, Domaine Robert Groffier, Dominique Laurent, Domaine Leroy, Domaine Hubert Lignier, Domaine Méo-Camuzet, Domaine Denis Mortet, Domaine Mugneret-Gibourg, Domaine de la Romanée-Conti,

Domaine Joseph Roty, Domaine Christian Sérafin, and Domaine Comte Georges de Vogüé

GOOD VALUES: LOOK FOR 1995 AND 1996
Bertrand Ambroise Nuits-St-Georges and Nuits-St-Georges Vieilles Vignes; Chopin-Groffier Côtes de Nuits-Villages and Nuits-St-Georges; Geantet Pansiot Gevrey-Chambertin Vieilles Vignes; Maison Vincent Girardin Maranges Clos de Loyères and Santenay Gravières; Robert Jayer-Gilles Hautes Côtes de Beaune, Hautes Côtes de Nuits, and Côte de Nuits-Villages; Fernand Lécheneaut et Fils Chambolle-Musigny, Vosne-Romanée, and Nuits-St-Georges; Perrot-Minot Chambolle-Musigny

White-Wine Producers and Their Wines

What to Buy: Chardonnay

1994	1995	1996	1997
C+	A-	A	B

DOMAINE LEFLAIVE ★★★★ $$$$ ❦❦
Puligny-Montrachet's most famous name, with high prices to match. After coasting through the 1980s, Leflaive is once again making highly concentrated wines that combine power and finesse. **LOOK FOR:** Puligny-Montrachet Folatières, Les Combettes, and Les Pucelles; Bâtard-Montrachet; and Chevalier-Montrachet.

DOMAINE SAUZET ★★★★ $$$$ ❦❦
Along with Leflaive, the other fabled name in Puligny-Montrachet. The style here tends toward generous, powerful, thoroughly ripe wines with clean, complex aromas and excellent clarity of flavor. **LOOK FOR:** Puligny-Montrachet Referts, Champs-Canet, and Combettes; and Bâtard-Montrachet.

VERGET ★★★★ $$$–$$$$ ❦❦
The *négociant* venture of the Mâconnais producer Jean-Marie Guffens, offering dramatic, full-blown Burgundies with extraordinarily rich mouth feel and uncanny persistence on the palate, from old vines all over the Côte d'Or. **LOOK FOR:** Meursault Rougeot, Porusots, and Les Charmes; Puligny-Montrachet Sous le Puits and Enseignères; Chassagne-Montrachet Remilly, Morgeot, and La Romanée; Corton-Charlemagne; and Bâtard-Montrachet.

DOMAINE JEAN-MARC BOILLOT ★★★ $$$$ ❦❦
Spicy wines characterized by orange-peel, peach, and dried-fruit aromas. Typically ripe verging on sweet but with sound balanc-

ing acidity. **LOOK FOR:** Puligny-Montrachet, Puligny-Montrachet Les Referts, Champs-Canet, Les Combettes, and La Truffière.

DOMAINE MICHEL COLIN-DELEGER ★★★ $$$$ ♥♥
Silky wines with the smoky, nutty notes that come from long contact with the lees. Archetypical Chassagne-Montrachet. **LOOK FOR:** St-Aubin Le Charmois; Chassagne-Montrachet Les Chaumées, Les Chenevottes, Remilly, Morgeot, and Les Vergers; Puligny-Montrachet La Truffière and Demoiselles.

DOMAINE BERNARD MOREY ★★★ $$$ – $$$$ ♥♥
Full-bodied rich Burgundies that offer early pleasure. Aromas and flavors tend to be rather honeyed and exotic, and acidity levels fairly low. **LOOK FOR:** St-Aubin Le Charmois; Chassagne-Montrachet Vieilles Vignes, Les Embrazées, Vide Bourse, and Caillerets; and Puligny-Montrachet La Truffière.

MAISON LOUIS JADOT ★★★ $$$-$$$$ ♥♥
Sharply focused, ageworthy white Burgundies whose crisp acidity often requires a few years of aging in the bottle. Aromas typically feature vibrant spiced apple, lemon-lime, and minerals. **LOOK FOR:** Chassagne-Montrachet (Duc de Magenta), Puligny-Montrachet Clos de la Garenne (Duc de Magenta), Meursault Perrières, Puligny-Montrachet Les Perrières, Corton-Charlemagne, and Chevalier-Montrachet Demoiselles.

MAISON OLIVIER LEFLAIVE FRERES ★★★ $$$-$$$$ ♥♥
Open, approachable wines maturing in the medium-term, true to their sites; never excessively oaky. **LOOK FOR:** St-Aubin Remilly; Meursault Clos des Perrières; Puligny-Montrachet and Puligny-Montrachet Folatières.

Ready, Set, Drink: White Burgundy

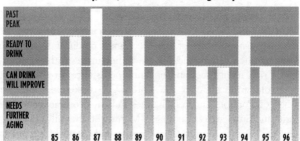

	85	86	87	88	89	90	91	92	93	94	95	96
PAST PEAK												
READY TO DRINK												
CAN DRINK WILL IMPROVE												
NEEDS FURTHER AGING												

ADDITIONAL TOP-NOTCH POSSIBILITIES: OFTEN EXPENSIVE
Domaine Guy Amiot et Fils, Domaine Carillon, Domaine Coche-

Dury (a Meursault superstar), *Domaine Patrick Javillier, Domaine des Comtes Lafon* (superb and scarce Meursaults), *Domaine Marc Morey, Domaine Michel Niellon, Domaine Paul Pernot, Domaine Jacques Prieur* (since 1994), *Domaine Ramonet*

COTE CHALONNAISE

The Côte Chalonnaise lies just south of the Côte d'Or, and international demand for the somewhat less refined wines of this district is not quite so frenzied. Of the Côte Chalonnaise area's four main appellations, two (Givry and Mercurey) are best known for their reds, one (Montagny) for its whites, and one (Rully) for both. Côte Chalonnaise wines are generally accessible earlier than those of the Côte d'Or, but are capable of aging gracefully in the bottle.

At the Table

Since most Côte Chalonnaise reds are drunk on the early side for their youthful fruit, they are well suited to aggressively seasoned dishes. Serve them with grilled duck or lamb, flavorful meats that complement the primal cherry/berry notes of young Pinot. Grilled salmon is another option, as is roasted chicken seasoned with tarragon or fennel. Côte Chalonnaise whites are flexible companions to lighter fish and poultry dishes, especially those that feature fruit as a flavor component.

The Bottom Line

Bottles from the most talented Côte Chalonnaise winemakers can offer some of Burgundy's best values. Though a destructive frost in the spring of 1998 has increased pressure on prices, they are rarely higher than those of simple village wines from the more hallowed *communes* of the Côte d'Or.

Producers and Their Wines

DOMAINE JOBLOT ★★★ $$ ♟♟
New-oaky, full-throttle Givry reds whose density and concentration of dark-berry fruit transcends the appellation. **LOOK FOR:** Givry Clos de la Servoisine and Clos de Cellier aux Moines.

MAISON FAIVELEY   ★★ $$–$$$ ♥♥

Richly fruity, solidly built, often meaty Mercureys that are rather
refined in the context of the appellation. **LOOK FOR:** Mercury
Clos du Roi and Clos des Myglands.

DOMAINE DELAUNAY   ★★ $$ ♥♥

Gutsy, traditionally made Mercureys; structure demands cellar-
ing. Slightly rustic dark-berry and tar aromas. **LOOK FOR:** Mercurey
Meix Foulot and Clos du Château de Montaigu.

DOMAINE MICHEL JUILLOT   ★★ $$ ♥♥

Vibrant, minerally white wines and supple reds with uncommon
depth and weight for Mercury. Both are unusually ageworthy.
LOOK FOR: Mercurey and Corton-Charlemagne among the
whites; Mercurey Clos des Barraults and Champs Martin and
Corton-Perrières among the reds.

MACONNAIS

The best Mâconnais (mah-cawn-nay) whites are among the
world's most compelling values in high-end Chardonnays.
Although generally a bit leaner and stonier than Chardonnay
from the Côte d'Or, they have good concentration and acidity,
and barrel-aged versions can be creamy and mouth-filling. In
the ripest years, these latter wines may show a honeyed tropical-
fruit character that calls to mind the richest California
Chardonnays.

Mâcon with the name of a village appended (such as
Mâcon-Clessé or Mâcon-Viré) is typically a better wine than simple Mâcon or Mâcon-Villages. The appellation called Pouilly-
Fuissé (poo-yee fwee-say) produces a somewhat richer (and
usually pricier) version of Chardonnay, while relatively inexpensive Saint-Véran is an excellent value.

At the Table

Less expensive Chardonnays from the Mâconnais can
be served alongside lighter fish and poultry dishes. But
the richest Pouilly-Fuissés have the body and often the
honeyed, tropical fruit character of big California
Chardonnays; pair them with richly sauced fish steaks,
lobster, and scallops, or with sweetbreads.

The Bottom Line

Mâcon supplies a less expensive version of white Burgundy. The best growers' wines are likely to set you back $20 to $25 or more; however these wines compare favorably to higher-priced Chardonnays. Wines from the local co-ops are generally cheaper, but quality is unreliable.

What to Buy: Mâconnais

1995	1996	1997
B+	A	B+

Producers and Their Wines

DOMAINE FERRET ★★★ $$$ ♟♟
Super-rich, large-scaled wines. They often show exotic aromas of honey and dried fruits. The wines from this producer can appear quite new-oaky in their youth, but they age gracefully. **LOOK FOR:** Pouilly-Fuissé Le Clos, Les Perrières, Tournant de Pouilly, and Menetrières.

DOMAINE DE LA BONGRAN– ★★★ $$ – $$$$ ♟♟
JEAN THEVENET Super-ripe, often downright honeyed wines from late-picked grapes. The wines are an idiosyncratic style of Chardonnay, remarkable in the years with noble rot (such as 1994 and, especially, 1995). **LOOK FOR:** Mâcon-Clessé Tradition and Mâcon-Clessé Le Vrouté.

DOMAINE DU VIEUX SAINT-SORLIN– ★★★ $$ – $$$ ♟♟
OLIVIER MERLIN Intensely flavored, smoky-rich wines given vivacity by underlying citric and mineral notes. These wines are better than most California Chardonnays that cost twice as much money. **LOOK FOR:** Mâcon La Roche Vineuse Les Cras and Vieilles Vignes.

VERGET ★★★ $$ ♟♟
This *négociant* firm is a terrific source for fat, silky, but focused Mâconnais wines that offer substantial early appeal. Excellent value. **LOOK FOR:** Saint-Véran Tête de Cuvée, Mâcon Tête de Cuvée, and Pouilly-Fuissé Tête de Cuvée.

ADDITIONAL TOP-NOTCH POSSIBILITIES
Domaine André Bonhomme, Château Fuissé, Domaine Henri Goyard, Domaine Guffens-Heynen, Domaine Robert-Dénogent, Domaine Valette

CHABLIS

When grown in the clay-and-chalk soils around the town of Chablis, Chardonnay is a cerebral elixir to which the American jug Chablis bears no relation. With its flinty minerality and penetrating acidity, Chablis has more in common with Sauvignon Blanc from the Loire Valley than with most New World Chardonnays. Chablis is typically more austere and delicate than white Burgundy from the Côte d'Or but just as long-lived.

At the Table
Brisk, minerally Chablis is ideal with shellfish. *Premier cru* Chablis and oysters is one of the all-time great matches: The best Chablis vineyards literally lie on soil made from decomposed oyster shells. Chablis also pairs well with white-fleshed fish like sole and lake trout; *grand cru* Chablis has the palate presence to stand up to fish preparations using richer sauces. Thanks to the steeliness and sheer grip of Chablis, these wines also perk up deep-fried foods and smoked salmon.

The Bottom Line
At $25 to $35 for *premiers crus* and $40 to $60 for *grands crus*, Chablis is about 33 to 50 percent less expensive than wines of similar pedigree from the Côte d'Or.

What to Buy: Chablis

1994	1995	1996	1997
C+	B+	A	B+

Producers and Their Wines

RENE ET VINCENT DAUVISSAT ★★★★ $$$ – $$$$ ♛♛
Consistently superb; extraordinary aromatic complexity, concentration, and richness. True to their *terroir* and long on personality. **LOOK FOR:** Chablis Sechets, Vaillons, Forêt, Preuses, and Clos.

VERGET ★★★★ $$$ – $$$$ ♛♛
Expressive, layered wines from old vines in the best sites. The

négociant Jean-Marie Guffens provides unusually dense, and somewhat controversial, wines due to his extensive use of the wines' lees. LOOK FOR: Chablis Vaillons, Montée de Tonnerre, Bougros, and Valmur.

J. MOREAU & FILS ★★★ $$$ – $$$$ ♥♥
A distinctly modern style of Chablis, showing more fruit than mineral austerity; no oak is used. LOOK FOR: Chablis Vaillons; *grands crus* Clos, Valmur, and Vaudésir.

LOUIS MICHEL ET FILS ★★★ $$$ – $$$$ ♥♥
The classic example of Chablis made entirely in stainless steel: minerally, bright, focused wines that often show more Chablis character early on than wines aged in oak. LOOK FOR: Chablis Vaillons, Montée de Tonnerre, Vaudésir, Grenouilles, and Clos.

BILLAUD-SIMON ★★★ $$ – $$$$ ♥♥
Minerally, stylish wines with sharply focused green-apple and citrus-fruit aromas and flavors. Much improved following a recent generational change. LOOK FOR: Chablis Mont de Milieu Vieilles Vignes, Montée de Tonnerre, Vaudésir, Preuses, and Clos.

ADDITIONAL TOP-NOTCH POSSIBILITIES
Domaine Adhémar Boudin, Domaine Jean Dauvissat, Domaine Jean-Paul Droin, Domaine Jean-Pierre Grossot, Domaine Jean-Marie Raveneau (superb but hard to find), *Domaine Vocoret et Fils*

BEAUJOLAIS

Beaujolais, made from the Gamay grape, is a fruit bomb in a bottle, an undemanding wine that has wide appeal. Its fresh acidity, mild tannins, and aromas and flavors of cherry, strawberry, and raspberry make it ideal for casual quaffing. Most Beaujolais is made via carbonic maceration, a fermentation technique that is designed to extract fruit flavor rather than tannins from the grapes.

On the Label
Beaujolais Nouveau is a modern marketing miracle, not the top designation of the wine. Here are the words you'll find on a Beaujolais bottle, in ascending order of desirability:
• **Beaujolais Nouveau,** released each November less than three months after the harvest, is a pale, unaged version of the finer Beaujolais that will be shipped months later.

- **Beaujolais** on the label with no further designation means the wine can come from anywhere in the region.
- **Beaujolais-Villages** is from one of a number of well-respected towns, most surrounded by granite-based soil, in the hillier, northern part of the region.
- **Cru Beaujolais** includes the top hillside villages, which can put their own names on the label: Brouilly, Côte de Brouilly, Chénas, Chiroubles, Fleurie, Juliénas, Morgon, Moulin-à-Vent, Régnié, and St-Amour. The best of these *crus* can gain in complexity with a few years of aging in the bottle.

At the Table

With its snappy fruit, bright acidity, and light tannins, Beaujolais is made for the table. This wine makes an excellent choice when a light red is appropriate, such as with salads, fish courses, Southwestern preparations with chiles or garlic, or even Asian fare such as beef or pork stir-fries. Roast chicken and Beaujolais is a classic pairing, but almost any poultry will be complemented by the wine. Beaujolais is also a perfect partner for richer foods that could be bogged down by a tannic or highly alcoholic wine; try beef stews or daubes or thick cuts of pork. The somewhat more serious and structured Beaujolais *crus* are compatible with game birds, grilled pork, or lighter beef and lamb main dishes that might otherwise demand a Pinot Noir or even a lighter Rhône wine. In the wine bars of Lyons, the French culinary capital just to the south of the Beaujolais region, these wines are perennial favorites drunk chilled with grilled sausages and charcuterie.

The Bottom Line

Basic Beaujolais is normally $8 to $12. The best *cru* bottlings from smaller growers are typically $15 to $20, but these wines can be more interesting, and more fun, than lesser red Burgundies at twice the price.

What to Buy: Beaujolais

1995	1996	1997	1998
A-	B-	B+	A-

Producers and Their Wines

HENRY FESSY ★★★ $ – $$ ❢❢
These are Beaujolais with complex aromatics, spicy fruit, and expressive floral tones. **LOOK FOR:** Beaujolais-Villages, Brouilly Cuvée du Plateau du Bel-Air, Chiroubles Cuvée Peyraud, and Morgon Calot.

TRENEL ★★★ $ – $$ ❢❢
Reliable, elegant, silky wines that emphasize red-fruit flavors. Trenel offers a consistently satisfying Nouveau. **LOOK FOR:** Beaujolais-Villages en Primeur, Chiroubles, Morgon Côte de Py, and Moulin-à-Vent Domaine de la Tour du Bief.

GEORGES DUBOEUF ★★ $ – $$ ❢❢❢
Refreshing, fruity wines well suited to uncritical quaffing. The best of them—worth a couple of extra bucks—are marketed under the names of individual domaines. **LOOK FOR:** Flower-label Juliénas, Fleurie, Moulin-à-Vent; Chiroubles Château de Javernand, Fleurie Château des Déduits and Clos des Quatre Vents, Morgon Domaine des Versauds and Jean Descombes, Moulin-à-Vent Domaine des Rosiers, and Domaine de la Tour du Bief.

MAISON LOUIS JADOT ★★ $ – $$ ❢❢
Substantial, serious examples of Beaujolais. In many instances a bit of up-front fruitiness has been sacrificed in favor of more weight and structure. **LOOK FOR:** Fleurie, Morgon, and Moulin-à-Vent.

ADDITIONAL TOP-NOTCH POSSIBILITIES
Guy Bréton (Morgon), *Domaine des Champs Grilles* (St-Amour), *Nicole Chanrion* (Côte de Brouilly), *Michel Chignard* (Fleurie Les Moriers), *Domaine Diochon* (Moulin-à-Vent Vieilles Vignes), *Domaine Laurent Dumas* (Fleurie), *Durdilly* (Beaujolais Nouveau, Beaujolais Les Grandes Coasses), *Jacky Janodet* (Moulin-à-Vent), *Jean Foillard* (Morgon Côte de Py), *Domaine du Granit* (Moulin-à-Vent), *M. Lapierre* (Morgon), *Domaine de la Madone* (Beaujolais-Villages Le Perréon), *Domaine Manoir du Carra* (Beaujolais-Villages), *Yvon Métras* (Fleurie), *Pierre Meziat* (Chiroubles Sélection Vieilles Vignes), *Joël Rochette* (Brouilly Pisse-Vieilles, Régnié Côtes des Braves), *Clos de la Roilette* (Fleurie), *Michel Tête* (Beaujolais-Villages, Juliénas, and Juliénas Cuvée Prestige), *Jean-Paul Thévenet* (Morgon Vieilles Vignes), *Georges Viornery* (Côte de Brouilly), *Domaine du Vissoux* (Beaujolais Primeur Pierre Chermette, Fleurie Poncié, and Moulin-à-Vent Rochegrès)

Champagne

Numerous countries make sparkling wine according to the Champagne method, but few imitators approach the complexity of the real article. True Champagne comes only from the Champagne region. It ranges from lemony and austere to rich and nutty. The grape varieties blended to make Champagne are both white and red: Chardonnay, Pinot Noir, and Pinot Meunier.

Because this northerly climate does not always provide the raw materials to make balanced, complete wines, most Champagne bottlings combine juice from two or more vintages. A relatively lean, high-acid vintage, for example, can be softened by the addition of mellower, riper wine from a warmer year.

·Reims

Seine

At the Table

Very dry, delicate Champagne makes the perfect aperitif; it also goes well with raw oysters and is lovely with hors d'oeuvres, particularly deep-fried or salty appetizers like squid and shrimp tempura, cheese *gougères*, and shrimp and pork dumplings. Creamy, delicately flavored cheeses like Coulommiers and Explorateur pair nicely with many lighter-bodied Champagnes, too. Richer examples marry beautifully with oily fish or fish served with a rich sauce. Rosé Champagne with sushi makes a pleasing combination; smoked ham is another good match. Very salty foods such as aged Parmesan or cheddar, cheese straws, and roasted nuts are perfect with Blanc de Blancs bottlings.

On the Label

• **Brut,** which literally means *raw*, signifies a wine that ranges from fairly dry to completely dry. Most Champagnes are bruts.

- **Extra dry, sec, demi-sec,** and **doux,** in increasing order of sweetness, are the designations found on slightly sweet to sweet wines.
- **Blanc de Blancs** is a brut Champagne made entirely from Chardonnay.
- **Rosé** is normally made by adding a small percentage of red wine early in the Champagne-making process.

The Bottom Line

Champagne is expensive to make, and even nonvintage bottlings generally sell for $25 or more. Fortunately, the better nonvintage Champagnes (designated NV in the notes below) are actually as good as most vintage wines. Vintage Champagnes generally fall in the $35 to $60 range, while prestige cuvées routinely sell for $60 to $80, and many retail for $100 or more. Some advice: Many big-name Champagnes are discounted at holiday time, and a little shopping around can turn up good deals. Wines featured below retail for $60 or less.

Pol Roger 1990 Brut Chardonnay ★★★★ $$$$ ♥♥♥

Flamboyant toasted, roasted aromas of citrus oil, butterscotch, and spice, with a yeasty complexity. Intense peach-pit flavor is quite dry and penetrating; bracing acidity makes this almost painful today. Unevolved and worth aging.

Veuve Clicquot 1990 Vintage Réserve ★★★★ $$$$ ♥♥♥

Complex aromas of apple, toast, vanilla, and melted butter. Rich apple, lemon, and spice flavors offer brilliant clarity and cut, thanks to strong acidity. Youthfully taut on the finish.

J. Lassalle 1992 Special Club Brut ★★★★ $$$$ ♥♥

Ripe aromas of peach, apple, and toffee. Rich, creamy, and rather full in the mouth, with ripe, bright flavors and superb intensity. Firm and fresh but gently styled and ideal for current consumption. Very long on the palate.

Legras NV Blanc de Blancs de Chouilly ★★★★ $$$ ♥♥

Crystalline, soil-inflected aromas of lemon, chalk, and stones. Very dry and lemony, with an almost saline impression of extract. Creamy and textured but tangy in the mouth. Very crisp, long finish shows a late flavor of fennel.

Billecart-Salmon NV Rosé Brut ★★★ $$$$ ♥♥♥

Delicate flowery nose hints at red berries. Fresh, creamy red-fruit palate offers subtle earth tones, lovely ripeness, and excellent texture. Long, subtle back end. Easygoing rosé.

Guy Larmandier NV Cramant Grand Cru ★★★ $$$$ ♥♥♥
Blanc de Blancs Very subtle lemony nose. Intensely flavored but quite light and elegant; a bone-dry Champagne offering lovely finesse in the middle palate and a persistent if slightly skinny finish. Very understated Champagne.

Pol Roger 1990 Brut Rosé ★★★ $$$$ ♥♥♥
Inviting aromas of strawberry, orange peel, earth, and brioche. Penetrating and quite dry in the mouth, with subtle orange-peel, red-berry, and earth notes. Finishes brisk and long. More serious than most rosés.

Taittinger 1992 Brut Millésime ★★★ $$$$ ♥♥♥
Aromas of lemon peel, fennel, Granny Smith apple, and chalk; showing its Chardonnay component. Dry, penetrating gin-and-tonic flavors are subtle and brisk. Should show more personality with another year or so in the bottle.

Taittinger NV Cuvée Prestige Rosé ★★★ $$$$ ♥♥♥
Orange-pink color. Perfumed raspberry, cherry, strawberry, and mint aromas. Strong acidity gives penetrating, clean red-fruit flavors a keen edge. Finishes with a refreshing note of tart red berries.

Veuve Clicquot NV Demi-Sec ★★★ $$$$ ♥♥♥
Aromas of toast, smoke, lemon, chalk, and earth are deep and complex. Very fresh and moderately sweet; rather exotic flavors of melon, peach, candied pear, and marzipan are balanced by ripe acidity. Long, strong, pineappley aftertaste.

Guy Larmandier NV Premier Cru Brut Rosé ★★★ $$$ ♥♥♥
Very ripe aromas of strawberry and raspberry. Intensely flavored and quite rich, but with sound supporting acidity. Atypically fat for this bottling. More a wine with bubbles than a Champagne.

Heidsieck & Co Monopole NV Blue Top Brut ★★★ $$$ ♥♥♥
Nose combines spice, lemon cream, apple, and minerals, plus floral and chalky notes. Quite dry and intensely flavored; gives an almost saline impression. Pristine, focused, and very long.

Lanson 1990 Brut ★★★ $$$ ♥♥♥
Bright, fruit-driven peach and apricot nose complicated by notes

of toast and coffee. Ripe, fairly dry, and light-to-medium-bodied, with good intensity and length. Finishes fresh and nutty.

Piper-Heidsieck NV Extra Dry ★★★ $$$ ♥♥♥
Highly aromatic lemon, biscuit, and mineral nose. Slightly sweet but fresh and focused, thanks to brisk acidity. Lovely fruit carries through to a ripe, very long aftertaste.

Vintage vs. Nonvintage Champagnes

The reputations of the major Champagne firms hinge on the quality and consistency of their nonvintage blends, which maintain the house style year in and year out and which are every bit as satisfying as most vintage bottlings. Usually only three to five vintages each decade are blessed with the favorable conditions necessary for making balanced, complete, vintage-designated wines. At the top of the Champagne hierarchy, at least in price, are the prestige bottlings, or *têtes de cuvées* (such as Moët & Chandon's Dom Pérignon and Roederer's Cristal). These are vintage wines made from the best grapes, using painstaking traditional methods and extra aging, not to mention fancy packaging.

Veuve Clicquot NV Brut ★★★ $$$ ♥♥♥
Pale color. Deeply pitched apple, spice, and toast nose. Full, rich, and ripe. Given focus and shape by sound lemony acidity. Quite dry and toasty. Unusually refined, lingering aftertaste.

Pierre Gimonnet NV Blanc de Blancs ★★★ $$ ♥♥
Premier Cru Lively aromas of citrus and spiced apple. Penetrating, high-pitched chalky, lemony flavor allied with a more mature, sweeter butterscotch element. Strong acidity holds the wine's disparate components together. A dinner-table Champagne.

Nicolas Feuillatte NV Brut Premier Cru ★★ $$ ♥♥♥
Fresh, gingery aromas of apple, pear, spice, and mint. Crisp and dry in the mouth, with flavors of lemon and ginger ale. Good

43

ripeness and penetrating flavor intensity prevent this very firm wine from coming across as austere.

Philipponnat NV Brut Royale Réserve   ★★ $$ ❦❦❦

Stony, toasty nose, with apple, pear, and spice notes. Fresh and medium-bodied, with slightly high-toned, tangy pear and spice flavor. Complicated by Chablis-like notes of stone and hay. Attractively fruity, lingering finish.

Languedoc-Roussillon

A sun-drenched area in the south of France, stretching from the Rhône river delta down to the Spanish border, the Languedoc-Roussillon (lahn-guh-doc roo-see-yohn) offers more delicious red wine for under $12 than any other grape-growing zone in the world. In recent years, heavy investment in modern wine-making equipment and more extensive use of noble grape varieties like Syrah and Cabernet Sauvignon have resulted in darker, fresher, longer-lasting wines. Happily for consumers, prices have not risen as dramatically as wine quality.

Some people mistakenly consider Languedoc Syrah-based wines knockoffs of northern Rhône wines. Not so—they are highly distinctive wines in their own right. More rustic red blends based on Grenache, Carignan, Syrah, and Mourvèdre, whether from Corbières, Minervois, or more generic appellations, are usually perfect for early consumption. White wines from indigenous varieties generally lack acidity, but recent plantings of Chardonnay, Sauvignon Blanc, and Viognier are producing competent wines. This part of France is also a good source of inexpensive rosés.

Most of Corbières, and parts of the Languedoc adjacent to the Mediterranean, are among France's hottest vineyard sites. But cooler hillside microclimates, as well as the more Atlantic-influenced Minervois appellation in general, typically yield less "roasted" and more aromatically complex wines.

Coteaux du Languedoc

Minervois

Rhône River Delta

Corbières

COTEAUX du LANGUEDOC

A cluster of grape-growing areas covering nearly 75 square miles, the Coteaux du Languedoc produces a host of spicy reds. The addition of Syrah and Mourvèdre to bottlings previously dominated by Carignan and Cinsault has resulted in wines that are more aromatically complex and better balanced than ever before. A handful of villages, mostly those in cooler hillside spots protected from hot winds off the Mediterranean, have been granted their own appellations.

At the Table

With their increasing emphasis on grapes with firm backbone like Syrah and Mourvèdre, these reds should be paired with hearty foods that can support their weight and tannic bite: grilled meats, robust stews, and full-flavored or mature cheeses. They are ideal with rich, slow-cooked dishes that feature root vegetables and aggressive herbs, spices, and garlic. Serve Languedoc reds alongside lamb stew with figs, garlic, and fennel; lamb-and-sausage cassoulet; rabbit with mustard; or pork loin with tamarind and orange-cranberry chutney.

The Bottom Line

This is the mother lode for assertive, concentrated red wines under $15, and the best wines costing a few dollars more generally justify their price tags.

What to Buy: Coteaux du Languedoc

1994	1995	1996	1997
B	A-	B	B

Château Lavabre 1996, Pic-Saint-Loup ★★★ $$ ♟♟
Tangy aromas of raspberry, violet, and Christmas spices. Spicy, supple, and concentrated. Thick fruit, nicely brightened by the oak. Snappy and intensely flavored. Finishes with dusty tannins.

Château La Roque 1996 Cupa Numismae, ★★★ $$ ♟♟
Pic-Saint-Loup Vibrant aromas of cassis, black cherry, violet, and smoke. This wine is dense, velvety, and mouth-filling, with

strong fruit that's brightened by firm acids. The finish is quite
suave, with palate-dusting, even tannins.

Domaine Clavel 1996 La Copa Santa, Méjanelle   ★★★ $$ ▼▼
Enticing, aromatic nose of raspberry, violet, pepper, and spice.
This is a thick and tactile wine, with deep berry flavor and a
firm, persistent finish.

Domaine de Poujol 1996, Coteaux du Languedoc   ★★★ $ ▼▼
Clean, fruity aromas of crushed berries and cherry. Thick, pliant,
and fresh in the mouth, with a restrained sweetness and strong,
ripe fruit. Generous and pliant. Dry, peppery finish.

Domaine de l'Hortus 1996 Grande Cuvée,   ★★ $$ ▼▼
Pic-Saint-Loup Deep ruby red. Wild aromas of game, bacon fat,
and smoky oak. Sweet, supple, and truffley on the palate, with
sound supporting acidity. Complex finish features a peppery
edge and a hint of woodsmoke.

Gilbert Alquier 1996, Faugères   ★★ $$ ▼▼
Raspberry, pepper, smoke, and garigue spices on the nose.
Supple, peppery red-fruit flavors have a juicy quality and spicy
fruit character that should make the wine versatile at the table.

Château Grande Cassagne 1997 Rosé,   ★★ $ ▼▼
Costières de Nîmes Red berries, cherry, and mint on the nose,
plus a faintly candied note. Round, fruity, pliant, and generous; a
nicely concentrated wine with harmonious, ripe acidity. Finishes
ripe and smooth.

Château Grande Cassagne 1997 Syrah,   ★★ $ ▼▼
Costières de Nîmes Spicy blackberry and woodsmoke aromas.
Rich, sweet, and concentrated, with velvety dark-berry flavors.
Distinct note of violet pastille. Finishes with fine tannins and
strong black-fruit flavor.

Château de Lascaux 1996, Coteaux du Languedoc   ★ $ ▼▼
Musky, gamy aroma of sandalwood, orange peel, and grilled
nuts. Slightly tart-edged and peppery; slightly dry on the finish.

Mas de Bressades 1997 Rosé, Costières de Nîmes   ★ $ ▼▼
Musky nose. Soft and round in the mouth, with good ripe fruit
but limited nuance and shape. Lacks real complexity but offers
good fruit intensity.

CORBIÈRES and MINERVOIS

Wines from Corbières and Minervois continue to undergo dramatic improvement, as the use of higher percentages of Syrah and Mourvèdre adds freshness and refinement to what were previously rather rustic wines.

At the Table

With their juicy, red-berry flavors, these wines pair beautifully with a variety of rich poultry dishes and with all but the heartiest red-meat preparations. Grenache- and Carignan-based wines, drunk young, are sufficiently brisk to cut through fairly heavy foods, especially those with modest fat; they work nicely, for example, with game pies and with sausages. As a general rule, spicy and grilled flavors match these wines well. Try grilled quail with braised apples and celery root or lamb chops with curried couscous or ratatouille.

The Bottom Line

Steady increases in wine quality have far outpaced price hikes, with the result that these wines can offer stunning value.

What to Buy: Corbières & Minervois

1994	1995	1996	1997
B	B+	B-	C+

Domaine de Fontsainte 1996, Corbières ★★★ $ ❦❦❦
Reticent aromas of raspberry, pepper, and woodsmoke. Ripe, pliant red-fruit flavor offers lovely sweetness and mouth-filling texture. Fat yet shapely. Finishes with ripe tannins.

Château d'Oupia 1995 Les Barons, Minervois ★★★ $ ❦❦
Super-ripe chocolate and game aromas. Then juicy, nicely defined currant, plum, and cherry flavors in the mouth, with complicating notes of venison and black olive. Smooth, spicy, and persistent on the finish.

Château Maris 1995 Comte Cathare Prestige, ★★ $$ ❦❦
Minervois Super-ripe, portlike aromas of chocolate, black cherry,

maple syrup, smoke, and game. Fat, lush, and peppery; very rich
and mouth-filling, with a restrained sweetness. Rather low acidity.

Domaine des Chandelles 1995, Corbières ★★ $$ ♥♥
Deep ruby red. Inky aromas of cassis, violet, pepper, and spice.
Sweet, dense, and intensely flavored; the bright violet, pepper,
and spice notes carry through to the persistent, very firm finish.
Very fresh.

Château La Baronne 1996 Montagne d'Alaric, ★★ $ ♥♥♥
Corbières Complex aromas and flavors of raspberry, sandalwood,
pepper, orange peel, and roasted coffee. Lush and smooth, but
juicy and vibrant. Tangy cherry and bitter chocolate on the finish.

Château d'Oupia 1996, Minervois ★★ $ ♥♥♥
Tangy, perfumed aromas of crushed red berries, violet, gunpowder,
and pepper. Juicy, fruity, and firm; high-pitched crushed berry
flavor is intense and penetrating. Finishes with very fine tannins.

Domaine de Villemajou 1995 Gold Label, ★★ $ ♥♥♥
Corbières Highly aromatic nose combines raspberry, smoke,
game, and spice. Supple, spicy flavors of sweet cherry and pepper; concentrated and layered. Finishes with light, fine tannins.

Etang du Moulin 1996 Reserve, Minervois ★★ $ ♥♥♥
Exotic aromas of orange peel, chocolate, black pepper, and
raisin. Strawberry and pepper flavors on the palate. A not especially complex but dense and snappy wine. Finishes firm,
peppery, and sweet.

Les Palais 1995 Cuvée Tradition, Corbières ★★ $ ♥♥♥
Super-ripe aromas of black cherry, licorice, mint, and garigue.
Fat, supple, and peppery, kept firm by juicy acidity. Fresh black-
cherry flavor leads to a tangy, satisfying finish.

Domaine Borie Maurel 1997 Syrah, Minervois ★★ $ ♥♥
Expressive aromas of raspberry, black olive, black pepper, and
garigue spices. Lush and smooth in the mouth, with harmonious
acidity. Finishes rather gentle and persistent.

Domaine de Fontsainte 1997 Gris de Gris, Corbières ★★ $ ♥♥
Perfumed, floral aromas of mandarin orange, red berries, thyme,
and mint. Dry and lively, with intense cherry and raspberry flavors
and firm acidity. An austere mineral note keeps this rosé brisk.

Domaine La Combe Blanche 1994 Tradition,   ★★ $ ♥♥
Minervois Perfumed nose combines raspberry, cherry, tar, and pepper. Juicy and fruity, with lively acidity and a suave texture. Finishes with fine, light tannins and a hint of damp earth.

VINS de PAYS
and OTHER WINES

The best of France's *vins de pays* (van duh peh-yee; VdP) are among the world's most extraordinary red-wine values; a high percentage of these country wines come from the vast Languedoc-Roussillon area. The availability of cheap land has enabled many outside investors to plant internationally favored varieties like Cabernet Sauvignon, Merlot, Chardonnay, and Sauvignon Blanc, and the better bottlings of these can be far more satisfying than inexpensive wines from most New World growing areas. But caveat emptor: There are also far too many pitifully thin *vins de pays* on the market.

At the Table
The straightforward, easy-to-drink red *vins du pays* can be as fruit driven as Beaujolais and are good choices for veal, pork, and most poultry. Stick to easygoing foods: roasted chicken with garlic mashed potatoes, grilled *merguez* sausage with couscous, or grilled-vegetable sandwiches with pesto mayonnaise. The red *vins du pays* of the Languedoc-Roussillon are perfect for picnics and go swimmingly with such fare as pizza, pasta and tomato sauce, or hamburgers.

The Bottom Line
A treasure trove of under-$10 wines.

RED WINES

Mas de Bressades 1996 Cabernet/Syrah,   ★★ $ ♥♥♥
VdP du Gard Black cherry, licorice, and an herbal nuance on the nose. Velvety, concentrated but still tightly wound. Brisk but nicely integrated acidity supports strong fruit. Good structure for aging.

Château Capendu 1997 Cabernet, VdP d'Oc　　★★ $ ❦❦
Cool aromas of black currant, strawberry, and tobacco leaf.
Supple, sweet flavors of plum, currant, and oak spice. Easygoing
and fairly rich. Finishes with dusty, smooth tannins.

Domaine de Montpezat 1996 Prestige, VdP d'Oc　　★★ $ ❦❦
Black-currant, cherry, tobacco, lead-pencil, and oak-spice
on the expressive nose. Lush but firm, with very good depth and
concentration of fruit. Fresh acidity gives sweet flavors clarity. A
blend of Cabernet and Syrah.

Domaine St-Martin de la Garrigue 1996 Bronzinelle,　★★ $ ❦❦
VdP de Coteaux de Bessilles　Cool, rather Bordeaux-like aromas
of black raspberry, red currant, chocolate, cedar, and underbrush. Expansive and supple, with bright, spicy currant flavor.
Lovely harmonious acidity and very good length.

Guilhem Durand 1996 Syrah, VdP des　　　★★ $ ❦❦
Coteaux de Lézignan　Smoky aroma of black raspberry and
leather. Supple, seamless, sweet fruit shows clear varietal notes
of leather and pepper and is supported by sound acids. Good
density and texture. Has plenty of personality.

Val d'Orbieu 1997 Château de Jau,　　　★ $ ❦❦❦
Côtes du Roussillon-Villages　Very ripe, smoky aromas of raspberry and cherry. Fruity and ripe in the mouth, with good weight
and intensity. Finishes with light tannins that will not deter
immediate consumption.

Val d'Orbieu 1997 Le Jaja de Jau Syrah/Grenache,　★ $ ❦❦❦
VdP d'Oc　Cherry and red currant on the nose. A sweet, pliant
mouthful of fruit with a slightly roasted quality. Not particularly
complex but soft on the finish.

Château de Campuget 1997 Merlot, VdP du Gard　★ $ ❦❦
Currant, cherry, and a whiff of meat on the nose. Lush and fruity
in the mouth; easygoing and harmonious. Sound varietal character. Finishes with soft tannins and lingering berry flavor.

Domaine Piquemal 1996 Merlot　　　　★ $ ❦❦
Cuvée Pierre Audonnet, VdP des Côtes Catalanes　Perfumed
raspberry and sandalwood aromas. Juicy, dry-edged raspberry
flavor is fresh and delineated. Not particularly sweet but firm,
shapely, and persistent.

WHITE WINES

Jacques & François Lurton 1997 Les Fumées ★★ $ ♥♥♥
Blanches Sauvignon Blanc, VdP d'Oc Aromas of melon, peach, lemon oil, smoke, and spice. Supple and melony, with good flavor intensity; almost Chardonnay-like in texture. Finishes with firm acidity that extends the fruit.

Val d'Orbieu 1997 Chardonnay Réserve St-Martin, ★ $ ♥♥♥
VdP d'Oc Tangy dried-fruit, apple, and spice aromas. Soft, smooth, ripe, and juicy; has a sweet melony flavor of decent intensity and good mouth feel. Brisk, firm finish.

Château de Campuget 1997 Viognier, VdP du Gard ★ $ ♥♥
Highly aromatic nose combines flowers, licorice, mint and other fresh herbs, and pineapple. Juicy and light, with nice lift on the palate. Dry, firm, and clean. Brisk on the finish.

Domaine de Coussergues 1997 Chardonnay, VdP d'Oc ★ $ ♥♥
Rather Sauvignon-like aromas of melon, ginger ale, and goose-berry. Fat and spicy, but quinine and grapefruit notes keep it fresh. Good flavor intensity and texture. Dusty, lively finish.

Domaine de Coussergues 1997 Sauvignon, VdP d'Oc ★ $ ♥♥
Ripe but brisk aromas of mint and other fresh herbs, lemon skin, and grapefruit. Smooth, ripe, intensely flavored, and satisfying; a very fresh, inexpensive Sauvignon Blanc.

Loire Valley

The popularity of Loire Valley wines was recently given a boost by the back-to-back outstanding vintages of 1995 and 1996. Even so, these aromatic, lively wines are generally more appreciated by sommeliers, who relish their vibrancy and their food-friendliness, than by the general wine-drinking population. The makers of most Loire Valley wines do not use new-oak barrels; therefore, the wines offer, first and foremost, the flavors of fresh fruit. They are typically light- to medium-bodied and are ready to drink young.

Four grape varieties, three white and one red, account for virtually all of the Loire Valley's good values. Chenin Blanc produces wines that range in style from austere, minerally, and bone-dry to very sweet, even nectarlike. At its best, Muscadet is a dry, bracing white. Sauvignon Blanc, which makes a refreshingly brisk warm-weather white, finds its greatest expression in Sancerre and Pouilly-Fumé. Cabernet Franc, the chief red grape of the region, becomes a fragrant, juicy wine in warm years but in others can be vegetal, if not downright under-ripe.

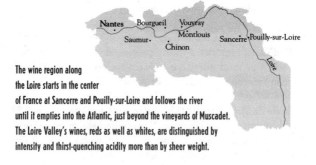

The wine region along
the Loire starts in the center
of France at Sancerre and Pouilly-sur-Loire and follows the river
until it empties into the Atlantic, just beyond the vineyards of Muscadet.
The Loire Valley's wines, reds as well as whites, are distinguished by
intensity and thirst-quenching acidity more than by sheer weight.

CHENIN BLANC

The rather unfashionable Chenin Blanc achieves greatness in the middle Loire Valley, producing ageworthy wines that range from entirely bone-dry to supersweet. Among the top examples: Vouvray and Montlouis, which, depending on the site, the weather, and the winemaker, may be dry (sec), off-dry (demi-sec), medium sweet (*moelleux*), or sweet and unctuous (doux, *liquoreux*); the steely, lemon-limey Savennières, often slightly sweet in warm years; and excellent sweet dessert wines in Coteaux du Layon.

At the Table

Crisp, minerally Savennières and Vouvray sec make refined aperitifs. Dry and off-dry Savennières complement lean fish, as well as crudités. Vouvray is even more flexible, pairing well with freshwater fish in lemon-based sauces or lobster with cream sauces. The acidity in Chenin Blanc cuts through oily fish and butter-based sauces. Try demi-sec Chenin Blanc with dishes that feature sweet spices, such as curried chicken or gingered shrimp. Moderately sweet Chenin is often paired with foie gras, while *moelleux* is a natural companion to fresh fruit and fruit desserts.

The Bottom Line

Dry and off-dry Vouvrays are good value at $15 to $18. The sweet wines of the Loire cost $20 to $30 in good years, but limited special bottlings from the greatest vintages seem to be priced according to rarity more than quality.

What to Buy: Dry Chenin Blanc

1994	1995	1996	1997
B-	A	A+	B+

What to Buy: Sweet Chenin Blanc

1994	1995	1996	1997
C-	A-	B+	A-

Domaine des Baumard 1996 Clos du Papillon,　★★★$$ ♈♈♈
Savennières Pale color. Truffle, lemon-lime, and game aromas. Explosively fruity in the mouth, with floral and honey flavors given superb clarity by limey acidity. Very ripe but thoroughly dry on the powerful, bracing aftertaste.

Pierre-Yves Tijou 1996 Clos des Perrières,　★★★$$ ♈♈♈
Savennières Pale color. Subdued nose hints at chalk and lime. Surprisingly juicy and ripe; intense flavors of minerals, lemon, lime, and toast. Rich, bright, very long, but quite unevolved today.

Champalou 1996, Vouvray　★★★$$ ♈♈
Green-tinged pale color. Steely, citric, and floral aromas. Perfumed flavors of apple and white flowers; slightly sweet and gentle, but succulent ripe acidity keeps the wine firm. Finishes very long and minerally, with a hint of fennel.

Domaine Foreau 1996 Sec, Vouvray　★★★$$ ♈♈
Bright, clean aromas of lime skin, minerals, and beeswax. Brisk lemon, lime, and chalk flavors currently disguise the wine's ripeness and richness. Finishes sleek and long, with notes of lime oil and white flowers.

Domaine de la Motte 1996,　★★★$ ♈♈
Coteaux du Layon-Rochefort Aromas of honey, toffee, and pear eau-de-vie. Moderately sweet, intense flavors of toffee apple and honeysuckle, plus floral and earth notes. Finishes quite strong, with notes of crème brûlée and white plum. Lovely dessert wine.

Bourillon-Dorléans 1997 Demi-Sec La Bourdonnerie, ★★ $$ ♟♟
Vouvray Floral peach and honeysuckle on the nose. All fruit in the mouth: juicy, minty peach flavor is moderately sweet but given lift and clarity by firm acidity. The wine finishes fairly long and slightly hard.

Domaine du Closel 1997 Clos du Papillon, ★★ $$ ♟♟
Savennières Low-toned nose of smoke, earth, resin, and hay. A fat and large-scaled wine, with exotic apricot and white-plum flavors along with a floral nuance. The bottlings are showing more sheer texture than intensity at this point; best right now on the long finish.

MUSCADET

Muscadet is a dry, bracing, low-alcohol white wine made around the city of Nantes, where the Loire River empties into the Atlantic Ocean. The best examples offer fresh lemon-lime tones and a saline, minerally scent of the sea. The words *sur lie* on the label signify a wine that was aged on its lees (see Glossary, page 221), a technique that adds complexity and preserves freshness.

At the Table
Muscadet makes a refreshing aperitif. It is also a classic partner for raw shellfish, especially clams and oysters: Its citric and mineral notes complement the tangy, briny taste of most bivalves. Try Muscadet with simply sautéed flounder finished with a splash of lemon or lime juice, lightly poached oysters or clams with Pernod and lemon, or seviche with cilantro and citrus vinaigrette. Examples that are slightly *pétillant*, or spritzy (see Glossary, page 222), are perfect with herb omelets.

The Bottom Line
At $8 to $12, the best Muscadets offer very good value.

What to Buy: Muscadet

1995	1996	1997
A	A+	B+

Louis Métaireau 1996 One ★★★ $$ ▼▼▼

Musky, gingery, mineral-infused nose. Intensely flavored and creamy, but lovely acidity provides the lime and mineral flavors with excellent definition. Quite dry, yet it is also rich. The finish is both ripe and very long. This wine merits its premium price.

Clos de la Senaigerie 1996 ★★★ $$ ▼▼

Musky, complex aromas of quinine, lime, minerals, and earth. Very bright lemon and lime flavors show excellent clarity, thanks to strong but ripe acidity. Firm, long, and precise on the aftertaste. Essence of Muscadet.

Domaine de la Borne 1996 ★★ $ ▼▼▼

Reticent aromas of lemon ice and minerals. Full, concentrated, and intensely flavored; a richer-styled Muscadet with more size than most. But shows slight alcohol on the finish. Needs to be served with food.

Château La Morinière 1996 ★★ $ ▼▼

Vibrant, precise lime-skin and mint aromas, along with a note of orange pith. Silky and ripe, with the orange-pith flavor repeating. The wine offers good texture and density and harmonious acidity.

Clos des Briords 1997 Cuvée Vieilles Vignes ★★ $ ▼▼

Ripe aromas of peach skin and orange peel. Very rich but very dry, with an almost chewy texture and a strong saline, minerally quality. Thick and ripe for Muscadet, but with good supporting acidity. Slightly earthy, long finish.

SAUVIGNON BLANC

The best Loire Valley Sauvignon Blancs are characterized by aromas and flavors of fresh herbs, citrus fruits, gooseberries, and minerals, as well as by vibrant acidity. In years that produce less-ripe grapes, the wines can be overtly vegetal (an asparagus aroma, for instance, is not uncommon), making them rough going for drinkers accustomed to lusher, fruitier wines like New World Chardonnays. Sancerre and Pouilly-Fumé, from villages that face each other across the Loire River, provide the finest and most concentrated examples of Sauvignon. Although good Loire Valley Sauvignon Blancs are capable of aging, they are generally best consumed when their youthful fruit and snap can be appreciated, within three years after the vintage.

At the Table

Loire Valley Sauvignon Blanc is a remarkably versatile wine alongside shellfish, river fish, and poultry, as well as with lighter dishes incorporating fresh herbs, fresh green vegetables, or citrus fruits. Their earth tones go especially well with sweet corn, and their bracing acidity provides a perfect foil to rich sauces. Other suitable mates include grilled shrimp with cilantro and lemongrass, pasta with spring greens, and even that known enemy to wine, asparagus with lemon. Sancerre and goat cheese is a classic local pairing, since both have a pungent mineral character and acidity.

The Bottom Line

Sancerre and Pouilly-Fumé don't come very cheap: Examples under $12 generally lack character. Still, relatively few of these wines exceed $20. Top growers in nearby, but lesser, appellations like Quincy frequently offer good alternatives at around $10.

What to Buy: Sauvignon Blanc

1995	1996	1997
A	A+	B

Hippolyte Reverdy 1997, Sancerre ★★★★ $$ ♟♟♟
Pungent, complex aromas of citrus oil, tarragon, ginger, and minerals. Similar flavors. Fat, rich, generous; harmonious acids keep flavors focused and firm. Very long finish of ginger and mineral dust.

Lucien Crochet 1996 La Croix du Roy, ★★★★ $$ ♟♟♟
Sancerre Subtle gooseberry, lemon, lime, and mineral aromas. Pristine, sharply etched citric and mineral flavors offer great finesse. Very clean and very long on the aftertaste, with finishing notes of licorice and grapefruit.

Lucien Crochet 1996 Le Chêne, Sancerre ★★★★ $$ ♟♟♟
Knockout nose features lime skin, orange peel, fennel, smoke, and chalk. Bursting with juicy pink-grapefruit flavor. Slow-building, very long, clinging finish of lemon, minerals, and chalk. Essence of Sancerre.

Patient Cottat 1996 Vieilles Vignes, Sancerre ★★★★ $$ ♟♟
Flamboyant aromas of truffle, dried fruits, rose petal, and lime.
Super-ripe and extremely concentrated, with juicy mandarin-
orange flavor intensified by brilliant framing acidity. Beautifully
balanced and focused. Great length.

André Neveu 1997 Les Manoirs Vieilles Vignes, ★★★ $$ ♟♟♟
Sancerre Bracing aromas of lime, spearmint, and tarragon. Rich
and supple, with good weight and texture. Sweetly citric fruit
offers good weight and texture. A rather thick, powerful style.

Célestin-Blondeau 1997 Les Rabichottes, ★★★ $$ ♟♟♟
Pouilly-Fumé Subdued but ripe aromas of lemon, sage, mint,
and Granny Smith apple. Lemony, bright, and crisp, with a com-
plicating note of Anjou pear. Very young today. Seemed to put
on flesh in the glass.

Ladoucette 1996, Pouilly-Fumé ★★★ $$ ♟♟♟
Ripe aromas of gooseberry and herbs, plus a hint of dried fruit.
Ripe and thick in the mouth; has an almost Chardonnay-like
richness but strong framing acids keep the wine in focus.

Marc Deschamps 1996 Cuvée des Porcheronnes, ★★★ $$ ♟♟♟
Pouilly-Fumé Ripe, grassy aromas of lemon drop and smoke.
Bright, crisp, and classic, with lemon and grapefruit flavors and a
suggestion of soil. The finish is ripe and long, with a bracing
touch of austerity.

Régis Minet 1996, Pouilly-Fumé ★★★ $$ ♟♟♟
Pungent aromas of chlorophyll, mint, tarragon, and grapefruit,
plus a hint of orange. Intense flavor of pink grapefruit is brisk
but not austere thanks to gentle, ripe acidity. Quite stylish.

Domaine Mardon 1997, Quincy ★★ $$ ♟♟
Fresh herbs, mint, and smoky soil tones on the nose. It's both
intensely flavored and smooth, with good texture and ripeness.
A rather stylish, supple wine, finishing with pleasant mint and
gooseberry notes.

Domaine des Corbillières 1997 Sauvignon, ★★ $ ♟♟♟
Touraine Bright, clean aromas of lime and pear. Brisk, chalky
flavors of lemon and lime. The ripe acids are in harmony with
the wine's fruit. Offers good texture and density and a very
supple finish.

Domaine des Huards 1997, Cheverny   ★★ $ ♛♛
Aroma of candied citrus peel. Fleshy but penetrating, with
rather complex, fresh flavors of mint, pear skin, minerals, and
fresh herbs. The aftertaste is firm and crisp for the vintage.

CABERNET FRANC

Cabernet Franc, generally blended with other red varieties in
Bordeaux and elsewhere, makes a good fruity wine on its own in
the Loire Valley. Cabernet Francs from the Loire typically display
aromas and flavors of bitter cherry, raspberry, and blackberry;
they can show a silky texture in warm years, but a markedly leafy,
herbaceous quality in less successful vintages. Chinon (shee-
nohn), Bourgueil (boor-guh'y), and Saumur-Champigny (saw-
muhr shahm-pee-n'yee) are the most famous appellations.

At the Table

With its intensity of flavor, firm acidity, and generally
lighter tannins, Loire Valley Cabernet Franc is ideal with
dishes that oaky, alcoholic, or harsh reds would overwhelm. It complements roast chicken or Cornish hen,
pork or poultry pâtés, and light meats, and its acidic bite
enables it to cut through rich foods like duck confit and
cold lamb salad. The sweet/bitter interplay of fruit flavors
in the wine also works well with dishes that feature complex flavor combinations, such as quail with figs and bitter greens or duck with cardamom. In multicourse
meals, Cabernet Franc provides an excellent lead-in to
richer, more powerful wines.

The Bottom Line

Chinon and Bourgueil are generally priced in the $15 to $25
range, and they offer reasonable value in the riper years. St-
Nicolas-de-Bourgueil is often a few dollars cheaper.

What to Buy: Cabernet Franc

1995	1996	1997
A-	A	B+

Pierre Bréton 1996, Bourgueil ★★★ $$ ❦❦
Very ripe, sappy aromas of raspberry and licorice. Rich and spicy in the mouth; rather full-bodied for Loire Valley Cabernet Franc thanks to very ripe acidity. Expansive, generous red-fruit flavors carry through to the finish.

Domaine de la Chanteleuserie 1996 Cuvée Alouettes, ★★★ $$ ❦❦
Bourgueil Sappy bitter-cherry, blackberry, licorice, and pepper aromas. Thick but bright, with intense raspberry and blackberry flavors. Finishes long and brisk, with fairly light tannins.

Joël Taluau 1996 Vieilles Vignes, ★★★ $$ ❦❦
St-Nicolas de Bourgueil Deep ruby-red color. Black-raspberry, bitter-chocolate, and gunflint aromas. Concentrated and quite dense, with deep flavors of cherry liqueur and Valrhona chocolate. Finishes very long, with chewy tannins buried by fruit.

Jean Gambier 1996, Bourgueil ★★★ $ ❦❦❦
Super-ripe aromas of bing cherry and spice. Spicy cherry, red-currant, and tart red-berry flavors in the mouth. Ripe and stylish, thanks to harmonious acidity. Finishes long, with fine tannins. Has a pliant texture like Burgundy.

Pierre Gauthier 1996 Les Caillots, Bourgueil ★★★ $ ❦❦
Black cherry, blackberry, and a note of smoked bacon on the nose. Dense and supple, with deep rich berry and licorice flavors. Finishes with a hint of leather and subtle length. Should age well.

Olek-Mery 1996 Cuvée des Tireaux, Chinon ★★ $$ ❦❦❦
Dark ruby red. Bitter cherry, cranberry, and cocoa-powder aromas. Cherry and licorice fruit is currently tightly wrapped and a bit tough, but this rather tannic, dry-edged wine has the concentration and acidity to reward aging.

Pierre Bréton 1996 Clos Sénéchal, Bourgueil ★★ $$ ❦❦❦
Dark ruby red. Reticent, floral aromas of licorice and cherry. Tightly wrapped and intense, with tart, sharply defined berry flavors of cranberry, red currant, and pomegranate. Finishes long and fresh, with firm tannins.

Couly-Dutheil 1997 Les Gravières, Chinon ★★ $$ ❦❦
Aromas of blackberry, smoke, licorice, and animal fur. Juicy, pungent red-berry, spice, and licorice flavors. A very young wine with a strong backbone and a firm finish.

Domaine de Bel Air 1997 La Fosse aux Prêtres,   ★★$ ❢❢
Chinon Perfumed aromas of black cherry and tar. Supple, ripe, and accessible; not especially complex but sappy and delineated, with a sweet cherry flavor and brisk but ripe acidity.

Philippe Delesvaux 1997, Anjou   ★★$ ❢❢
Highly aromatic raspberry and sandalwood nose. A real fruit bomb in the mouth, with sappy, rich, spicy red-fruit and pepper flavors and good density. Finishes with dusty, ripe tannins and very good length.

Provence

Provence's dry, sunny climate produces rich, spicy red wines and crisp, sophisticated rosés. The whites of Provence, however, too often lack freshness. If the wines of this region have one common theme, it is the influence of garigue, the wild, pungently spicy brush that dots rocks and hillsides along France's Mediterranean coast. Typical garigue notes include thyme, rosemary, basil, sage, lavender, wild mint, and fennel.

Except for the Mourvèdre-based wines of Bandol, Provençal wines have traditionally been based on classic southern French grape varieties like Grenache, Carignan, and Cinsault. But many interesting newer wines feature sizable percentages of Syrah and Cabernet Sauvignon.

This sun-drenched region features a surprising range of microclimates, depending on the elevation of vineyards and their proximity to the sea or the cooling influence of mountains. Provence has historically been a hotbed of organic viticulture thanks to its extremely dry climate, which minimizes the risk of fungal diseases of the vine.

Les Baux-
de-Provence

Marseilles

Bandol

BANDOL

This small appellation on the seacoast southeast of Marseilles makes Mediterranean France's most serious and ageworthy red wines. In vintages blessed by abundant heat and sunshine, the late-ripening Mourvèdre grape delivers deep color; complex, smoky/meaty aromas of black fruits, licorice, and leather; and a firm tannin and acid backbone. In cooler years, however, Bandols can be astringent and hard.

At the Table

Bandols should be served with richly flavored or highly seasoned dishes that can stand up to their earthy and gamy flavors and their tannic bite: Think grilled food, game, and garlic. Try a youngish Bandol with lamb daube, rabbit stew with prunes, or roast pork loin with sage and onions, or with virtually any barbecued meat. The serious tannins of Bandols are buffered by the richness of duck confit.

The Bottom Line

Considering the fact that most ageworthy wines command a premium, Bandol at $20 to $30 is fairly priced.

What to Buy: Bandol

1994	1995	1996	1997
B-	B+	B	B+

Château de Pibarnon 1995   ★★★★$$ ♟♟
Spicy aromas of red berries, tree bark, and pepper. Supple and generously flavored; notes of cherry and cinnamon apple. Easygoing and immediate, finishing with ripe tannins and good length.

Château Pradeaux 1993   ★★★★$$ ♟♟
Roasted aromas of stewed tomato and cinnamon. Dense, smooth, and rich, but quite powerful and tough today, with flavors of earth, smoke, and tobacco. Strong tannins coat the teeth. Needs bottle aging.

La Bastide Blanche 1995   ★★★$$ ♟♟
Wild aromas of mocha, iron, leather, and brown spices. Large-framed, sweet, and young. Lush and fat, but has the structure to age. Finishes with pepper and iron notes.

Domaine la Suffrène 1996 Cuvée Les Lauves   ★★$$ ♟
Aromatic, complex nose combines cherry, tree bark, and mint. Juicy, penetrating, and youthful; rather reserved and somewhat dry today but shows good ripeness and backbone.

OTHER RED WINES

After Bandol, the best Provençal reds generally come from cooler microclimates, where fruit ripens slowly and evenly. In windswept Les Baux-de-Provence, for example, the harvest frequently does not begin until the first of October. Many of the best wines feature a high percentage of Cabernet Sauvignon and/or Syrah.

At the Table

These red wines tend to be more directly fruity than Bandol, with gentler tannins but sound acidity. Serve them with hearty poultry dishes such as braised chicken thighs with garlic and olives, as well as with light red-meat preparations or mixed grills. Their garigue character nicely echoes the herbal notes in such dishes as sautéed chicken with fennel or lamb ragout with rosemary.

The Bottom Line

Prices are generally in the $12 to $20 range, and the better wines offer very good value.

What to Buy: Other Red Wines

1994	1995	1996	1997
B	B+	B	B

Domaine de Trévallon 1995, VdP des Bouches- ★★★ $$$ 🍷🍷
du-Rhône Deep ruby red. Aromas of black-raspberry preserves, dark chocolate, black pepper, and game. Dense and highly concentrated, but already shows lovely inner-mouth perfume. Dark-berry flavor explodes on the tannic finish.

Commanderie de Peyrassol 1993 Cuvée ★★ $$ 🍷🍷
Marie-Estelle, Côtes de Provence Aromas of black cherry, chocolate, roast chestnut, and fresh herbs. Supple, pliant berry and pepper flavors offer subtle intensity. Finishes with dusty, fine tannins.

Domaine Richeaume 1995 Cabernet Sauvignon, ★★ $$ 🍷🍷
Côtes de Provence Currant, smoky oak, and menthol aromas. Fresh and concentrated; vibrant crushed-currant taste. Generous, smooth, with good underlying acid and tannin structure.

Mas de Gourgonnier 1996, Les Baux-de-Provence   ★★ $$ ❦❦
Super-ripe aromas of cherry, plum, and smoke. Supple and ripe
in the mouth, with a flavor of dried cherry and a jammy quality.
Fruity yet thoroughly dry.

Domaine Sorin 1996 Cuvée Privée, Côtes de Provence ★★ $ ❦❦
Cassis, blackberry, violet, and oak-spice aromas. Supple, juicy, fruit-
driven flavors of cassis, black cherry, and mint. Intensely flavored
and lively, with sound acidity. Youthfully exuberant; firmly tannic.

Château Calisse 1997, Coteaux Varois   ★★ $ ❦
Raspberry, game, and leather on the nose. Supple and fruity, with
black-cherry and berry flavors and a slight green edge. Gently
styled, nicely balanced, with modest complexity and persistence.

ROSÉ WINES

Provence's crisp, dry rosés, with their delicate red-fruit and soil
notes, are the finest, most grown-up blush wines in the world.
Though rosés are usually drunk within a year following their
release, those from Bandol benefit from a couple years of aging.

At the Table

Provençal rosés make refreshing aperitifs, especially dur-
ing the warm months. The wines are also extremely flex-
ible at the table. They are de rigueur with bouillabaisse
in the restaurants of the region and are crisp enough to
cleanse the palate of just about any garlicky, salty, or oily
fish preparation. Rosés are also excellent with grilled
poultry, as well as with pasta or light meat dishes fla-
vored with garlic or fresh herbs. These fruity, penetrating
wines have the intensity to bridge the gap between
lighter dishes early in a meal and richer main courses.
Perfect pairings include: warm mussel salad with toma-
toes, grilled eggplant with black-olive stuffing, and
grilled chicken with ratatouille.

The Bottom Line

Seldom cheap (generally in the $12 to $20 range), but the best
merit their price premium over other rosés.

Château Calisse 1997, Coteaux Varois   ★★★ $ ❦❦

Reticent aromas of strawberry, thyme, and lavender. Fresh, brisk, and supple, with intense raspberry and watermelon flavors. At once strongly fruity and delicate. Finishes brisk and flowery.

Château Pradeaux 1997, Bandol   ★★ $$ ❦❦

Deep strawberry, smoke, earth, and iced-tea aromas. Big, rich, ripe, and dry; plenty of texture. Rather earthy flavors and a slight dry edge make it better suited to drink with a meal than as an aperitif.

Domaine Richeaume 1997, Côtes de Provence   ★★ $$ ❦❦

Pale color. Delicate aromas of apple and mandarin orange. Juicy and dry, with sound acids and very good flavor intensity. Very refreshing rosé, with a note of strawberry on the finish.

Château Revelette 1997, Coteaux d'Aix-en-Provence ★★ $ ❦❦

Fruity cherry, raspberry, strawberry, mint, and earth aromas. Bright and very dry on the palate, with attractive, delicate red-fruit flavors. Firm, lingering finish.

Commanderie de Peyrassol 1997 Cuvée Eperon d'Or, ★★ $ ❦❦
Côtes de Provence Lively aromas of orange pith, lemon, minerals, and red berries. Intensely flavored, supple, and dry in the mouth, with the orange note repeating. Clean, precise, and fresh.

Château Routas 1997 Rouvière, Coteaux Varois   ★ $ ❦❦

Orange-red color. Red fruit and mint on the nose. Quite dry and brisk, with cherry and mint flavors and good texture. Finishes with a note of cherry and a suggestion of alcohol.

Rhône Valley

Stretching from just south of Burgundy all the way to Provence, the Rhône Valley includes two very different winegrowing areas. In the north, steep vineyards yield some of the world's greatest ageworthy reds from the Syrah grape. This area is also the true home of the now-fashionable Viognier grape, a white variety that shows to best advantage in the exotically scented wine called Condrieu. The Mediterranean-influenced southern Rhône produces flamboyantly aromatic, lushly fruity wines from a blend of grapes dominated by Grenache.

The Rhône Valley is really two distinctly different regions. Syrah rules in the north, home to Côte-Rôtie, Hermitage, and Cornas. Châteauneuf-du-Pape and Côtes-du-Rhône come from the south, where most wines are blends of three or more warm-climate grapes.

NORTHERN RHONE RED WINES

The greatest Syrah wines of the northern Rhône, Côte-Rôtie and Hermitage, are the model for many other Syrahs. Côte-Rôtie is the more perfumed, in part because many contain a small percentage of Viognier. The best Côte-Rôties have floral, spicy aromas of raspberry, violet, black pepper, and smoked meat; a velvety texture; and spicy fruit. Hermitage, usually made entirely from Syrah, is one of the longest-lived wines anywhere. Top Hermitages offer blackcurrant, meat, licorice, and spice aromas and a tannic backbone. The more rustic Syrah called Cornas has dark-berry, black-olive, and leather aromas and a solid tannic spine. St-Joseph is a lighter, generally faster-maturing Syrah with the scented character of Côte-Rôtie, while Crozes-Hermitage is like a junior version of Hermitage.

At the Table

Serve robust Hermitage with full-flavored dishes like rare steak, venison, and saddle of hare. The more peppery, equally tannic Cornas is a perfect accompaniment to hearty stews and daubes. Côte-Rôtie, with its sweet, gamy perfume, matches beautifully with game birds. The typically lighter wines from St-Joseph and Crozes-Hermitage are good with pork, duck, lamb, and beef, as well as with recipes including wild mushrooms. Northern Rhône Syrahs are also frequently served with hard or semihard cheeses like cheddar, Morbier, and Manchego.

The Bottom Line

Production of Côte-Rôtie and Hermitage is extremely limited, and strong worldwide demand has pushed prices to the $30 to $60 range. But wines from the top producers offer at least as much individuality as most Bordeaux and Burgundies at similar prices. The best examples of St-Joseph and Crozes-Hermitage are considerably cheaper and provide the additional advantage of earlier drinkability.

What to Buy: Northern Rhône Red Wines

1994	1995	1996	1997
B	A-	B-	B+

Jean-Louis Chave 1996, Hermitage ★★★★ $$$$🍷🍷
Pungent aromas of dark berries, licorice, smoked meat, and spices. Supple but vibrant dark-berry and mineral flavors, with lovely sweetness in the middle. Tannins are firm but not tough. Deceptively accessible, but built to age.

Chapoutier 1995 La Sizeranne, Hermitage ★★★ $$$$🍷🍷🍷
Pungent aromas of smoke, game, black currant, and caramel. Supple and medium-bodied, with bright framing acidity. Notes of mint and licorice. A polite, fruity style of Hermitage.

Jaboulet 1996 La Chapelle, Hermitage ★★★ $$$$🍷🍷
Dark ruby to the rim. Sweet, pungent aromas of blackberry, black cherry, cassis, mint, vanilla, toasty oak, and licorice. High-pitched and very intensely flavored, with lively acidity. Very long finish features fine tannins.

Guigal 1995 Brune & Blonde, Côte-Rôtie ★★★ $$$🍷🍷🍷
Spicy raspberry, violet, and smoky oak on the nose. Plump and thoroughly ripe, with lovely depth of flavor and a rather gentle structure. Not a powerhouse but deep and harmonious. Lingering, ripely tannic finish.

Albert Belle 1996, Hermitage ★★★ $$$🍷🍷
Very dark ruby. Cool yet ripe aromas of black raspberry, licorice, coffee, and chocolate. Vibrant, spicy, cassis-flavored fruit, complicated by a gamy nuance. Very fresh and firmly tannic; built to age.

Bernard Levet 1995, Côte-Rôtie ★★★ $$$🍷🍷
Smoky, raspberry-scented nose. Sweet and lush but rather

unevolved—not yet showing its deep fruit. Finishes with substantial chewy tannins. Will reward a couple more years in the cellar.

Cave de St-Désirat 1995 Cuvée des Meriniers, ★★★ $$$ ♥♥
St-Joseph Roasted cherry, black pepper, and a musky, floral component on the nose. Supple and lush, with an almost Côte-Rôtie-like weight and sweetness. Long pepper-and-raspberry finish.

Gilles Barge 1996 Côte Brune, Côte-Rôtie ★★★ $$$ ♥♥
Reticent, brooding aromas of black fruit, spice, and licorice. Sappy and concentrated, with intense dark-berry and spice flavors. Sound acidity and strong structure give this firmly tannic wine very good grip.

Jean-Luc & Jean-Paul Jamet 1996, Côte-Rôtie ★★★ $$$ ♥♥
Black raspberry, black cherry, licorice, and smoke on the nose, plus a faint gamy quality. Firm but sweet, with a pliant texture and lively dark berry flavors. Solidly tannic but not tough.

Michel Ogier 1996, Côte-Rôtie ★★★ $$$ ♥♥
Vibrant, expressive aromas of cassis, red currant, licorice, and smoked meat. Lively and stylish, with dark berry flavors. Finishes with rather fine tannins and notes of licorice and pepper.

Auguste Clape 1996, Cornas ★★★ $$ ♥♥
Aromas of blackberry, black cherry, violet, and licorice. Densely packed, with a creamy texture but very firm acidity. Rather stylish for Cornas. Finishes with strong but fine tannins.

Jaboulet 1996, Cornas ★★ $$$ ♥♥♥
Fresh, high-pitched aromas of black olives, dark berries, and licorice, with a seductive floral aspect. Bright, sharply defined black-fruit flavors. Quite youthful today. Tart-edged, fruity finish.

Domaine de Rochevine 1995, St-Joseph ★★ $$ ♥♥♥
Perfumed aromas of raspberry, violet, bacon fat, and sandalwood, rather like Côte-Rotie. Sweet, fruity and peppery in the mouth; not quite as rich as the nose suggests. But finishes with good length and ripe tannins.

Jaboulet 1996 Domaine de Thalabert, ★★ $$ ♥♥♥
Crozes-Hermitage Black cherry, tar, and shoe-polish aromas, plus a whiff of stewed tomato. Fairly dense and ripe; good backbone. Hint of licorice; finishes firm, with a note of espresso.

Albert Belle 1996 Cuvée Louis Belle, ★★ $$ ♥♥
Crozes-Hermitage Dark berries, smoke, and animal fur on the nose. Intensely flavored, rich, and fat, with a deep, plummy ripeness and a silky texture. Finishes with substantial tannins.

Michel Ferraton 1995 La Matinière, ★★ $$ ♥♥
Crozes-Hermitage Smoky aromas of raw meat, coffee, and leather. Peppery and bright; good flavor intensity and firm-edged acids. Harmonious combination of soil and dark-berry flavors.

Yves Cuilleron 1996 L'Amarybelle, St-Joseph ★★ $$ ♥♥
Enticing aromas of black raspberry, cherry, licorice, and spice, plus a vague animal nuance. Very good intensity and concentration; on the lean side, but has penetrating flavor.

Alain Graillot 1996, Crozes-Hermitage ★★ $$ ♥
Cassis, black cherry, licorice, and roast coffee on the nose. Sweetly spicy and supple, with modest fat and gentle fruit. Slightly dry on the finish. Finishes with a faintly resiny quality.

Ready, Set, Drink: Northern Rhône Red Wines

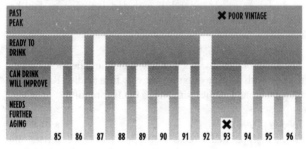

CONDRIEU
A Noteworthy Northern Rhône White Wine

The greatest manifestation of Viognier is an utterly distinctive drink from the tiny appellation of Condrieu. Unfortunately, inconsistency is one of the hallmarks of this wine. Often bottlings are thin, extremely alcoholic, or lacking in acidity. But the best show stunningly perfumed aromas of spring flowers, honeysuckle, peach, and citrus fruits, and they manage to maintain a sense of delicacy even when they possess head-spinning alcohol. To enjoy their explosive fruit, drink Viogniers within two or three years of the vintage.

At the Table

Condrieu may be shown to greatest advantage along-side dishes that allow its complexity and exotic fruit character to shine. Among the best choices are simply prepared fish, shellfish, and poultry dishes that incorporate tropical fruits. At the same time, Condrieu tends toward low acidity, which enables the wine to temper more pungent flavors, such as those found in sautéed shrimp with cumin and pineapple salsa, scallop or lobster and saffron risotto, or foie gras terrine with quince.

The Bottom Line

Due to extremely limited production and steadily rising demand, Condrieu is expensive, typically in the $30 to $50 range.

What to Buy: Condrieu

1995	1996	1997
B	B-	B

Christophe Pichon 1996   ★★★ $$$ ♛♛
Pungent grapefruit, fresh herb, and gooseberry aromas are rather like Sauvignon Blanc. Bracingly fresh, very youthful flavors of gooseberry and grass. Light but quite penetrating.

Guigal 1996   ★★★ $$$ ♛♛
Subtle aromas of grapefruit skin, smoke, and licorice. Round and supple, but youthfully unevolved; minerally and true to its soil. Finishes with pear and apricot notes. Ageworthy Condrieu.

Yves Cuilleron 1996 La Petite Côte   ★★★ $$$ ♛♛
Spicy, smoky aromas of peach and litchi. Rich, creamy, and smooth; flavors of spice, flowers, and ginger. Textbook Condrieu; holds its shape nicely on the fresh, clean finish.

SOUTHERN RHONE RED WINES

The star appellation in the southern Rhône is Châteauneuf-du-Pape, which produces wines ranging from soft, fruity, and uncomplicated to massive, with an alcohol content of 14 percent or even higher. Although wines of the latter style improve in the bottle for a decade or more, young Châteauneuf-du-Papes are rarely too tough to drink, thanks to their sweetness of fruit and absence of harsh tannins.

Gigondas is a similarly sturdy, spicy red with high alcohol and mouth-filling texture. The better examples can rival Châteauneuf for aromatic character and chewy texture.

Bottles that are labeled simply Côtes-du-Rhône, or Côtes-du-Rhône followed by the name of a village, are generally immediately accessible wines with peppery cherry and raspberry flavors and soft tannins. The appellation Côtes du Ventoux produces quite similar wines.

Grenache, a grape that produces robust, full-bodied wines with high alcohol and low acidity, dominates most southern Rhône Valley blends, but use of up to 12 other grape varieties is permitted. Most Châteauneuf-du-Papes, for example, consist chiefly of Grenache supplemented by small percentages of Syrah and Mourvèdre. However, the trend today at many of the southern Rhône's best estates is toward greater use of these latter two varieties, which contribute deep color, fine aromatic character, and the acids and tannins that counteract Grenache's tendency to oxidize quickly.

At the Table

The southern Rhône is close to Provence; thus its spicy, substantial reds naturally complement the herbs and spices and garlic-rich preparations native to the Mediterranean. Serve Châteauneuf-du-Pape with game or with cassoulet; you can't go wrong with dishes such as grilled saddle of lamb with garlic and Moroccan spices or duck with wild mushrooms and thyme. Lighter, less flamboyant Côtes-du-Rhônes are more appropriate alongside simpler meat dishes or grilled sausages.

The Bottom Line

The better Châteauneuf-du-Papes in the $25 to $30 range remain reasonably priced for their high quality, even if they are not the great deals they used to be. At $15 to $20, Gigondas can offer better value. The Côtes-du-Rhône category is one of France's top sources for bargain-priced (i.e., under $15) reds.

What to Buy: Southern Rhône Red Wines

1995	1996	1997
A-	C+	B

Château Mont-Redon 1996, ★★★ $$$🍷🍷🍷
Châteauneuf-du-Pape Cool, spicy cassis and blueberry nose has a perfumed quality, along with complicating spice and coffee notes. Sweet, supple, and elegantly styled, with a lovely core of spice. Subtle, fine finish. Rather gently styled.

Clos des Papes 1996, Châteauneuf-du-Pape ★★★ $$$🍷🍷🍷
Aromas of black currant, black cherry, herbs, and pepper, plus a note of earth. Rich, fat, and concentrated, but not a blockbuster. Stylish, mouth-filling, and nicely balanced. Finishes with fine tannins and a hint of chocolate.

Château La Nerthe 1995, ★★★ $$$🍷🍷
Châteauneuf-du-Pape Super-ripe raspberry, smoke, and coffee nose. Fat and dense, but wears its 14.5 percent alcohol gracefully. Classic roasted Châteauneuf character. Finishes with strong but sweet tannins and persistent raspberry and black-cherry flavor.

Château du Trignon 1995, Gigondas ★★★ $$🍷🍷🍷
Roasted aromas of plum and soy sauce; extremely ripe though not quite raisiny. Lush, layered, and very rich, but the lively acidity and a peppery quality keep it fresh. Finishes clean, firm, and long.

Domaine du Cayron 1995, Gigondas ★★★ $$🍷🍷🍷
Pepper, smoke, and beefsteak tomato on the exotic nose. Very intense, pungent fruit offers superb sweetness and texture. Really tangy and fresh for a wine so ripe. Long, ripely tannic finish. From an excellent vintage, and it shows.

Guigal 1995, Châteauneuf-du-Pape ★★★ $$🍷🍷🍷
Spicy aromas of game, pepper, tar, and tree bark. Expansive and ripe in the mouth, with deep flavors of woodsmoke and pepper. Serious rather than simply ripe and sweet. Firmly structured.

Lucien Barrot 1995, Châteauneuf-du-Pape ★★★ $$🍷🍷🍷
Flamboyantly ripe nose of roasted red berries and pepper. Urgent flavors of plum, pepper, smoke, leather, and Cuban cigar tobacco. Lovely sweetness in the mouth. Finishes long and peppery.

Domaine Saint-Benoit 1996 Cuvée de Grande Garde, ★★★ $$ ♥♥
Châteauneuf-du-Pape Youthful aromas of red currant, raspberry, and woodsmoke. Fresh and unevolved; a serious, faintly gamy wine with very good peppery length and even tannins.

Château Fortia 1996, Châteauneuf-du-Pape ★★ $$ ♥♥♥
Expressive aromas of raspberry, cassis, game, leather, and smoke. Offers an enticing gamy flavor and noteworthy inner-mouth complexity. Rather low acidity and gentle tannins give this wine considerable early appeal.

Clos du Caillou 1996, Châteauneuf-du-Pape ★★ $$ ♥♥♥
Slightly high-toned aromas of cherry, mint, and other herbs, with a floral nuance. Sweet and youthful, with very good flavor intensity and focus. Firm, persistent finish features smooth tannins.

Domaine de la Vieille Julienne 1996, ★★ $$ ♥♥♥
Châteauneuf-du-Pape Black-cherry, mineral, and menthol aromas; hint of nutty oak. Fresh, ripe, and fairly intense cassis and blackberry flavors. Complicated by mineral note. Firm, sweet finish.

Guigal 1995, Gigondas ★★ $$ ♥♥♥
Reticent, slightly roasted aromas of plum, cherry, earth, and pepper. Fresh and peppery in the mouth; sound acidity gives the fruit a juicy quality. Not especially dense but rather stylish for Gigondas.

Vieux Télégraphe 1996, Châteauneuf-du-Pape ★★ $$ ♥♥♥
Reticent nose hints at gunflint, smoke, and licorice. Sweet and supple in the mouth, with good ripeness and an impression of rather low acidity. The fruit lingers before the ripe tannins kick in. Finishing flavors of violet and licorice.

Clos du Mont-Olivet 1996, Châteauneuf-du-Pape ★★ $$ ♥♥
Cassis, raspberry, game, black pepper, and animal fur on the complex nose. Firm but expressive in the mouth. Rather low in acidity and thus lacking a bit of thrust, but quite persistent.

Château Mont-Redon 1997, Côtes-du-Rhône ★★ $ ♥♥♥
Tangy, slightly candied aromas of cherry, red berries, and gingerbread. Sweet, supple, and seamless in the mouth, with flavors of strawberry, smoke, cranberry, and earth. Creamy and firm.

Domaine Gramenon 1996 Le Gramenon, ★★ $ ♥♥♥
Côtes-du-Rhône Pungent aromas of red berries and cracked

pepper. Juicy, intensely flavored and very fresh, with vibrant acidity giving the wine a penetrating, food-friendly quality.

Domaine Saint-Luc 1996, Coteaux du Tricastin ★★ $ ♥♥♥
Smoke, black-cherry, and garigue aromas, plus a whiff of hot stones. Supple and dense, but firm acidity keeps the super-ripe black-cherry flavors bright. Finishes with a note of exotic fruit and ripe, substantial tannins.

Domaine le Sang des Cailloux 1996, ★★ $ ♥♥♥
Côtes-du-Rhône
Impressive red-ruby color. Super-ripe aromas of blackberry, black raspberry, eucalyptus, tar, and pepper. Dense, spicy, herbal; urgent fruit framed by fresh acidity. Tangy, persistent, and food-friendly.

Domaine de la Solitude 1997, Côtes-du-Rhône ★★ $ ♥♥♥
Exotic aromas of dried red berries, smoke, and pepper; just short of over-ripe. Lush, sweet, and harmonious, with a suave, velvety texture and almost raisiny ripeness. Sound acidity extends the finish.

Château Valcombe 1997 Signature, Côtes du Ventoux ★★ $ ♥♥
Smoky aromas of cherry, tar, and pepper. Smooth and fruity in the mouth, with a flavor of raspberry. Finishes with a kick of candied raspberry and boysenberry jam.

Domaine de l'Ameillaud 1996 Cairanne, ★★ $ ♥♥
Côtes-du-Rhône-Villages
Deep red ruby. Sappy aromas of plum, cherry, and pepper. Supple, juicy, and fresh, with intense berry and cherry flavors. Crisp acidity gives the wine good structure. Finishes with slightly dry tannins.

Domaine d'Andézon 1996, Vieilles Vignes, ★★ $ ♥♥
Côtes-du-Rhône
Deep color. High-pitched aromas of raspberry, violet, and bacon fat. Concentrated raspberry flavor has an urgent quality thanks to penetrating acidity. Firmly structured, with slightly drying tannins

Domaine Grand Veneur 1995 Vieilles Vignes, ★★ $ ♥♥
Côtes-du-Rhône-Villages
Spicy raspberry and licorice nose. Rich, tangy red-fruit flavor in the mouth; smooth, spicy, and faintly herbal. Finishes sweet and very persistent, with ripe tannins.

ITALY

ITALY'S MOST SOUGHT-AFTER WINES—ESPECIALLY Barolo, Barbaresco, and Brunello di Montalcino—carry high price tags. But Italy, the world's largest producer and exporter of wine, is also one of the richest sources of distinctive wines at modest prices. A revolution in vineyard management and wine-making technique has swept the country over the past 20 years, and today's Italian wines have greater international appeal than ever before.

Grapes & Styles

Most of Italy's world-class wines are hearty, full-flavored reds, such as those made from Nebbiolo (Barolo and Barbaresco) and Sangiovese (Chianti and Brunello di Montalcino). Italy also produces a host of lighter reds ideal for immediate consumption as well as a full range of whites, including sweet and sparkling wines.

On the Label

Although some of Italy's bottles are labeled by grape variety (Pinot Grigio, for example), many of the country's most famous wines bear the name of their place of origin and may consist of either one variety of grape or a blend. And there are a panoply of varieties—French, German, and indigenous. In light of the bewildering array of wine styles and local specialties, it isn't surprising that wine consumers abroad keep reaching for a few familiar bottles like Chianti, Soave, Orvieto, and Valpolicella. But these wines barely hint at the riches Italy has to offer today.

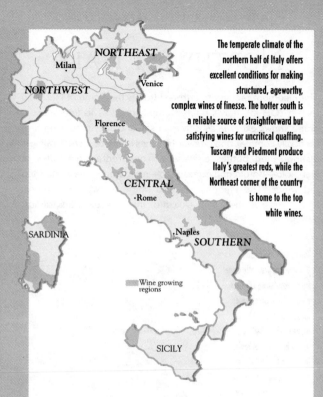

The temperate climate of the northern half of Italy offers excellent conditions for making structured, ageworthy, complex wines of finesse. The hotter south is a reliable source of straightforward but satisfying wines for uncritical quaffing. Tuscany and Piedmont produce Italy's greatest reds, while the Northeast corner of the country is home to the top white wines.

Though Italy has **Denominazione di Origine Controllata** (DOC), or controlled denomination of origin, laws similar to France's AOC rules (see page 8), the rigidity of the Italian system, established in the 1960s, frequently stifled experimentation. During the 1970s and 1980s, many of Italy's most progressive producers rejected the DOC and started making proprietary wines that were labeled only **vino da tavola** (VdT), or table wine. Ironically, these include some of the country's finest bottlings, often commanding prices higher than their regions' officially designated wines. Recent changes in labeling law have made a more specific designation, **Indicazione Geografica Tipica** (IGT), available to many of these producers in an attempt to bring them into the DOC system.

NORTHWEST ITALY

The Piedmont region of northwest Italy is the home of Nebbiolo (neb-b'YOH-lo), Italy's noblest grape variety. This late-ripening grape shows extreme sensitivity to soil and site, producing aromatically complex and ageworthy wines in the best spots but less distinguished bottles elsewhere. The greatest examples of Nebbiolo—Barolo and Barbaresco—rank among the world's top red wines. The Piedmont is also home to two considerably lighter reds, Barbera and Dolcetto, that can be drunk almost immediately.

The finest Barolos and Barbarescos generally come from south-facing hill sites around Alba. Other wines made from the Nebbiolo grape (such as Gattinara) grown in subalpine regions farther to the north typically offer less density and aromatic complexity.

BAROLO and BARBARESCO

The exceptional Barolo and Barbaresco wines are both made in the vineyards around Alba, which is also Italy's white-truffle capital. Barbaresco is marginally less powerful but is often more elegant than Barolo; still, the similarities between the two wines generally outweigh the differences.

Nebbiolo grown in the areas around Barolo and Barbaresco (the two wine zones take their names from villages within them) produces bottlings with strong acidity and a firm tannic spine. Until the 1980s, Barolo tended to be an austere, macho wine whose fierce tannins made it virtually unapproachable in the first decade of its life. But the recent trend has been toward wines with riper tannins and fresher fruit (typically cherry, raspberry, and strawberry complicated by notes of dried flowers and violet). These smoother new-wave wines are still powerful, full-bodied, and capable of a decade or two of development in the bottle.

At the Table

Barolo and Barbaresco make classic matches for roast meats and game, especially venison. The smoke and earth qualities of the wines are complemented by dishes that incorporate or suggest these elements; truffle-infused dishes pair nicely with Barolo and Barbaresco, as do porcini mushrooms. Try these wines also with Parmigiano-Reggiano and Fontina, or cheeses with a pronounced earthiness, like Fontina Val d'Aosta or Toma di Carmagnola from the Piedmont. Although the new-wave wines are intensely flavored and fairly large-scaled, they are also highly nuanced and delicately perfumed, so rich or strongly seasoned foods can overwhelm them.

The Bottom Line

Quantities of the best Barolos and Barbarescos are extremely limited, and strong worldwide demand has sent prices soaring. Even basic bottlings typically cost $30 or more, while vineyard-designated releases are often $40 to $60, if not higher. (Note that the 1995 Barolos and the 1996 Barbarescos can't legally be released until January 1, 1999.)

What to Buy: Barolo & Barbaresco

1990	1991	1992	1993
A	B	C-	B
1994	1995	1996	1997
C+	A-	A	A

Producers and Their Wines

ALDO CONTERNO   ★★★★ $$$$ ❦❦

Marvelous Barolos that provide an uncanny combination of *terroir* character and rich, dense, inviting fruit. From an enlightened traditionalist who avoids heavy tannins and believes that the aromas of new French barrels would overwhelm the delicate Nebbiolo perfume. **LOOK FOR:** Barolo Bussia Soprana, Barolo Vigna Colonnello, and Barolo Vigna Cicala.

CANTINA VIETTI ★★★★ $$$$ ⟁⟁
Robust wines that have impressive density, accurate site speci-
ficity, and powerful tannic structure, as well as superb aging
potential. The producer can be described as an open-minded
traditionalist who does not hesitate to take advantage of modern
techniques. **LOOK FOR:** Barbaresco Masseria, Barolo Brunate,
Lazzarito, and Rocche.

DOMENICO CLERICO ★★★★ $$$–$$$$ ⟁⟁
Harmonious, ripe, intensely fruity Barolos with the fruit to support their substantial tannins. Aged in a high percentage of new
oak, these wines offer early appeal, but they also capable of aging
gracefully in the bottle. **LOOK FOR:** Barolo Ciabot Mentin
Ginestra and Pajana.

Ready, Set, Drink: Barolo & Barbaresco

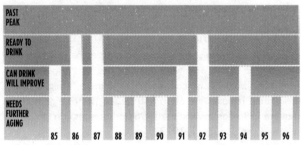

MAURO MASCARELLO ★★★ $$$$ ⟁⟁
Very rich, traditionally made Barolos that frequently show an
almost exotic floral perfume on release but require long aging to
resolve their tannins. The immensely rich and stylish
Monprivato is consistently outstanding. **LOOK FOR:** Barolo Santo
Stefano, Bricco, and Monprivato.

CERETTO ★★★ $$$–$$$$ ⟁⟁
A wide array of modern-style Barolos and Barbarescos that offer
early accessibility and medium-term ageability. **LOOK FOR:** Barolo
Prapò and Brunate; Barbaresco Bricco Asili; and Barbaresco Asij
for value.

PAOLO SCAVINO ★★★ $$$–$$$$ ⟁⟁
Rich, often oaky wines with tangy black-cherry, dark-berry, and
spice flavors and superb generosity of flavor. Another modern-
style producer whose gentle extraction of tannins results in
wines with considerable early appeal. **LOOK FOR:** Barolo Bric del
Fiasc, Cannubi, and Rocche.

PRUNOTTO   ★★★ $$$–$$$$♥♥

Elegant, supple Barolos with good depth and backbone. Under new ownership, the winery's bottlings have been decidedly fresher and sweeter and considerably more consistent since the late 1980s. **LOOK FOR:** Barbaresco Montestefano, Barolo Bussia, and Barolo Cannubi.

RENATO RATTI   ★★★ $$$–$$$$♥♥

Silky Barolos with red-fruit, smoke, and earth aromas that call to mind red Burgundy. The wines are approachable early but are good agers as well. Renato Ratti created the modern style of Barolo back in the 1960s. **LOOK FOR:** Barolo Marcenasco and Marcenasco Rocche.

ALBINO ROCCA   ★★★ $$$♥♥

Supple, lush, fruit-driven wines that frequently show an ineffable violet perfume, from a rising star in Barbaresco. The Barbaresco called Bric Ronchi is made entirely in small French *barriques* (see Glossary page 219). **LOOK FOR:** Barbaresco Vigneto Bric Ronchi and Vigneto Loreto.

CARRETTA   ★★★ $$–$$$♥♥

Medium-bodied, slightly austere wines of finesse; less dense than some, but the aromas are clean and complex, and the tannins are a bit gentler since the early 1990s. Good value. **LOOK FOR:** Barolo Cannubi.

ADDITIONAL TOP-NOTCH POSSIBILITIES

Elio Altare, Brovia, Michele Chiarlo, Cigliuti, Giacomo Conterno, Conterno-Fantino, Corino, Angelo Gaja, Bruno Giacosa, Manzone, Marcarini, Bartolo Mascarello, Moccagatta, Parusso, Giuseppe Rinaldi, Luciano Sandrone, Seghesio, Roberto Voerzio

OTHER NEBBIOLO WINES

Most Barolo and Barbaresco producers also make a lighter, earlier-bottled version of Nebbiolo. These wines are labeled simply Nebbiolo d'Alba, and they offer much of this variety's complexity and character in a more accessible and far less expensive package. In addition, the Piedmont region produces several other Nebbiolo wines, including Gattinara, from north of Alba (where the variety goes by the name Spanna). These wines show Nebbiolo's earthy perfume, but they rarely compete with Barolo and Barbaresco either for sound acidity or for sheer palate impact.

At the Table

Lighter-weight Nebbiolos go with pheasant, duck, and grilled chicken, as well as with meat-based pasta sauces. As these wines are generally less complex than Barolos and Barbarescos, they are good alongside grilled or assertively seasoned dishes. Or try a lighter-styled Nebbiolo with mushroom risotto; the earth notes marry perfectly with the forest-floor scents of the mushrooms, while the fresh, sweet fruit of the young wine harmonizes with the Parmesan and butter. Some additional recommendations: roast squab with chestnuts, grilled polenta with wild mushrooms and thyme, or red-wine risotto. Young Nebbiolos also pair nicely with sharp, aged cheeses.

The Bottom Line

At prices generally in the $15 to $30 range, the best of these Nebbiolo bottlings offer considerable complexity and character for the money.

What to Buy: Other Nebbiolo Wines

1994	1995	1996	1997
C+	A-	A-	A

Prunotto 1996 Occhetti, Nebbiolo d'Alba ★★★ $$ ♟♟
Very fresh, fruit-driven aromas of red cherry, rose petal, and licorice. Velvety and sweet, with bracing acidity augmenting the wine's flavor intensity. A fruit bomb of a Nebbiolo, finishing with dusty tannins and excellent grip.

Bruno Giacosa 1996 Valmaggiore, Nebbiolo d'Alba ★★ $$ ♟♟
Cherry, plum, raspberry, and smoky oak aromas. Rich, concentrated, and vibrant, with an almost Barolo-like structure. Firmly tannic and long, but rather tough today; needs some bottle aging.

Nervi 1991 Gattinara ★★ $$ ♟♟
Perfumed aromas of raspberry, plum, almond, and tobacco. Supple and rather lush in the mouth despite its firm acid backbone. Not especially complex, but, thanks to its smooth tannins, less gritty than most Gattinaras.

DOLCETTO and BARBERA

The Piedmont's lighter-bodied and immediately accessible reds, Dolcetto and Barbera, are the wines the locals drink every day, reserving Barolo and Barbaresco for special occasions. Dolcetto is easygoing, supple, and intensely fruity, while Barbera is leaner and more penetrating, relying almost entirely on its acidity, rather than its tannins, for structure.

At the Table

Dolcetto is an excellent first red wine of the meal, served with a pasta course or with an antipasto of cured meats. In the Piedmont, the wine is commonly served alongside fritto misto (fried vegetables, meat, cheese, and even fruit). Lightly chilled, Dolcetto is also an ideal companion for simply prepared dishes such as roast chicken. Thanks to its tart acidity and bracing flavors of bitter cherry and cranberry, Barbera is a perfect palate-cleanser with rich foods, especially fatty meats and the funkier flavors of game and organ meats. Barbera is also well suited to pizza, pasta in tomato-based sauces, and beef cooked in red-wine sauce. Strong-smelling, aged cheeses such as Gorgonzola are another possible match.

The Bottom Line

The better examples of Dolcetto and Barbera, generally $14 to $18, are very good value.

What to Buy: Dolcetto & Barbera

1994	1995	1996	1997
C+	A-	A	A

Albino Rocca 1997 Vignalunga, Dolcetto d'Alba ★★★ $$ ♥♥
Vivid, youthful aromas of black cherry, cassis, violet, and licorice. Rich and very concentrated, with fat, strong fruit enlivened by sound acidity. Larger-than-life Dolcetto.

Prunotto 1995 Pian Romualdo, Barbera d'Alba ★★★ $$ ♥♥
Inviting aromas of cherry, violet, and oak spice. Rich, lush, and

harmonious, with more than enough deep fruit to buffer the wine's firm acidity. Impressively structured for Barbera. Finishes with chewy, ripe tannins.

Icardi 1996 Surì di Mù, Barbera d'Alba   ★★ $$♥♥♥
Cherry and cinnamon spice on the nose. Juicy bitter-cherry flavor complicated by a meaty nuance. Impressive middle-palate texture for young Barbera. Strongly spicy aftertaste.

Albino Rocca 1996 Gepin, Barbera d'Alba   ★★ $$♥♥
Vibrant cassis and berry nose. Classic high-acid, tightly wound Barbera; very young but shows good underlying sweetness. Intensely flavored but on the lean side. Brisk and very firm finish.

Clerico 1997 Dolcetto d'Alba   ★★ $$♥♥
Subtle aromas of tart black cherry, blackberry, and rose petal. Big, rich, and concentrated, with juicy acidity giving the wine good flavor definition and a layered texture.

Francesco Boschis 1997 Pianezzo,   ★★ $$♥♥
Dolcetto di Dogliani Exotic aromas of strawberry, peach, and white flowers. More classic flavors of black fruits and violet, with the floral character adding complexity. Penetrating and long on the palate. Should make a particularly flexible food wine.

Carretta 1997 Dolcetto d'Alba   ★★ $♥♥♥
Perfumed nose of berries, violet, licorice, smoke, and caraway seed. Slightly dry-edged but fruity, with solid underlying structure and good balance. Finishes brisk, with a flavor of raspberry.

Prunotto 1997 Fiulot, Barbera d'Asti   ★★ $♥♥♥
Roasted cherry and licorice on the nose. Fresh and fruity, with rather modest acidity for Barbera. Not especially fleshy or nuanced, but offers good flavor intensity. Light tannins.

WHITE WINES of
NORTHWEST ITALY

The area's most serious white is Gavi, a crisp, very dry wine made from the Cortese grape. The Arneis grape yields a perfumed, softer wine for early consumption. Muscat is responsible for the low-alcohol Asti, the popular, sweet sparkling wine of the Piedmont, as well as for a host of other light, grapey Moscatos.

At the Table

The dry white wines of the northwest, Gavi and Arneis, are commonly served with raw vegetables or other antipasti; they pair well with hearty but straightforward fare like pea-and-fava-bean soup or onion foccacia. As these wines are usually meant to be consumed soon after their release, they should be poured with foods that complement their crisp, clean, fresh flavors. Try them with asparagus or figs wrapped with prosciutto or braised chicken with cinnamon and cloves. Muscat-based wines make refreshing aperitifs but are equally satisfying with sweet preparations, especially those incorporating fruit like apricots or peaches.

The Bottom Line

White wines from northwest Italy are generally reasonably priced but rarely offer compelling value.

Broglia 1997 La Meirana, Gavi di Gavi   ★★★ $$ ▼▼▼

Fresh herbs and apple on the nose. Rich to the point of thick in the mouth; offers uncanny density and fat for Gavi. Ripe flavor of pear. Finishes very long, with expressive sweet fruit.

Ca' dei Frati 1996 I Frati, Lugana   ★★ $$ ▼▼▼

Aromas of lemon custard and hazelnut. Fresh, ripe lemon and mineral flavors are given good structural underpinning and cut by strong ripe acids. Shows a distinctly stony quality. The acidity keeps the finish dry and brisk.

Icardi 1997 Moscato d'Asti   ★★ $$ ▼▼▼

Perfumed peach and honeysuckle nose. Sweet, frothy, and vibrant in the mouth; has the sappy thickness of apricot nectar. Explosively fruity, with just enough balancing acidity to maintain its freshness. Very long, sweet-but-firm aftertaste.

La Scolca 1996 Gavi   ★★ $$ ▼▼▼

Stony, bracing aromas of grapefruit and lemon skin, white flowers, and almond. Dense, concentrated grapefruit-flavored fruit is kept quite brisk by a strong spine of acidity. This is a Gavi with unusual flavor intensity.

Bruno Giacosa 1997 Roero Arneis ★★ $$ ♉♉

Pear, peach, and almond aromas border on tropical. Fat and rich in the mouth, with sweet peach and nut flavors and a blossomy pear scent. Just enough finishing dryness to give it grip.

Bera 1997 Moscato d'Asti ★★ $ ♉♉♉

Reticent aromas of peach and honey. Then explosively sweet and full in the mouth, with a super-ripe flavor of apple. Atypically large-scaled for Moscato. Slightly sugary but persistent on the finish.

Icardi 1997 Cortese L'Aurora ★★ $ ♉♉♉

Ripe, nutty aromas of peach, orange, and honeysuckle. Fat, silky, and harmonious in the mouth, with soft acidity and considerable richness. A note of pear skin keeps the finish firm.

NORTHEAST ITALY

The temperate northeast part of Italy, which includes the regions of Friuli-Venezia Giulia, Veneto, and Trentino-Alto Adige, provides ideal conditions for making fresh, fruity white wines. In recent years, numerous vintners have taken steps to make wines with more texture, richness, and flavor intensity than the bottlings of the region have ever had in the past.

In Friuli, the stars are primarily white wines like Pinot Bianco (Pinot Blanc), Pinot Grigio (Pinot Gris), and Tocai Friulano. Lately, increasingly interesting and flavorful Merlots and Cabernets have been coming from this area. The best white wines from Trentino-Alto Adige can rival Friuli's for flavor intensity and accurate varietal character. The region also produces some interesting indigenous reds, including Teroldego.

The Veneto's Soave, as its name suggests, is a softer style of white wine. Valpolicella is one of the Veneto's most important reds. Look for the word Classico on the label (as in Soave Classico or Valpolicella Classico): This indicates that the wines come from their area's best hillside vineyards. The Veneto is also the home of recioto wines, sweet reds and whites made using grapes that have been dried to concentrate their sugar content. Amarone (ah-mah-ROE-neh) is a dry red version of this style, with all of its sugar fermented to alcohol, resulting in a wine with head-spinning alcoholic content.

Northeast Italy's moderate climate enables numerous white and red grape varieties to ripen slowly and develop superb flavor intensity. The hillier eastern side of Friuli provides excellent soils and microclimates for making what are considered the most important white wines of Italy.

At the Table

The subtly flavorful whites of northeast Italy are refreshing on their own before a meal, but they are also perfect with simply prepared fish or shellfish. In the restaurants of Venice, these wines are paired with the delicate sea creatures native to the Adriatic, which might be swallowed up by a big, oaky Chardonnay, for instance. The generally sound acidity of the northeastern wines even allows them to stand up to vinaigrette-dressed salads. Some more specific matches: soft-shelled crabs with lemon, mussels in white wine, pasta or risotto primavera. The region's reds go well with meat antipasti, such as salami and prosciutto, and with veal or lamb dishes, especially those served at room temperature.

The Bottom Line

The northeast is the source of Italy's most intensely flavored and refined white wines, but prices for these gems can be high. Still, there are sound values to be found in the $12 to $20 range. Only the most concentrated of the region's red wines offer true value.

What to Buy: Wines from the Northeast

1995	1996	1997
B	B	B+

WHITE WINES

Scubla 1997 Tocai Friulano,   ★★★ **$$** ♆♆♆
Colli Orientali del Friuli Nuanced, pure aromas of melon, flowers, mint and other fresh herbs, and smoke. Fresh, rich, and melony in the mouth, with sharply delineated, very ripe flavors and solid underlying structure. Slightly tart-edged, youthful finish.

La Cadalora 1997 Vallagarina Chardonnay,   ★★★ **$$** ♆♆
Trento Thoroughly ripe aromas of pineapple, grapefruit, and melon. Rich, layered, and ripe; tangy acidity gives the fruit a three-dimensional texture. Really explodes on the rich finish.

Renato Keber 1996 Pinot Bianco, Collio   ★★★ **$$** ♆♆
Nuanced aromas of tangerine, orange blossom, and acacia honey. Ripe and chewy in the mouth; strong acidity gives the wine terrific lift. Long, dry, tangerine-flavored finish.

Puiatti 1997 Pinot Grigio, Collio   ★★ **$$** ♆♆♆
Aromatic nose of grapefruit skin, pear blossom, peach, and lemon thyme. Rich, dense, fat, and mouth-filling; mature flavors make this thoroughly ripe wine perfect for immediate consumption.

Pojer & Sandri 1996 Chardonnay, Trentino   ★★ **$$** ♆♆
Aroma of white grapefruit. Firm, spicy, citric, and pure in the mouth; subdued but penetrating fruit carries through to a lively, youthful finish. A far cry from oaky California Chardonnay.

Pojer & Sandri 1996 Nosiola, Trentino   ★★ **$$** ♆♆
Lemon, fresh-herb, and licorice aromas. Intensely flavored and dominated by grapefruit; a pithy bitterness is mitigated by sneaky, ripe finishing flavor. Like a citric soft drink without the sugar.

Anselmi 1997 Soave San Vincenzo, Veneto   ★★ **$** ♆♆♆
Nuanced nose hints at spices, lemon, fresh herbs, and banana. Fat, sweet fruit is tactile and mouth-filling; a lemony flavor contributes freshness. Impressively long for a wine of this price.

Az. Agr. Forchi 1997 Villa del Borgo Chardonnay,   ★★ **$** ♆♆♆
Friuli Orange and tangerine aroma complicated by a fresh herbal note. Brisk, juicy flavors of lemon and mint. No shortage of intensity. Finishes firm and persistent. A lot of Chardonnay for $7!

Cavalchina 1997 Bianco di Custoza   ★★ **$** ♆♆♆
Very pale color. Dusty aromas of lime, mint, talc, and fresh

herbs. Strong acidity gives the floral, lemony fruit a juicy crispness and very good intensity. Lime-skin and quinine notes leave the finish particularly refreshing.

Prà 1997 Soave Classico Superiore, Veneto ★★ $♥♥♥

Vibrant aromas of grapefruit, lemon, peach, mint, and licorice. Spicy, bright, and quite dry, with exotic peachy fruit complemented by a minerally nuance. Some lingering CO_2 adds freshness. Dry, persistent, spicy aftertaste.

Tiefenbrunner 1997 Pinot Grigio, Alto Adige ★★ $♥♥♥

Laid-back aromas of pear, herbs, and spices, plus a positive earthy character. Sweet and round, showing good weight in the mouth. Sound supporting acidity gives shape to the floral, fruity flavors.

Zemmer 1997 Chardonnay, Alto Adige ★★ $♥♥♥

Subdued aromas of pepper, talc, and grapefruit. Spicy, juicy, and floral, with ripe peach and melon flavor firmed by pepper and mineral notes. Finish is slightly tart, but with very good thrust.

Castel San Valentino 1997 Pinot Grigio, Alto Adige ★★ $♥♥

Vibrant, musky aromas of lemon, flowers, ginger, and minerals. Fat and dense but quite dry, with flavors of ginger, pear skin, and quince. Offers a chewy texture and a clinging aftertaste.

RED WINES

Acinum 1993 Amarone Classico Superiore, ★★★ $$$♥♥♥
Veneto   Saturated red ruby. Exotic fruits, citrus skin, clove, and a hint of prune on the nose. Velvety yet vibrant, with moderately sweet, intense flavor of dried apricot. Harmonious acidity enlivens the strong finishing flavors.

Masi 1994 Amarone della Valpolicella, Veneto ★★★ $$$♥♥♥

Pure aromas of cherry, rose petal, violet, spearmint, and espresso. Fat, thick, seamless, and dry. Fresh flavors avoid the cooked quality of so much Amarone. Finishes very long and firmly tannic, with a late burst of maraschino cherry.

Santi 1993 Amarone della Valpolicella, Veneto ★★★ $$$♥♥♥

Intriguing nose combines cherry, bitter almond, violet, and a mineral tang. Super-ripe but not raisiny; really stuffed with cherry and mineral flavor. Shows very firm structure and noteworthy freshness. Long, sweet, powerful finish.

Zenato 1991 Amarone, Veneto ★★★ $$$ ❢❢
Enticing aromas of dried berries, raspberry, smoke, and vanilla. Very sweet, thick and fruity, with a note of chocolate; firm acids keep the flavors fresh. Concentrated and powerful.

Zeni 1996 Teroldego Rotaliano, Trentino ★★★ $$ ❢❢❢
Perfumed, highly aromatic nose of crushed blackberry, violet, and meat. Lush, smooth, and peppery in the mouth, with insinuating spice and cooked-strawberry flavor. Lively acids carry the fruit.

Allegrini 1995 La Grola, Veneto ★★★ $$ ❢❢
Spicy-cherry and damp-earth aromas. Dense and sweet, with terrific intensity and depth of berry and plum flavor. Seamless and complex. Finishes firm and very long. Strong juice.

Foradori 1997 Teroldego Rotaliano, Trentino ★★★ $$ ❢❢
Knockout aromas of crystallized berries, violet, smoked meat, and cinnamon. Smoky and velvety; violet-tinged dark-berry flavors offer density and thrust. Tannins are firm yet suave.

Mazzi 1996 Valpolicella Classico Superiore, Veneto ★★ $$ ❢❢❢
Complex nose combines strawberry, raspberry, earth, and cracked black pepper. Spicy and sappy in the mouth, with pepper and underbrush flavors. Finishes slightly dry and firm, with a flavor of singed red fruits.

Masi 1996 Valpolicella Classico Superiore, Veneto ★★ $$ ❢❢❢
Bitter cherry, strawberry, and cinnamon on the nose. Round, fruity, and generous, with tangy red-fruit flavors complicated by floral and earthy nuances. Slightly dry-edged but ripe finish. Attractive wine, and terrific value.

Zenato 1995 Valpolicella Classico Superiore, Veneto ★★ $ ❢❢❢
Plum, cherry, spice, and curry powder aromas. Sweet and fruity, with a hint of vanilla; a strong spine of acidity clarifies and extends the flavors through to the firm, lingering finish.

CENTRAL ITALY

This is red-wine country. Tuscany, the best-known wine region within central Italy, sets the pace for other areas with its ever-finer Chiantis. Some whites, notably Orvieto and Verdicchio, add to the luster of the area.

Tuscany's rolling hills and summer sunshine provide ideal conditions for the Sangiovese grape, the basis of the region's best reds. The Marches, Umbria, and Latium are known for white wines such as Verdicchio, Orvieto, and Frascati, respectively.

Tuscany

If Piedmont resembles Burgundy, with its small estates producing limited quantities of wine from favored hillside vineyards, then Tuscany is more like Bordeaux. Here castles and villas have achieved the grandeur of Bordeaux châteaux. The late-ripening Sangiovese (san-joh-VAY-zeh) grape, the most widely planted variety in Italy, is the foundation for Chianti, as well as for nearly all of the other best Tuscan reds.

CHIANTI

Italy's single most important wine area, Chianti is the heart of Tuscany. Today's Chiantis are fresher and more concentrated than ever before, thanks to stricter regulations on permitted vineyard yields and sharp reductions in the percentage of white grapes that must be included in the blend.

Sangiovese is the backbone of Chianti, although it has traditionally been blended with at least three other grapes, including small percentages of Canaiolo and the white grapes Trebbiano and Malvasia. The better wines are dry but flavorful, with tart, spicy cherry and plum fruit; nuances of tar, dried flowers, and woodsmoke; and a firm spine of tannin and acidity. Chianti can be enjoyed young for its fresh fruit but can also age admirably in the bottle for a decade or more. Chiantis labeled *Riserva* have received longer aging in barrel and typically come from the estate's best grapes in the strongest vintages.

The Chianti Classico area is the center of the Chianti zone and, following a revival that began in the late 1970s, Italy's most reliable source of high-quality wine. New legislation now allows Chianti Classico to be made from 100 percent Sangiovese. Chianti Rùfina, east of Florence, produces a less dense but equally fine version of Chianti. Less frequently seen in the U.S. are Chianti Colli Fiorentini, Chianti Colli Senesi, and Chianti Colli Aretini, named after the hills surrounding Florence, Siena, and Arezzo.

At the Table

Chianti's sweetness and richness of fruit are well suited to rich meats, especially beef. Chianti also is good with mixed grills, hamburgers, and pastas with tomato sauce. In the restaurants of Tuscany, Chianti is frequently paired with osso buco, *bistecca alla fiorentina*, *bollito misto*, and stuffed peppers, as well as with dry cheeses like Parmigiano-Reggiano, Pecorino, and aged goat cheese. Some other recommended selections: roasted quail with tarragon, lamb-and-artichoke stew, or roasted chicken stuffed with sweet sausage.

The Bottom Line

On release, most basic Chiantis fall between $6 and $7, with Classicos normally $10 to $15. The best are good value. Riserva bottlings start at $15; those $40 or more are often overpriced.

What to Buy: Chianti

1990	1991	1992	1993
A+	B-	C-	B+
1994	1995	1996	1997
B-	A	B-	A

Rocca di Castagnoli 1995   ★★★ $$$ ▼▼▼
Chianti Classico Riserva Poggio a Frati High-toned aromas of black currant, plum, and leather. Dense and lush, but strong

framing acids give the fruit a penetrating quality. Offers lovely sweetness and depth of flavor. Tannins are dusty but even.

Antinori 1995 Chianti Classico ★★★ $$ ♥♥♥
Villa Antinori Riserva Refined aromas of red currant, tobacco, and dried flowers. Dense, silky, and very concentrated; red-fruit flavors are strong and focused. Finishes with terrific persistence and very fine tannins. A wine of impressive finesse.

Badia a Coltibuono 1996 Chianti Classico ★★★ $$ ♥♥♥
Cool aromas of red berry, violet, tar, and spicy oak. Fat with fruit; rich black-cherry flavor is framed and intensified by fresh acidity. Has the sheer fruit to support its substantial ripe tannins.

Castello di Volpaia 1994 ★★★ $$ ♥♥♥
Chianti Classico Riserva Showing perfumed aromas of black raspberry, dried flowers, game, and gingerbread. This Chianti is round, supple, and deep, with smoky cherry and currant flavors and a generous texture. The dusty tannins are in perfect harmony with the wine's fruit.

Felsina 1995 Chianti Classico Riserva ★★★ $$ ♥♥♥
High-toned aromas of violet, dried flowers, and spearmint. Ripe, juicy red-berry flavors are given clarity by sound acids. Intriguing peppery note. Quite long on the aftertaste, with firm but very smooth tannins.

Casaloste 1995 Chianti Classico ★★★ $$ ♥♥
Spicy aromas of red currant, cinnamon, and tobacco leaf. Lush, rich, and very ripe, with deep, generous flavors of red currant and tobacco. Subtle oak contributes to this organically made wine's appeal. Very ripe tannins.

Dievole 1995 Chianti Classico Novecento ★★★ $$ ♥♥
Roasted aromas of dark berries, violet, and meat, plus an exotic oak-spice component. Creamy-rich and inviting; bitter-cherry flavor is complicated by grilled nuts and vanilla bean. Finishes with tongue-dusting but ripe tannins.

Fattoria del Piazzano 1995 Chianti Riserva ★★★ $$ ♥♥
Super-ripe aromas of strawberry, cherry, dried currant, and earth. Lush, generous, and pliant, with compelling, sappy sweetness supported by sound tannic structure. No rough edges. The flavors really saturate the palate.

Antinori 1995 Chianti Classico Pèppoli ★★ **$$** ♟♟♟
Complex nose of bitter cherry, iodine, tobacco, and loam. Peppery
but smooth on the palate. Good concentration, restrained sweet-
ness, and firm framing acidity. Classic Chianti with character.

Fontodi 1996 Chianti Classico ★★ **$$** ♟♟♟
Deep red-ruby color. Expressive nose combines black cherry,
leather, tar, dark chocolate, and pepper. Supple, slightly floral
cherry and berry flavors are at once sweet and penetrating.
Finishes with good length and ripe tannins.

Frescobaldi 1995 Chianti Rùfina ★★ **$$** ♟♟♟
Nipozzano Riserva Super-ripe aromas of plum, cherry, and cur-
rant. Big, rich, and expansive on the palate, but with tangy berry
flavors and a firm acid spine. Finishes with ripe tannins and
notes of cherry and red berries.

Nozzole 1994 Chianti Classico Riserva ★★ **$$** ♟♟♟
Red-fruit aromas of cherry, raspberry, cranberry, and plum. Lush,
round, and seamless; rather developed plummy flavor offers sneaky
intensity. Finishes ripe and satisfying. Rather elegantly styled.

Ruffino 1995 Chianti Classico Riserva Ducale ★★ **$$** ♟♟♟
Aromatic red-currant, tobacco, and mint nose. Sweet, round,
and pliant, with a flavor of cooked strawberry. But has enough
harmonious acidity for balance. Offers good weight in the
mouth and a smooth, ripe finish.

Colognole 1995 Chianti Rùfina ★★ **$** ♟♟♟
Smoky red-berry, cassis, and leather aromas. Round and easy-
going, with noteworthy depth of flavor. Rather fat and sweet for
Rùfina; balanced for early drinking. Finishes with a refreshing
berry skin character and good length.

Poliziano 1997 Chianti Colli Senesi ★★ **$** ♟♟♟
Cherry, smoke, and tar nose. Juicy, bright flavors of pomegranate,
cherry, and spice. Youthfully firm but tangy and enticing. Finishes
with firm acids and tannins and sweet, lingering red-fruit flavors.

Tenuta le Calcinaie 1997 Chianti Colle Senesi ★★ **$** ♟♟
Vibrant cherry, raspberry, sandalwood, and meat aromas. Juicy,
brisk, and intense in the mouth; urgent berry flavor has a strong
spiciness. Not particularly fleshy but very attractive. Finishes
with more acidity than tannins.

OTHER WINES BASED on SANGIOVESE

Brunello di Montalcino, considered one of Italy's greatest reds, comes from vineyards around the town of Montalcino, south of Siena. This wine offers a concentrated, full-bodied, slow-aging version of Sangiovese. Vino Nobile di Montepulciano is a San-giovese wine closer in weight to Chianti than to Brunello. Rosso di Montalcino and Rosso di Montepulciano are lighter, earlier-bottled versions of wine from these two areas. Carmignano, a small zone west of Florence, broke off from Chianti in the 1970s due to the desire of its producers to blend some Cabernet Sauvignon with their Sangiovese. Carmignano is typically a rounder, richer wine than Chianti, with slightly lower acidity.

At the Table

Brunello is usually fuller than Chianti, with less acid bite and more substantial tannins. It is thus well-suited to rich and strong-flavored red-meat preparations. Uncomplicated meat dishes will enable these wines to show their complexity. Brunello also goes well with aged but not pungent cheeses. Carmignano can be paired with the same kinds of dishes as Chianti, but its some-what richer texture goes especially well with the cuts of beef that have the most internal fat, such as hanger steak, or with the most assertively flavored cuts, like beef shank and oxtail. Serve Rosso di Montalcino and Rosso di Montepulciano with game birds or lighter beef dishes.

The Bottom Line

Brunello di Montalcino is Tuscany's most expensive wine, and only the finest examples from the best vintages justify their high prices (look for the very good 1993s). Tariffs generally begin at $25 to $30 and can easily reach $50 or more. Vino Nobile di Montepulciano is less expensive than Brunello, though rarely compelling. But Rosso di Montalcino and, occasionally, Rosso di Montepulciano can provide quite a mouthful for $15 to $25. Carmignano tends to be undervalued at around $18 for basic wines and up to $30 for Riserva bottlings.

What to Buy: Other Wines Based on Sangiovese

1992	1993	1994	1995	1996	1997
C-	B+	B-	A	B	A

Caprili 1993 Brunello di Montalcino ★★★ $$$$ ♥♥
Snappy aromas of black raspberry, cherry, cola, and minerals. Lush, dense, and intensely flavored, but extremely young today and dominated by its very firm structure. Very long, classy aftertaste.

Pertimali 1995 Brunello di Montalcino ★★★ $$$$ ♥♥
Perfumed cherry-berry and licorice nose, plus a whiff of leather. Sweet, ripe, and stylish; the cherry-berry flavors are complemented by a lively minerality and sound acids. Ripe tannins harmonize nicely with the wine's fruit.

Argiano 1993 Brunello di Montalcino ★★★ $$$ ♥♥♥
Sweet aromas of plum, cedar, vanilla, and earth, plus a faint roasted quality. Concentrated, sweet flavors of cherry, plum, and red currant, plus exotic suggestions of clove and orange peel.

Avignonesi 1995 Vino Nobile di Montepulciano ★★★ $$$ ♥♥♥
Aromas of cherry, red currant, and roasted plum. Dense and full, with woodsmoke and plum flavors and a strong spine. At once seamless and powerfully built. Long, ripely tannic aftertaste.

Nottola 1995 Vino Nobile di Montepulciano ★★★ $$ ♥♥♥
Cherry, red currant, and almond on the nose. Big, rich, and ripe; packs a major wallop of fruit over a sound structural underpinning. Finishes quite long, with substantial chewy but ripe tannins.

Dei 1995 Vino Nobile di Montepulciano ★★★ $$ ♥♥
Nose combines black cherry, black raspberry, and minerals. Juicy, pure, and penetrating, with excellent intensity and compelling inner-mouth floral perfume. Structured, firm, and long.

Gorelli 1996 Rosso di Montalcino ★★★ $$ ♥♥
Sappy aroma of crystallized red fruits and grilled nuts. Lush and dense in the mouth; cherry and currant flavors are complicated by a vibrant mineral note. Intensely flavored and quite suave. Finishes firm, long, and a bit peppery.

Dei 1997 Rosso di Montepulciano ★★ $$ ♥♥♥
Bright, floral nose combines red currant, mint, ginger, and nut-

meg. Fat and spicy in the mouth, but ripe acidity gives this youthful wine a firm backbone. Dry and flavorful.

La Braccesca 1995 Vino Nobile di Montepulciano ★★ $$ ❢❢❢
Black-cherry and fresh-herb aromas, along with a floral top note. Dense and thick, with notes of earth, tobacco, and dried herbs. Currently rather tannic and in need of patience.

Lisini 1996 Rosso di Montalcino ★★ $$ ❢❢❢
Warm aromas of currant, plum, cherry, and leather. Round and ripe in the mouth, with harmonious acidity and very good, fleshy depth of flavor. Finishes ripely tannic, with a peppery nuance.

Ambra 1995 Carmignano ★★ $$ ❢❢
Aromas of cassis, spearmint, and oak spice. Firm, gutsy, and solidly built; cherry, licorice, mint, and roasted-coffee flavors offer good intensity but come across as slightly tough today. Firm finish.

San Fabiano Calcinaia 1995 Cerviolo, Rosso di ★★ $$ ❢❢
Toscana Raspberry and smoky, nutty oak on the nose. Dense and thick; complex, strong, almost syrupy flavors of red currant, bitter cherry, toffee, and espresso. Very firm backbone. Finishes with bitter red-berry notes.

La Costa 1995 Rosso di Toscana ★★ $ ❢❢❢
Smoky aromas of cherry, raspberry, roasted coffee, and tobacco. Cool, nicely delineated red-berry flavors are supported by bright acids and firm tannic structure. Slightly dry but flavorful finish.

Altesino 1996 Rosso di Altesino ★★ $ ❢❢
Pungent, fruit-driven aromas of spicy raspberry and cranberry. Firm acidity gives the sweet red-fruit flavor unusual brightness and cut. Finishes with firm tannins and a hint of bitter almond.

SUPER-TUSCANS

Super-Tuscan is a term frequently used for a category of bold, attention-grabbing Tuscan wines labeled *vino da tavola* (VdT), or table wine. In recent years, many of these wines have been granted the right to use the more specific designation IGT, or Indicazione Geografica Tipica (see On the Label, page 74). Super-Tuscans originally were not permitted to carry a specific appellation because they were technically made outside the system—that is, they did not meet local requirements governing permitted grape varieties, the type of vessel used to age the wines, or the length of aging time prior to release. Because of their richness and early accessibility, the best of the super-Tuscans have become extremely popular—and expensive—inside and outside Italy.

At the Table

These large-scaled, fruit-loaded wines will stand up to powerful food. Their smoky notes ask for grilled red meats or dishes that incorporate wild mushrooms. The slight sweetness that results from aging in small oak barrels also complements grilled meat, and roasts, too. Or serve super-Tuscans with rich cow's-milk cheeses like Toma di Carmagnola and Vacherin.

The Bottom Line

The prices of the most sought-after super-Tuscans often reflect their rarity rather than their quality: Many bottles now sell for $50 or more. Although there are some very good wines in the $20 to $30 range, this category is not normally a place to look for top values.

What to Buy: Super-Tuscans

1993	1994	1995	1996	1997
B+	B-	A-	B-	A

Antinori 1995 Tignanello, IGT ★★★★ $$$$ ♥♥♥
Blackberry, cassis, and cedar on the nose. Thick and very concentrated; flavors of dark berries, grilled nuts, and vanilla. Suave, sweet, and mouth-filling. Finishes with terrific grip and even, tongue-coating tannins.

Ciacci Piccolomini d'Aragona 1995 Ateo, VdT ★★★ $$$ ♥♥
Nuanced nose of currant, game, maple syrup, and gunflint. Silky and tactile in the mouth; impressively deep and intensely flavored. Seamless and long, with integrated acids and tannins.

La Quadratura del Cerchio 1995, VdT ★★★ $$ ♥♥♥
Dark berries, violet, pepper, and thyme on the nose. Lush, sweet, and very concentrated; notes of violet and pepper repeat in the mouth. Pliant, long finish. Quite stylish.

Castello di Fonterutoli 1996 Badiola Poggio, IGT   ★★ **\$\$** ♥♥
Blackberry, cocoa powder, and cappuccino on the nose. Ripe, gamy, and supple, with a hint of rose petal and good weight in the mouth. Finishes slightly dry-edged, with a note of pepper.

Piazzano 1995 Rosso dei Colli, VdT   ★★ **\$\$** ♥♥
Expressive, super-ripe aromas of red currant and sweet vanillin oak. Lush and oaky in the mouth; shows an exotic, raisiny, dried-grape character. Strong inner-mouth floral tones.

Monte Antico 1995 Rosso, VdT   ★ **\$** ♥♥♥
Slightly rustic but inviting nose combines plum, red currant, leather, and tobacco. Similar flavors in the mouth; silky, ripe, and textured. Finishes with substantial dusty tannins.

Other Central Italian Wine Regions

Like Tuscany, the rest of central Italy is best known for its red wines, but most of these are lesser versions of Sangiovese that cannot compete with the better examples from Chianti or Montalcino. Here are the wines you're most likely to encounter on retail shelves, presented by region:

Abruzzi is the home of easygoing, rather soft, red Montepulciano d'Abruzzo, typically a wine of modest concentration. White Trebbiano also comes from here.

Emilia-Romagna sends forth a flood of lightweight Sangiovese as well as white wines—often vapid and characterless—made from Trebbiano. This is also the source of Lambrusco, which is generally a fizzy, rather sweet, low-alcohol wine in a screw-top bottle.

Latium, or Lazio in Italian, produces Frascati (based on the Malvasia and Trebbiano grapes), which is a white wine that typically shows more texture than flavor.

Marches makes Verdicchio, a white that is usually reasonably priced. Only the best bottles offer real flavor intensity.

Umbria, the most important wine region in central Italy after Tuscany, is best known for Orvieto, a sometimes slightly sweet white blend with substantial palate impact. Like Verdicchio,

Orvieto is being revitalized by growers who own vineyards in the most favored spots. Umbria also features some good varietal wines, including Chardonnay.

At the Table

Crisp, clean Verdicchio, from the Marches, with its nutty undertones, matches up with cold fish and vegetable dishes, as well as with composed salads. The rather straightforward white wines of Umbria work with lighter poultry dishes and with most fish courses but may not have the oomph to stand up to the richest preparations or to fish cooked on the grill. Lush Montepulciano d'Abruzzo bottlings pair nicely with simply grilled, straightforward preparations (try them with peppery steak or grilled portobello mushrooms). The lighter Sangiovese wines from Emilia-Romagna go well with quail and chicken.

The Bottom Line

Prices are generally quite reasonable for these wines, but only the best examples in each category merit the interest of discriminating drinkers.

WHITE WINES

Palazzone 1997 Orvieto Classico Superiore, ★★ **$$** ❣❣❣
Terre Vineate, Umbria Expressive aromas of pineapple, pear, smoke, honey, and talc. Fat, dense, and large-scaled for Orvieto, with impressive palate impact. Shows the full ripeness of the year. Slight youthful harshness on the finish.

Boccadigabbia 1997 La Castelletta Pinot Grigio, ★★ **$$** ❣❣
Marches Complex aromas of lemon and grapefruit pith, spice, and almond. Rich, round, and satisfyingly mouth-filling; a flavor of super-ripe pear is perked up by a spicy note of cinnamon toast. Spicy long aftertaste.

Antinori 1997 Castello della Sala Chardonnay, ★★ **$** ❣❣❣
Umbria Ripe nose of peach, nutmeg, and coconut cream pie. Dense, ripe, and full; pineapple and peach flavors are kept firm and focused by a mineral edge and lovely tangy acids. Very good length. Superb $12 Chardonnay.

Boccadigabbia 1997 Garbì Bianco, Marches   ★★ $ ♟♟♟
Subdued, musky aromas of lime, licorice, and spice. Densely packed
but quite dry, with a subtle nut-skin flavor contributing complexity. The fruit carries well through the palate-dusting finish.

Falesco 1997 Poggio dei Gelsi Est! Est!! Est!!!   ★★ $ ♟♟♟
Lazio Floral, almond-scented nose. Sweet honey and peach fla-
vors show unusual intensity and palate presence for the category.
Texture is almost Chardonnay-like. Finishes firm and persistent.

La Carraia 1997 Orvieto Classico Poggio Calvelli,   ★★ $ ♟♟♟
Umbria Bright, expressive aromas of honeysuckle, peach, and
lemon. Sweet, round fruit boasts spicy intensity and a lemony
underpinning. Juicy, bitter-edged finish calls for food.

Sartarelli 1997 Verdicchio dei Castelli di Jesi Classico, ★★ $ ♟♟♟
Marches Aromas of apricot, vanilla, smoke, and nuts. Lush
stone-fruit flavors enlivened by pineapple and grapefruit. Fat
and ripe for Verdicchio, but finishes with a refreshing bitter edge.

RED WINES

Cataldi Madonna 1991 Toni, Abruzzi   ★★★ $$$ ♟♟
Flamboyant aromas of currant, truffle, game, cedar, and spice.
Silky and lush in the mouth, with strong acidity and intense
spiciness giving the deep flavors firm shape. Excellent balance.
Finishes very long, with rather suave tannins.

Colli Amerini 1996 Carbio, Umbria   ★★★ $$ ♟♟♟
Crushed red berries, raw meat, and peppery Mediterranean
spices on the nose. Compellingly sweet fruit is fresh, intense,
and long on personality. Finishes firm, with ripe, dusty tannins.

Cataldi Madonna 1996 Montepulciano d'Abruzzo ★★ $$ ♟♟♟
Wild aromas of currant, truffle, game, and tobacco. Mouth-filling,
concentrated cherry and red-berry flavors maintain freshness
and good delineation. Distinctly firm on the finish, which fea-
tures moderate dusty tannins.

Falesco 1997 Merlot, Umbria   ★★ $$ ♟♟
Saturated ruby color. Fresh, spicy aromas of blackberry, wood-
smoke, and menthol. Fat, concentrated, and powerful, with lush
fruit supported by firm underlying structure. Finishes with chewy
but ripe tannins.

Falesco 1997 Vitiano, Lazio   ★★ $ 🍷🍷🍷
Aromas of red currant, coffee, smoke, and stewed tomato. Plump,
sweet, and packed with super-ripe black-cherry fruit. Hint of oak
spice. Finishes with slightly dusty tannins and moderate length.

Pieve del Vescovo 1997, Umbria   ★★ $ 🍷🍷🍷
Crushed berries, game, and violet on the nose. Round and layered
in the mouth; leads with its spicy, youthful dark-berry flavors.
Not especially long but gentle on the aftertaste.

Umani Ronchi 1995 Rosso Conero San Lorenzo,   ★★ $ 🍷🍷
Marches Sappy, vibrant aromas of black cherry and spicy oak.
Intense cherry flavor is juicy and penetrating, with harmonious
acidity giving the fruit noteworthy lift and brightness.

Tollo 1996 Montepulciano d'Abruzzo   ★ $ 🍷🍷🍷
Sappy, sweet, cherry-scented nose shows a smoky complexity.
Soft, fat, and rather full, with perfumed cherry flavor.

SOUTHERN ITALY

The southern third of Italy is just beginning to capitalize on its
huge potential for producing quality wines at reasonable prices.
By planting vines on cooler hillsides or in areas where the sea
tempers summer heat, growers can get sufficient buildup of flavor before sugar content soars and the grapes turn to raisins.

Apulia (Puglia in Italian) counts Salice Salentino, a full-bodied,
roasted red made from Negroamaro, as its most important wine.

Basilicata is the home of the tannic, slow-aging red wine
called Aglianico del Vulture.

Campania produces southern Italy's most serious reds, largely
from the late-ripening Aglianico grape. Campania also makes two
distinctive and ageworthy dry whites: the rich, almond-scented
Greco di Tufo and the more delicate Fiano di Avellino.

Sardinia bottles light, aromatic wines from the white grape
Vermentino; its reds are based mainly on the Carignan,
Grenache, and Mourvèdre varieties.

Sicily is famous for Marsala, made by a variant of the
Madeira method, and for sweet wines based on versions of the
Muscat grape. More sophisticated winemaking has led to
increasingly satisfying table wines as well.

Altitude and exposure to the sea are more important determinants of wine quality and style than southern Italy's relentless sunshine. Even sun-drenched Sicily produces good wines with surprisingly fresh acidity.

At the Table

Red wines based on Aglianico, with their rich but fresh flavors, complement roasted or lightly grilled meats and game. The larger-scaled reds of Sardinia are locally favored with roasted, herb-suffused meats; try them also with braised pork and olives or sweet-and-sour braised rabbit. Greco di Tufo is an excellent match for grilled fish, as well as for shellfish pastas, while Fiano di Avellino works with antipasti, grilled fish, chicken, including that in tomato-based sauces, pork, and veal. White wines based on Vermentino can be served with antipasti, pasta, fish, and lighter poultry dishes; their more assertive flavors work well with herbs (grilled chicken with fresh bay leaves, for example).

The Bottom Line

Southern Italy's better wines offer better price/quality rapport than any of Italy's other major wine areas.

RED WINES

Librandi 1993 Duca San Felice Riserva, Calabria   ★★ **$$** 🍷🍷🍷
Aromatic nose of roasted plum, chocolate, leather, and Mediter-

101

ranean spices. Full, tactile, and sweet; the flavors are warm and
spicy. Finishes with ripe, tongue-coating tannins.

Molettieri 1996 Irpinia Rosso, Campania   ★★ $$ ♥♥♥
Black fruit, coffee, meat, and cracked black pepper on the nose.
Rich, inviting, distinctly warm flavors of super-ripe currants and
pepper. Ripely tannic, persistent finish.

Ocono 1994 Aglianice del Taburno, Campania   ★★ $$ ♥♥
Jammy aromas of dried rose and red berries; ripe but not quite
roasted. Bright red-berry fruit is buttressed by a firm peppery
edge. Good texture and freshness. Lively finishing flavors.

Villa Matilde 1995 Falerno del Massico Classico,   ★★ $$ ♥♥
Falerno Wild aromas of fresh dark berries, violet, woodsmoke,
game, and mint. A smooth, rich midweight that shows claretlike
vibrancy. Finishes with substantial palate-dusting tannins.

Argiolas 1996 Costera, Sardinia   ★★ $ ♥♥♥
Super-ripe, roasted aroma of cherry and nuts. Fat with cherry
and raspberry fruit; dense, sweet, and easygoing, with a touch of
oak. A southern wine that's not pruney.

Cantele 1996 Primitivo, Puglia   ★★ $ ♥♥♥
Dark red-ruby color. Aromas of blackberry, black raspberry, and
licorice, plus a faint note of raisin. Dense, sweet, and fat, but
bright acidity frames the strong fruit. Finishes with attractive
sweetness and tongue-dusting tannins.

Cantine Botromagno 1993 Pier delle Vigne, Puglia   ★★ $ ♥♥♥
Red-berry nose shows a slightly roasted plum and raisin charac-
ter. Super-ripe but firm-edged, with somewhat rustic flavors similar
to the aromas. Finishes with round tannins and some acid bite.

Regaleali 1996 Rosso, Sicily   ★★ $ ♥♥♥
Spicy, grapey aromas of blueberry, black raspberry, and almond.
Fat, rich, and layered, with soft acids and fine, dusty tannins.
Shows a faint gamy nuance.

WHITE WINES

Clelia Romana 1997 Colli di Lapio   ★★★ $$ ♥♥
Fiano di Avellino, Campania Perfumed nose combines peach,
pear, honey, and licorice. Extremely fruity with notes of ripe

peach, Granny Smith apple, and grapefruit, with licorice, mineral dust, and mint. Sharply focused, complex, and very long.

Terre Dora di Paolo 1997 Fiano di Avellino,   ★★★ **$$** ❦❦
Campania Fragrant aromas of honey, fig, pear, and hazelnut. Super-ripe and generous on the palate. Noteworthy depth of fruit and underlying structure. Finishes very long, with dusty texture.

Feudi di San Gregorio 1996 Greco di Tufo,   ★★ **$$** ❦❦❦
Campania Inviting aromas of almond oil, truffle, and dried fruits. Full, ripe, and satisfying, with a flavor of bitter almond. Finishes with good grip and subtle, lingering fruit.

Planeta 1997 La Segreta Bianco, Sicily   ★★ **$$** ❦
Nuts and figs complement aromas of orange, tangerine, and tropical fruits. Lushly textured and very ripe, with strong peach and apricot flavors and a faintly gamy nuance. Firm-edged, very long, fruity aftertaste.

Argiolas 1997 Bianco, Sardinia   ★★ **$** ❦❦❦
Clean aromas of smoke, spice, and citrus fruits. Supple and ripe but quite fresh on the palate; flavors of lemon, apple, and nuts. A substantial wine with a firm, lingering finish.

Two Tips for Ordering Wine in Restaurants

1. Avoid the cheapest wines on the list. Most restaurants add a flat handling and storing charge to the price of each bottle, and this amount will naturally represent a larger percentage of the cost of an inexpensive wine. Also, restaurants tend to calculate markups on a sliding scale, and these are almost always highest for the least costly choices.

2. Avoid the most expensive wines on the list. Wine-savvy diners can find relative bargains at the high end. But proceed with caution if you are uncertain about whether you are getting good value. Some restaurants apply exorbitant markups on scarce, prestigious wines.

SPAIN

TRADITIONALLY RIOJA AND SHERRY WERE THE CHIEF exports from Spain. Now, many once obscure regions have emerged as sources of quality wines, including improved versions of rustic blends as well as internationally popular varietals.

GALICIA

NAVARRE

RIOJA

Ebro

CATALONIA

Barcelona

Duero

RIBERA DEL DUERO

PENEDES

RUEDA

PRIORATO

• Madrid

Tagus

Most of Spain's finest reds come from the north central areas of Ribera del Duero, Rioja, and Navarre. The northwest produces intensely flavored white wines. Sherry is produced in the southwest.

Guadalquivir

ANDALUSIA

JEREZ

Jerez de la Frontera Málaga

Wine growing regions

Grapes & Styles
Riojas and Ribera del Dueros are based on the Tempranillo grape. Garnacha is widely planted, while Cabernet Sauvignon and Merlot are increasing in acreage. Spain also offers intensely flavored whites, the sparkling cava, and excellent rosés.

On the Label
The finest reds, labeled *Gran Reserva*, spend at least two years in barrel and three in the bottle. Crianza and Reserva wines age in oak casks for a minimum of one year, followed by three or four years in the bottle.

Rioja

The most prized Riojas (ree-OH-has) are dry but fragrant and mellow wines that derive much of their character from slow aging in small oak barrels; the longer the wines age, the more their fruit flavors—black cherry, black currant, and plum—are softened and augmented by notes of tobacco, cinnamon, roast coffee, cedar, and vanilla. They are generally ready to drink upon release. These wines offer remarkable complexity and depth of flavor. The finest red Riojas are blends based on the Tempranillo grape, which contributes deep color, good acidity, and firm tannin; some jammy Garnacha (Grenache in France) is usually included for alcoholic strength. While white wines from Rioja are also popular in Spain, they have not yet gained much popularity outside the country due to their frequently excessively oaky, rather oxidized aromas.

At the Table

With their clarity of flavor, definite but not excessive tannin, and moderate alcohol, red Riojas are flexible food wines. In Spain, they traditionally accompany roasted meats (in the Riojan restaurants called *asadores*, lamb is the specialty). Other local pairings for Rioja include lamb chops grilled over vine cuttings and *patatas a la riojanas* (potato-and-chorizo stew). They also go well with meat and chicken stews, light game birds, and barbecued ribs. Mature Rioja has a mellowness that perfectly complements filet mignon; the older wine's woodsy sweetness also marries well with mushrooms.

The Bottom Line

Rioja is no longer cheap, but many excellent values can be found in the Crianza and Reserva categories, the former wines generally under $15, the latter $15 to $25.

What to Buy: Rioja

1991	1992	1993	1994	1995	1996
B+	C	C-	A	A-	B+

Bodegas Muga 1994 Reserva ★★★★ $$ ❢❢❢
Complex aromas of currant, roasted plum, cedar, game, and leather. Lush and silky, with terrific penetrating flavor. Impeccably balanced for early drinking, but has the structure to age. Finishes with ripe, dusty tannins.

Remelluri 1995 Crianza ★★★★ $$ ❢❢
Violet, cassis, licorice, and black-pepper aromas. Very concentrated and deep; explosive fruit expands to fill the mouth. Flavors are extremely youthful and the texture suave. Very long finish features ripe, dusty tannins.

Bodegas López de Herédia 1991 Viña Tondonia ★★★ $$ ❢❢❢
Reserva Ripe strawberry, plum, game, and leather nose complicated by earth and herbal nuances. Plummy, rich, and concentrated; quickly maturing flavors offer lovely inner-mouth sweetness. Velvety and long, with bright but harmonious acidity.

Bodegas Marqués de Cáceres 1991 Reserva ★★★ $$ ❢❢❢
Deep red-ruby color. Fresh aromas of cassis, licorice, and chocolate. Bracing flavors of bitter cherry, wood spice, and espresso. Still quite young. Finishes with tongue-dusting tannins.

Bodegas Montecillo 1989 Viña Monty Gran ★★★ $$ ❢❢❢
Reserva Pungent aromas of strawberry, tar, minerals, and cedar. Similar flavors in the mouth; tangy, fresh acidity gives the wine terrific firmness and grip. Finishes very long, with dusty, even tannins.

Bodegas Marqués de Cáceres 1994 ★★★ $ ❢❢❢
Tangy, fruit-driven aromas of raspberry, cherry, strawberry, and vanillin oak. Spicy and seamless in the mouth, with generous, easygoing fruit, lush texture, and beautifully integrated acidity. Concentrated and long.

Bodegas Bréton 1995 Loriñon ★★ $ ❢❢❢
Fresh aromas of cherry, cinnamon, and underbrush. Rich, soft, and oaky, with intensely fruity red-currant, cherry, tar, and leather flavors supported by ripe acidity. Lovely sweet, lingering aftertaste.

Bodegas López de Herédia 1994 Viña Cubillo ★★ $ ❢❢❢
Tawny-red color. Exotic aromas of oak, cinnamon, and orange peel. Juicy and firm-edged, with enough fresh cherry and strawberry flavor to balance the oak spice and vanilla.

Bodegas Montecillo 1995 Viña Cumbrero   ★★ $ ♈♈♈
Meaty aromas of red currant, pepper, and leather. Supple, sweet fruit shows meat and leather elements, but firm acids and notes of pepper and licorice keep it brisk and firm on the palate and finish.

Bodegas Sierra Cantabria 1995 Crianza   ★★ $ ♈♈♈
Aromas of plum and tobacco. Tart red-berry fruit on the palate; dry and restrained. Finishes firm, with slightly dry tannins.

Ribera del Duero

If Riojas are Bordeaux-like, Ribera del Duero (ree-BAIR-ah del doo-EH-ro) wines are more akin to California Cabernet. Here, winemakers bottle and release their rather full-bodied wines earlier to retain deep color and youthful fruit, using small oak barrels to tame the tannins and acidity rather than to add flavor. Ribera del Duero reds are generally based on Tempranillo, sometimes with Cabernet Sauvignon and Merlot added.

At the Table

The larger-scaled, tannic reds of Ribera del Duero stand up to assertive meats better than Rioja. Roast lamb is the specialty of the region, but *morcilla* (blood sausage made with rice) and rich suckling pig also buffer the tannin of Ribera del Dueros. They are paired with sheep's-milk cheeses, like the local Zamorano and Queso de Burgos, or Manchego and Idiazábal. Try them alongside roasted rack of venison with herbed polenta crust or grilled shell steaks with smoked eggplant.

The Bottom Line

Price tags can be steep for the region's better wines, but there are excellent values to be found at every quality level.

What to Buy: Ribera del Duero

1993	1994	1995	1996	1997
C-	A	A-	A	B

Bodegas Reyes 1996 Téofilo Reyes   ★★★★ $$$ ❧❧
Chocolatey ripe aromas of black raspberry, smoke, and animal fur, with a floral nuance. A super-ripe, spicy wave of dark-berry fruit; thick and fleshy, but firm acidity keeps it firm and shapely.

Bodegas Alejandro Fernández 1996 Tinto   ★★★★ $$ ❧❧❧
Pesquera Subdued, nuanced aromas of black raspberry, espresso, smoke, and earth. Like liquid silk in the mouth; sappy berry and milk-chocolate flavors perked up by lively acidity. Superbly structured. Explosively fruity and long on the finish.

Bodegas Alión 1994 Cosecha   ★★★ $$ ❧❧❧
Aromas of smoky oak, red currant, raspberry, tobacco, lead pencil, and loam. Silky, slightly dry-edged raspberry flavor is supported by a firm acid spine. Laid-back and young today. Finishes with substantial dusty tannins.

Bodegas Candado de Haza 1996 Tinto   ★★★ $$ ❧❧❧
Deep ruby red. Complex aromas of black raspberry, espresso, cinnamon, and charred oak. Seamless, lively red-berry flavors supported by fresh acidity and firm tannic spine. Youthfully unevolved but already quite long on the finish.

Bodegas y Viñedos Valtravieso 1994 Crianza   ★★★ $$ ❧❧
Complex aromas of crushed raspberry, gunflint, and smoky oak. Sweet, thick, palate-caressing flavors of red berry and game, with complicating iron and tobacco notes. Finishes long, with ripe tannins and a hint of framboise.

OTHER RED WINES

Navarre (Navarra in Spainish) is currently the happening region: Tempranillo and Garnacha dominate, but Cabernet and Merlot also figure prominently. Excellent wines come from Catalonia, too, especially the Penedès region. In recent years, the Priorato area of Catalonia has emerged with super-rich but generally pricey blockbusters in the style of the brawniest Châteauneuf-du-Papes.

Abadia Retuerta 1996, Sardon de Duero   ★★★ $$ ❧❧
Dark ruby color. Penetrating black-currant, floral, and oak-spice nose, with suggestions of dark chocolate and crystallized fruit. Lush but penetrating, with strong black-fruit flavors clarified by firm acidity. Very long finish.

Bodegas Agapito Rico 1997 Carchelo Monastrell, ★★★ $ ♥♥♥
Jumilla Enticing aromas of black raspberry, pipe tobacco, pepper, and tree bark. A burst of creamy, intense fruit in the mouth. At once tangy and velvety. Finishes long and ripely tannic.

Bodegas Guelbenzu 1996 Tinto, Navarra ★★ $ ♥♥♥
Currant, tobacco, and earth on the nose. Fat and full, with sweet, seamless red-currant flavor kept fresh by harmonious acidity. Finishes firm and long, with smooth, ripe tannins.

Bodegas Nekeas 1996 Vega Sindoa ★★ $ ♥♥♥
Cabernet-Tempranillo, Navarra Perfumed, floral aromas of red currant, plum, mint, and spicy oak. Silky in the mouth, but lively and firm, with tart red-berry flavors and enticing sweetness. Finishes with firm, suave tannins.

Bodegas Nekeas 1996 Vega Sindoa Merlot, ★★ $ ♥♥♥
Navarra Aromatic nose of plum, raspberry, and spicy oak. Lush and soft, with a restrained sweetness, modest complexity, and good concentration. Finishes with easygoing tannins.

Bodegas Ochoa 1995 Merlot, Navarra ★★ $ ♥♥♥
Aromas of raspberry, plum, and woodsmoke, plus a pungent whiff of grapefruit. Lush, sweet flavors of raspberry, currant, and tobacco. Stuffed with fruit. Finishes with dusty, even tannins and a hint of pepper.

Miguel Torres 1995 Coronas, Penedès ★★ $ ♥♥♥
Warm, complex aromas of black currant, plum, meat, pepper, and spicy, cedary oak. Sweet and lush in the mouth, with sound acidity but a complete absence of rough edges. Lingering, peppery finish. Mostly Tempranillo.

Vínicola del Priorat 1997 Onix, Priorato ★★ $ ♥♥♥
Pungently sweet aromas of raspberry, cassis, tar, and Christmas spices. Sweet and lush in the mouth, with ripe fruit flavors of moderate intensity and complexity. Fruity, ripely tannic finish.

ROSÉ WINES

Spain provides some of the world's best dry, flavorful rosés (*rosado* in Spanish). Compared to the rosés of Provence, those from Spain tend to be fuller and more pliant, often giving an impression of sweetness even when they are technically dry. The top source is Navarre, but excellent rosés are also made in Rioja and Ribera del Duero.

At the Table

In Spain, rosés are served virtually any time a white wine is called for, especially with salty and spicy dishes. In Navarre, rosés are enjoyed with asparagus, in Rioja with tapas, and in Málaga with fried fish. Fruity and vivacious, these wines are perfect with ham, fish soup, and *salade niçoise*. Try them as an accompaniment to tuna tartare with chile mayonnaise, prosciutto risotto, or barbecued baby back ribs with ginger-and-scallion sauce.

The Bottom Line

Don't eschew rosés. Spain's best examples, usually priced under $12, offer remarkable value.

What to Buy: Rosé Wines

1995	1996	1997
A-	B	B+

Bodegas Marqués de Cáceres 1997, Rioja ★★★ $ ♟♟♟
Delicate aromas of strawberry, rhubarb, rose petal, and earth. Rich and ripe, with unusual texture and depth for a rosé. Boasts terrific fruit intensity. Finishes vibrant, strong, and very long.

Bodegas Martínez Bujanda 1997 ★★ $ ♟♟♟
Conde de Valdemar, Rioja Ripe aromas of raspberry, smoke, and earth. Ripe and fairly large-scaled, with good volume in the mouth. Just enough acidity to give shape to the raspberry flavor. Better suited alongside food than as an aperitif.

Bodegas Muga 1997, Rioja ★★ $ ♟♟♟
Musky aromas of earth and smoke. Earthy and dense, but rather penetrating on the palate. Some oak influence. Finishes quite dry. Needs to be served with food.

Bodegas Sierra Cantabria 1997 Codice Rosado, ★★ $ ♟♟♟
Rioja Pale watermelon color. Strawberry, raspberry, and a whiff

of smoke on the nose. Rich, soft, ripe, and gentle on the palate.
A serious dry wine with good texture and length.

WHITE WINES

Northwestern Spain, especially coastal Galicia, produces Spain's
freshest white wines. The best are the vibrant, minerally examples from the Albariño grape. Similarly crisp but more substantial wines come from Rueda and its Verdejo grape. Chardonnay
and Sauvignon Blanc are increasingly being planted.

At the Table
Albariño is a nearly perfect shellfish wine. In Galicia, it
accompanies cockles, raw clams, both bay and sea scallops, and the local crab and lobster, as well as shellfish
empanadas. Albariño is also a good match for most
fried or grilled fish of other types (local favorites include
skate, *merluza* or hake, and octopus). These brisk wines
provide an excellent contrast to Chinese dishes with
sweet sauces, not just those based on fish, but chicken
and pork dishes, too. Albariño is equally successful with
sushi. The dry whites of Rueda pair well with garlicky
seafood but also go with ham, chicken, and omelets.

The Bottom Line
Albariño is not cheap, but the best are reasonably priced for
their high quality. Other Spanish whites can be great bargains.

What to Buy: White Wines

1995	1996	1997
A-	B	B+

Bodegas de Vilariño-Cambados 1997 Martin ★★★ $$ ❜❜❜
Codax, Rias Baixas Pineapple, grapefruit, and spice on the
nose. Dense, firm, and concentrated, with refreshing, sharply
delineated flavors. Very well-structured white wine.

Bodegas As Laxas 1997 Bagoa do Miño, ★★★ $$ ❜❜
Rias Baixas Ripe but restrained aromas of mint, minerals, and

curry powder. Very dry, intensely flavored and sinewy; the wine's taut structure currently hides its richness. Finishes very subtle, long, and vibrant. Distinctly ageworthy.

Bodegas Nekeas 1997 Chardonnay Vega Sindoa, ★★★ $$ ♥♥
Navarra Spicy, smoky nose of noteworthy complexity. Thick, tactile, and quite rich, but firm acidity keeps the fruit fresh and firm. Very long, spicy aftertaste.

Godeval 1997, Valdeorras ★★★ $$ ♥♥
Restrained aromas of spiced apple, honeysuckle, and minerals. Good concentration and intensity of flavor; firm acidity keeps the flavors very fresh. Finishes with subtle persistence.

Lusco 1997 Albariño, Rias Baixas ★★★ $$ ♥♥
Musky, gingery aromas convey an impression of dusty stone. Concentrated, rich, and sharply delineated; offers superb inner-mouth perfume and lift. Slightly tart-edged gingery fruit. Very long, bracing aftertaste.

Morgadío 1997 Albariño, Rias Baixas ★★★ $$ ♥♥
Perfumed, floral aromas of lime, fresh apple, and mint. Ripe entry, then lemony and minty, with vibrant citric acidity framing the fresh, youthful fruit. Finishes with lemon and stone notes and terrific length.

Condes de Albarei 1997 Albariño Clásico, ★★ $$ ♥♥♥
Rias Baixas Complex, ripe aromas of quinine, mint, and flowers, plus smoky and stony notes. Quite dry but rich, with strong, bright, spicy fruit. A subtle suggestion of oak adds to its appeal.

Lagar de Cervera 1997 Albariño, Rias Baixas ★★ $$ ♥♥♥
Musky, perfumed aromas of ginger, grapefruit, flowers, and minerals. Densely packed and very fresh, with intense lemon and ginger flavors. Suggestion of pineapple ripeness on the firm, persistent finish. Really clings to the palate.

Pazo de Señorans 1997 Albariño, Rias Baixas ★★ $$ ♥♥
Delicately perfumed pear-blossom, apple, and litchi aromas. Stylish and lively, with beguiling fruit. At once dense and light on its feet. Finishes dry but not austere, with persistent flavor.

Bodegas de Vilariño-Cambados 1997 Burgans ★★ $ ♥♥♥
Albariño, Rias Baixas Extravagant banana, apple, and peach

nose, plus a chalky suggestion of soil. Fat, soft, and mouth-filling, with a slight impression of sweetness. Holds its shape nicely.

Martinsancho 1997 Verdejo, Rueda ★★ $ ♟♟♟
Honeydew melon, smoke, and a subtle floral note on the nose. Gentle, ripe, and mouth-filling, but a grassy nuance and tangy acidity keep the wine fresh. Finishes with impressive length.

CAVA

Cava is a sparkling wine made using the Champagne method. Nonvintage (NV) is most commonly available. The greatest quantity comes from Catalonia and is made from indigenous Spanish grapes, but Chardonnay is increasingly finding its way into these blends. Today's cavas are cleaner and fresher than ever.

At the Table
In Barcelona, this extremely popular wine is consumed all day long as well as at both ends of the meal, with appetizers and desserts. The Spanish enjoy it with tapas, chicken, and sausage. Serve cava with young Manchego cheese, smoked salmon, garlicky shrimp, seviche, and almost any fried appetizer. Like other sparkling wines, cava works well with egg dishes. Catalonians frequently drink slightly sweet versions (labeled *seco*) with cookies or cake.

The Bottom Line
The best cavas, rarely priced higher than $12, rank among the world's great buys in sparkling wine.

Huguet 1993 Gran Reserva Brut Nature ★★★ $$ ♟♟
Precise, stony aromas of fresh apple, lemon, and peppermint. Quite full and concentrated but elegantly styled and totally dry. An uncompromising style of cava, with a very long, bracing finish.

Cristalino NV Brut ★★ $ ♟♟♟
Yeasty, spicy, Champagne-like aromas of baked apple, pear, and minerals. Toasty, spicy, and very fresh in the mouth; round but dry. Lively flavors of apple and nutmeg. Finishes with a refreshing musky quality.

Mont-Marçal NV Brut Reserva ★★ $ ▼▼▼

Very pale color. Crab apple, pear, and fresh mint on the nose. Fresh, brisk, and light-textured in the mouth, with a flavor of Golden Delicious apple. A restrained, stylish cava that's quite dry on the aftertaste.

Sumarocca NV Brut ★★ $ ▼▼▼

Subtle aromas of white flowers, lemon, and smoke. Good texture and roundness in the mouth; ripe, intense flavors of toast and lemon. Dry but not at all hard. A perfect cheap alternative to Champagne.

El Cep S.A. 1995 Marqués de Gelida ★ $ ▼▼▼

Lemon and earth aromas. Slightly sweet and soft, with a creamy texture and somewhat rustic flavors. But finishes dry, with surprising length.

Freixenet Cordon Negro NV Brut ★ $ ▼▼▼

Subdued, faintly yeasty aroma of lemon peel. Fresh flavors of lemon, apple, pear, and chalk. Soft and fairly full in the mouth, but finishes with a refreshingly bitter edge.

SHERRY

Sherry-style wines are produced in a number of countries, but the most refined and nuanced examples come from the area of Andalusia around Jerez de la Frontera. Eminently versatile, sherry runs the gamut from absolutely dry to literally (and deliciously) sticky sweet.

The best sherries are made from the Palomino grape grown on chalky soil. In theory at least, the finest raw materials are reserved for the dry sherries: fino, manzanilla, and amontillado. These wines get a modest amount of fortification with grape spirits to boost their alcohol levels and are not sweetened. Olorosos and cream sherries *are* sweetened and therefore are generally speaking more user-friendly. These may serve as better introductions for newcomers.

With few exceptions, sherry is an amalgam of vintages, produced through a blending and aging process called the *solera* system, in which more mature barrels are continually topped up with younger wines of the same sort and quality to ensure a consistency of style for the various sherry types offered by that particular *bodega*, or winery.

On the Label
• **Fino** (fee-no) is a subtly almond-scented, dry wine that generally carries 16 to 18 percent alcohol. It is typically rather ethereal, but the city of Jerez produces a number of excellent fuller-bodied examples.

• **Manzanilla** (mahn-thah-NEE-yah) is an even more delicate, though bracing, sherry aged in the seaport of Sanlúcar de Barrameda.

• **Amontillado** (ah-mon-tee-YAH-doh) is basically an aged fino that has developed fuller body and flavor.

• **Palo Cortado** (PAH-lo cor-TAH-do), usually slightly to moderately sweet, combines the nutty aromas of amontillado with the deeper color and fuller body of oloroso.

• **Oloroso** (o-lo-RO-so) is made from base materials that are not as refined as those used for fino but are believed to have greater aging potential. Most oloroso is sweetened to some degree.

• **Cream sherries** are olorosos mellowed by Pedro Ximénez grapes and tend to be even sweeter. As a rule, cream sherries begin with more heavily fortified base wines and carry alcohol in the 18 to 23 percent range.

• **Montilla** (mawn-TEE-yah), a wine very similar to sherry, is produced around the town of Montilla. It is made in the full range of sherry styles.

At the Table
The driest sherries make refreshing aperitifs but are also superb with shellfish, olives, eggs, pâtés, and hors d'oeuvres and dishes with vinaigrette sauces. In the seafood restaurants of Sanlúcar de Barrameda, boiled shrimp practically requires a glass of Manzanilla. Drier amontillados and olorosos can be paired with fried foods, almonds, and olives; in Spain, they are popular with black-bean soup and with powerful cheeses. Sweetened olorosos and cream sherries are good with espresso; the most unctuous examples are among the few wines that can stand up to chocolate desserts.

The Bottom Line
Sherry is incredibly underpriced, with many outstanding examples selling for less than $15 a bottle.

DRY SHERRY

Alvear Solera Abuelo Diego Amontillado, ★★★★ **\$\$** ▼▼▼
Montilla Nuanced aromas of orange peel, toasted almond, coffee, and woodsmoke. Sharply defined, powerful flavors. An uncompromising, authentic Amontillado, finishing with notes of citrus skin and walnut.

Valdespino Inocente Fino ★★★★ **\$\$** ▼▼
Subtle minerally, saline aromas. Big, rich, and powerful, but extraordinarily subtle and fine in the mouth. Has a glycerol richness but lemony acidity and strong soil tones leave the palate refreshed. Great length and individuality.

Vinicola Hidalgo Jerez Cortadó ★★★★ **\$\$** ▼▼
Subtle, slightly high-toned walnut aroma. Very rich and velvety but totally dry. A tangy, slightly salty quality keeps it lively on the palate. The salty, walnut-skin finish has an almost crystalline precision and builds slowly on the palate.

Vinicola Hidalgo Napoléon Amontillado ★★★★ **\$\$** ▼▼
Aromas of walnut, maple sugar, vanilla bean, and toffee. Rich and mellow, with warm, refined flavors enlivened by a citric, saline edge. Very long finish displays an almost painful intensity.

Vinicola Hidalgo Manzanilla Fina La Gitana ★★★★ **\$** ▼▼
Yeasty, fresh aromas of almond and apple. Silky yet tangy flavors of almond, apple, and olive. A lightly yeasty/smoky quality and hints of apple and citrus peel contribute to its complexity. Very long, salty aftertaste.

Alvear Fino, Montilla ★★★ **\$** ▼▼▼
Toasty, yeasty nose hints at pear and apple. Brisk and pungent yet rather elegant in the mouth, with almond and wood flavors and a long, fresh, olive-tinged finish.

Emilio Lustau Light Fino Jarana ★★ **\$** ▼▼▼
Salty, nutty aroma shows a lemon-limey fruitiness. Apple and mineral flavors fill the mouth. Quite penetrating but silky and accessible thanks to its impeccable balance. Minerals and smoked meat on the slow-building finish.

Hartley & Gibson Manzanilla Fine Very Pale ★★ **\$** ▼▼▼
Extra Dry Slightly high-toned nutty, yeasty aroma, with a resiny

nuance. Silky-smooth and rather rich for Manzanilla, with substantial flavor interest. Easy to drink for such a dry sherry.

SLIGHTLY SWEET TO VERY SWEET SHERRY

Emilio Lustau Moscatel Emilin ★★★★ $$ ♥♥♥
Knockout nose combines cassis, licorice, game, spearmint, and rye flour. Thick and supersweet yet almost miraculously fresh and invigorating; distinctly fruity flavors of licorice, fig, and orange peel. Very long, very sweet finish.

Emilio Lustau Rare Cream Solera Superior ★★★★ $$ ♥♥♥
Deep, complex aromas of crème caramel, spice, and tobacco. Very sweet, concentrated, and powerful; displays great weight and thrust. Supersweet yet tangy finishing flavors of walnut, almond, and toffee go on and on.

Vinicola Hidalgo Napoleón Cream Sherry ★★★★ $ ♥♥♥
Deep aromas of nuts, raisins, coffee, and maple syrup. Moderately sweet and very rich in the mouth; silky texture gives this wine a lovely lightness of touch. Impeccably balanced. Dry-edged, long finish hints at almond.

Emilio Lustau Deluxe Cream Capataz Andrés ★★★ $$ ♥♥♥
Deeply pitched aromas of apple, vanilla, clove, and marzipan. Very sweet and thick in the mouth, with portlike flavors of raisin, date, chocolate, and walnut. But a minerally aftertaste gives this wine a superb penetrating quality.

Alvear Festival Pale Cream, Montilla ★★★ $ ♥♥♥
The color of white wine. Fascinating aromas of quince, peach, and marzipan; has a tangy, yeasty nuance. Medium sweet, with apricot and lemon flavors and juicy acidity. A fascinating low-alcohol fino that features added grape must.

Hartley & Gibson Oloroso Superior Medium Dry ★★ $ ♥♥♥
Toasted nuts and a suggestion of dried apricot on the nose. Smooth, harmonious, and very easy to drink; slightly sweet flavors of dried fruits, chocolate, coffee, and toasted nuts. Finishes virtually dry.

PORTUGAL

PORTUGAL PRODUCES TWO OF THE WORLD'S greatest fortified wines, port and Madeira, and is also an excellent source of inexpensive, and steadily improving, table wines—both red and white.

The Atlantic coast of Portugal provides a temperate climate for grape growing, while the interior of the country is much hotter and drier. For example, port is made in the baking mountainside vineyards along the Douro River. Barely 100 miles to the west lies the Vinho Verde region, home of Portugal's vibrant, high-acid white-wine specialty.

VINHO VERDE
DOURO VALLEY
Oporto
DAO
BAIRRADA
Lisbon
Wine growing regions
ALENTEJO

Grapes & Styles

Most of Portugal's best reds are blends of indigenous grapes, such as Periquita and Baga, or varieties used in the production of port, though use of Cabernet Sauvignon and Merlot is increasing to satisfy world markets. The bracing Vinho Verde remains Portugal's most important white. Red Vinho Verde exists, but is best avoided.

On the Label

A wine labeled *garrafeira* (wine cellar) is one that a producer feels is of exceptional quality and therefore worthy of extra aging in both the cask and the bottle. By law, *garrafeira* reds must be left in cask at least two years and be aged in the bottle for another year prior to being released. Reserva should also designate a better wine, but this term carries no legal weight. Whatever quality designations appear on the label, if a variety is not indicated, the wine is probably a blend of grapes.

RED WINES

Today's Portuguese reds boast fresher fruit and gentler tannins than the traditional rougher, more rustic examples. In fact, these wines are often more distinctive than Cabernet and Merlot.

At the Table

By and large, Portuguese reds are medium-bodied wines with sound acidity levels; their assertive flavors call for strong and straightforward food. Most of these wines are ideal with lighter meat preparations (especially pork and veal) and richer poultry and game birds. In Portugal, fried pork loin, wild rabbit, and game pâtés are traditionally paired with Dão reds, while Douro reds are frequently served with sausages. The Baga grape on which most Bairrada reds are based has the penetrating acidity to cut through the fat of suckling pig. Mature reds from Alentejo, Douro, and Dão are often matched with game birds, like partridge, pigeon, and guinea fowl, that have been cooked in wine sauce.

The Bottom Line

While a growing number of Portuguese reds have passed the $20 barrier, most can be found for $12 or less.

J. P. Vinhos 1995 Quinta da Bacalhoa   ★★★ $$ 🍷🍷🍷
Cabernet Sauvignon, Terras do Sado Super-ripe, multifaceted nose combines black raspberry, plum, tar, coffee, and cinnamon. Lush, rich, and full in the mouth, with assertive flavors of cassis, spice, and game. Finishes very ripe and very long.

Niepoort 1994 Redoma, Douro   ★★★ $$ 🍷🍷
Dark red-ruby color. Sweet aromas of black raspberry, currant, leather, cocoa, and spice. Quite concentrated and solidly structured, with penetrating spicy fruit, fresh acidity, and substantial tongue-dusting tannins.

José Maria da Fonseca 1995 Periquita,   ★★★ $ 🍷🍷🍷
Terras do Sado Super-ripe, sappy aromas of red fruits, maple syrup, leather, and iron. Spicy red-fruit flavors are tangy, fresh,

and sharply delineated. Vibrant and light on its feet. Finishes with hints of iron and raisin.

Quinta da Lagoalva de Cima 1994 Quinta ★★ $$ ♟♟♟
da Lagoalva, Ribatejo Ripe aromas of smoke, grilled nuts, and currant. A velvety midweight with generous texture, perked up by firm acidity and spicy character. Spicy, youthful, and quite long.

J. P. Vinhos 1994 Herdade de Santa Marta, ★★ $ ♟♟♟
Alentejo Deep, spicy aromas of plum, raspberry, cassis, and tobacco. Sweet, concentrated, and harmonious, with brisk acids extending the berry flavors through a slightly roasted, long finish.

J. P. Vinhos 1992 Tinto da Anfora, Alentejo ★★ $ ♟♟♟
Meat, plum, smoke, and hot stones on the nose. Supple and sweet, with tobacco and mineral notes. Flavors are complex and warm. Finishes with a roasted note and ripe, smooth tannins.

Sogrape 1995 Reserva, Douro ★★ $ ♟♟♟
Spicy cherry and cassis aromas, with a faintly medicinal note and pepper and licorice nuances. Fresh red-berry flavor is given shape and grip by firm acids. Finishes with raisiny ripeness.

Quinta do Crasto 1995, Douro ★★ $ ♟♟
Cassis, cherry, flowers, game, mint, and oak spice on the nose. Velvety, sweet, and oaky in the mouth; stuffed with fruit, but an edge of acidity keeps the wine firm. Finishes with very good length and dusty, fine tannins.

Caves Aliança 1994 Aliança Particular, Dão ★ $ ♟♟♟
Deep plum, currant, and woodsmoke aromas. Supple, gentle, and nicely balanced, with fairly intense plum and currant flavors and sound supporting acidity. Finishes with even, slightly dry tannins.

Caves São João 1995 Porta dos Cavaleiros, Dão ★ $ ♟♟♟
Subdued but ripe aromas of cherry, dark berries, tobacco, licorice, and earth. Berry and earth flavors are given definition by solid ripe acidity. Good texture. Finishes with lingering fruit.

Quinta da Lagoalva de Cima 1995 Cima, Ribatejo ★ $ ♟♟♟
Red currant, spice, tar, and licorice on the nose. Supple and sweet; spice and red-currant flavors could use a bit more delineation. Finishes with light, even tannins and surprising persistence.

WHITE WINES

Vinho Verde (VEEN-ho VAIR-day), called green wine because it's meant to be consumed young, is Portugal's most famous white. Classic Vinho Verde possesses high acidity, low alcohol (about 9 percent), and a slight fizz; it is typically bone-dry and vibrant, with notes of lemon, lime, minerals, and earth. Other white wines produced from local grape varieties are livelier than ever, thanks to careful vinification techniques.

At the Table

Vinho Verde makes a stimulating aperitif but is also a perfect lunch or picnic wine served alongside shellfish and other seafood dishes. In Portugal, it traditionally accompanies boiled shrimp, lobster, and crabs; steamed mussels and clams; and the country's ubiquitous codfish preparations. The wine's combination of vivid fruit and sharp acidity works beautifully with Thai and Vietnamese fish specialities, as well as with sushi. Vinho Verde also pairs nicely with salty foods and with dishes that include olives. It is one of the few wines that can tame the acidic bite of salad dressings such as vinaigrette (try it with *salade niçoise*). Other unoaked Portuguese white wines are similarly flexible with a wide range of shellfish and finfish dishes.

The Bottom Line

Generally less than $8, Vinho Verde is one of the world's extraordinary wine bargains. Other Portuguese whites are also aggressively priced and well worth investigating.

Niepoort 1995 Redoma, Douro   ★★ $$ ♀♀♀
Minerals, fresh apple, and oak spice on the nose. Silky and rather suave in the mouth, with very good texture, attractive ripeness, and oak notes of cinnamon, clove, and butterscotch. Minerals and spice on the lingering finish.

Caves Aliança 1996 Galeria Chardonnay, Beiras   ★★ $ ♀♀♀
The floral, spicy nose hints at pineapple and peach liqueur. New-oak notes are nicely supported by deep, spicy fruit-salad

flavors. This is a well-balanced, lighter Chardonnay with a nice, entirely subtle sweetness.

P.V.Q. 1996 Quinta de Pancas Chardonnay, Estremadura ★★ $ 🍷🍷🍷 Musky, gingery aromas of mango and oak spice. Fat and rich, but spicy and bright. Offers impressive weight and palate presence. Finishes with firm, apple-tinged flavors.

Quinta da Aveleda 1997 Aveleda, Vinho Verde ★★ $ 🍷🍷🍷
Complex aromas of lemon, thyme, honeysuckle, and earth, plus a whiff of cured ham. Intensely flavored, very fresh, and fairly dry, with moderate fizziness and a flavor of ginger ale.

Quinta da Aveleda 1997 Trajadura, Vinho Verde ★★ $ 🍷🍷🍷
Bracing aromas of spearmint, lemon, and melon. Very dry and penetrating, with sharply focused lemon and fresh-herb flavors. Finishes bracing but not austere, with a chalky suggestion of soil.

Casa de Santar 1997, Dão ★ $ 🍷🍷🍷
Very aromatic nose of flowers and pear eau-de-vie. Reasonably intense cinnamon and spiced-apple flavors, with sound supporting acids. Dry but not austere on the rather subtle aftertaste.

J. P. Vinhos 1996 Catarina, Terras do Sado ★ $ 🍷🍷🍷
Aromas of citrus oil, lemon skin, mint, and oak. Apple flavor framed by spicy oak. Not especially complex, but fresh and firm.

Montéz Champalimaud 1996 Paço do Teixeiró, Vinho Verde ★ $ 🍷🍷🍷 Floral, grassy aromas of apple, lemon, and spice. Supple and lemony in the mouth, with harmonious acidity and good clarity of flavor. Slightly tart on the aftertaste.

PORT

Port is a fortified wine made by adding grape spirits to fermenting wine, a step that halts the fermentation and results in significant residual sweetness and a high alcohol content. Although port-style wines are produced all over the world, the real thing is always from Portugal.

On the Label

- **Ruby ports** are dark in color and usually quite sweet, with an aggressive, almost peppery fruitiness.

•**Tawny ports**, confusingly, can be inexpensive wines made by mixing white and red port, or they can be complex, mellow wines kept long enough in wood to fade to a golden color. Aged tawnies are silkier, generally less fruity, and more aromatically complex than rubies. Tawnies and rubies are wood ports: they age in barrel.

•**Vintage ports** are bottle ports: They spend a short time in barrel and require years of aging in bottle. Classic vintage port is made from superior grapes grown in the finest vineyards and is made only in years when the wines show exceptional depth and structure.

•**Late Bottled Vintage** (LBV) ports are relatively affordable wines from a single vintage, usually an unexceptional one, bottled four to six years after the harvest.

At the Table

Ports have the sweetness and tannic structure to stand up to a range of flavors, including some that would overwhelm most table wines: chocolate, caramel, vanilla, nuts (especially hazelnuts, almonds, and walnuts), coffee, and blue cheeses. Basic tawny ports, or tawnies up to 20 years old, are perfect with a slice of Stilton or a dish of nuts. Mature vintage ports, or older tawnies, are a refined way to extend a meal, savored on their own following dessert—traditionally, with a good cigar.

The Bottom Line

Classic vintage port is one of the world's most collectible wines and is priced accordingly: Today, many of the best values in port are offered by nonvintage (NV) tawnies and rubies, which deliver immediate drinkability and can be found for as little as $10.

What to Buy: Vintage Port

1982	1983	1984	1985	1986
B	B+	NV*	A	NV*
1987	1988	1989	1990	1991
NV*	NV*	NV*	NV*	B+
1992	1993	1994	1995	1996
B	NV*	A	B+	B

* Vintage not declared by most major port shippers.

WOOD PORT

Dow's Twenty-Year-Old NV Tawny ★★★ $$$ ❣❣❣
Aromas of toffee, roasted nuts, lead pencil, orange peel, and caraway seed. Intensely flavored fruit is silky but delineated and vibrant, with a fresh orange-peel flavor. Finishes clean and long, with hints of smoked nuts and marzipan.

Osborne Twenty-Year-Old NV Tawny ★★★ $$$ ❣❣❣
Very pale, orange-tinted tawny. Restrained aromas of rose petal, clarified butter, duck fat, bacon, nutmeg, and bitter cherry. Subtle in the mouth; notes of nuts and toffee. Finishes with bright acids. Delicious.

Warre's Nimrod Finest Rare NV Tawny ★★★ $$$ ❣❣
High-toned aromas of walnut, fig, and maple syrup, plus a hint of spiced apple. Very sweet, rich, and supple, with the maple-syrup quality complicated by a meaty nuance. Finishes subtle and long, with notes of raisin and walnut skin.

Ferreira Dona Antonia NV Tawny ★★★ $$ ❣❣
Aromas of walnut, raisin, smoke, minerals, and exotic fruits. Very sweet, lush, and thick in the mouth, with complex flavors of currant, orange peel, and maple syrup. Sweet finish dominated by walnut and hazelnut notes.

Graham's Six Grapes NV ★★★ $ ❣❣❣
Youthful aromas of cassis, licorice, chocolate, herbs, and damp earth. Very intense, sweet flavors of chocolate and dark berries. Robust yet smooth and not obviously alcoholic. Superb fruit is brightened by firm acids.

Fonseca Bin 27 NV ★★ $$ ❣❣❣
Aromas of red fruits, tar, and smoked meat. Fat, lush, and sweet; flavors of black cherry and earth. Slightly alcoholic but persistent back end.

Smith Woodhouse Lodge NV Reserve ★★ $$ ❣❣
Vintage Character Fruity aromas of cassis, black cherry, and dried herbs. Very rich, deep, and sweet, verging on raisiny. Round in the mouth, then finishes fairly dry and quite firm. A mélange of spices, raisins, and nuts on the aftertaste.

Cockburn Fine NV Ruby ★★ $ ❣❣❣
Laid-back, rather complex aromas of black raspberry, maple

syrup, and golden raisins. Smooth, nicely concentrated, rich flavors of maple syrup and fresh berries. Finishes slightly fiery but long, with a suggestion of raisin.

Osborne Original NV Tawny ★★ $ 🍷🍷🍷

Toasty, spicy, nutty nose. Baked cherry and spice on the palate; not weighty but offers plenty of flavor. Acidity is nicely integrated. Finishes with notes of toffee and brown butter and a dry, nutty quality that suggests Madeira.

BOTTLE PORT

Smith Woodhouse 1982 Madalena ★★★ $$$$ 🍷🍷
Single-Quinta
Sweet, perfumed aromas of red fruit and rose. Elegant, deep, and concentrated, without obvious weight or fat. Hints of honey, toffee, and smoke, plus a spicy nutmeg and mace character. Complex and refined.

Ferreira 1995 ★★★ $$$ 🍷🍷🍷

Slightly high-toned nose of black raspberry, cassis, caramel, and menthol. Very sweet and concentrated; a wave of youthful black-cherry, dark-berry, and herbal flavors supported by firm acids. Serious tannins will require extended aging.

Graham's 1995 Malvedos ★★★ $$$ 🍷🍷🍷

Super-ripe, exotic aromas of cassis and woodsmoke. Incredibly sweet and viscous on the palate; very concentrated, deep, and strong in extract. A fruit bomb of a port. Extremely long and powerful.

Dow's 1995 Quinta do Bomfin ★★★ $$$ 🍷🍷

Aromas of cassis, molasses, and sassafras. Smooth, elegant, and intensely flavored; in the classic crisp, drier Dow's style. Very stylish port, finishing long, firm, and minerally.

Duff Gordon 1995 ★★★ $$$ 🍷🍷

Saturated purple color. Deep, slightly raisiny aromas of cherry, blackberry, and boysenberry. Rich, thick, and verging on jammy, but clean and bright, with roasted red-berry flavors. Brisk cranberry and pomegranate finishing flavors.

Ramos-Pinto 1989 LBV ★★★ $$ 🍷🍷🍷

Aromas of black fruit, licorice, and herbs. Slightly medicinal cherry flavor offers moderate sweetness, excellent depth, and plenty of personality. The flavors are brisk yet mellow, the finish youthful and long.

Taylor 1991 LBV ★★★ $$ 🍷🍷🍷

Pungent, spicy nose features black cherry, minerals, and mocha. Very sweet and fruity, with dark-berry flavors perked up by lively acids. Thick and concentrated but shapely. The fruit builds on the long, powerful finish.

Dow's 1991 LBV ★★ $$ 🍷🍷🍷

Lively aromas of plums, smoke, and nuts. Juicy, delineated dark-berry flavors complicated by notes of toffee and nuts. Moderately sweet. Crisp acids keep the finish quite firm. An elegantly styled port.

Fonseca 1992 LBV ★★ $$ 🍷🍷🍷

Mint and fresh herbs on the nose. Flavors of bitter cherry, blackberry, and maple syrup; in the exotic style of this house. Jammy, dense, and sweet, with soft acidity. The finish is long, plump, and satisfying.

MADEIRA

The four styles of Madeira are named after their traditional grape varieties. From driest to sweetest, they are Sercial, Verdelho, Bual, and Malmsey. But even the sweet Buals and Malmseys are rarely cloying, due to their high natural acidity.

At the Table

In Portugal, Madeira is generally enjoyed before or after the meal, though Verdelho is frequently paired with fish and shellfish soups. The tangy Sercial makes a fine aperitif, especially when served with nuts or olives, since its pronounced acidity complements salty foods. As a rule, Sercial and Verdelho have surprisingly dry aftertastes that work well with young chèvres and also with double- or triple-cream cheeses. Buals and Malmseys are best consumed with nut-based desserts or, better yet, after dinner on their own.

The Bottom Line

Vintage Madeiras are rare and extremely expensive, up to several hundred dollars a bottle for wines from the nineteenth century. Much better value, and far easier to find, are five-year-old reserve bottlings (generally $18 to $20) or the even more harmonious ten-year-old special reserves ($30 to $35), which usually merit their price premium.

Blandy Ten-Year-Old Malmsey ★★★ $$$ ♛♛

Slightly high-toned aromas of smoke, raisin, and exotic fruits. Very sweet and concentrated; flavors are enticingly fresh though not especially complex. But long and fruity on the aftertaste, with no sign of alcohol.

Cossart Gordon Ten-Year-Old Bual ★★★ $$$ ♛♛

Complex aromas of prune, tar, and bonfire. Very rich and intensely flavored; the brisk acids temper the wine's strong sweetness. Subtle, long, and quite juicy on the finish. Very attractive, highly nuanced Madeira.

Colombo Old Reserve Ten-Year-Old Sweet ★★★ $$ ♛♛♛

Rich, nutty aromas of maple syrup and coffee bean. Silky-sweet but penetrating, with perfectly integrated acidity. Wears its alcohol gracefully. Very long and bright on the firm finish.

Blandy Five-Year-Old Verdelho ★★ $$ ♛♛

Bright aromas of smoke and orange peel. Intensely flavored and moderately rich, with bright framing acids. Finishes persistently fruity, subtle, and long.

Colombo Old Reserve Ten-Year-Old Medium Dry ★★ $$ ♛♛

Roast coffee, clove, orange peel, and smoked nuts on the nose. Intense fig and smoke flavors retain a vibrancy thanks to penetrating acidity and an edge of orange peel. Dry finishing note of walnut skin.

Leacock Rainwater Medium Dry ★★ $ ♛♛♛

Light, lively aromas of nuts, maple syrup, and game. Juicy and fruity in the mouth, with lemon, orange-peel, and honey tones. Comes across as only slightly sweet due to strong acidity. Finishes bright, spicy and long.

GERMANY

AMERICANS HAVE GIVEN THE WINES OF GERMANY A bum rap. They're often thought to be sugary sweet. In fact, even when they possess moderate residual sugar, the best German whites, especially Rieslings, are blazingly fresh, complex, and loaded with character. These wines strike a magical balance between sweetness and acidity; they are as deliciously refreshing as the perfect peach.

Grapes & Styles

Virtually all of Germany's finest wines are white, and most of these are made from the Riesling grape. German wines get their sweetness in one of two ways: Either the fermentation is stopped before all the grape sugar has been changed to alcohol or the winemaker allows the wine to finish its fermentation and then adds back some unfermented grape juice. The producer's goal is to find the right level of sweetness for the wine's typically strong natural acidity. This combination of sugar and bracing acidity is what allows the best Rieslings to gain complexity with age.

On the Label

German wine labels provide a wealth of information. Besides showing the name of the producer and the vintage, they indicate the type of grapes, their origin (region, district, vineyard site), and how ripe they were they were when harvested.

In addition, the word *trocken* (TRAW-ken) may appear on the label, signifying a very dry wine.

The more intensely flavored examples of most grape varieties are made at the extreme northern (or southern) limits at which the grapes are able to ripen. It's no coincidence that Germany produces some of the world's greatest Riesling: at a latitude of 50°, the country's best vineyards lie as far north as Winnipeg, Canada.

Wine growing regions

MOSEL-SAAR-RUWER

Bonn

NAHE   RHEINGAU

Frankfurt

RHEINHESSEN

Stuttgart

PFALZ

Mosel

Saar

Rhine

A bottle labeled *halbtrocken* (HALB-traw-ken), or half-dry, will be technically slightly sweet, but its acidity will make it taste dry to many drinkers, especially those accustomed to New World whites. Wines without these designations can be assumed to have perceptible sweetness.

The word *Qualitätswein* is found on the labels of better German wines. The bottles may also bear one of the following six designations, depending upon the level of sugar in the grapes when harvested:

•**Kabinett** (kah-bee-NET) indicates a wine made from grapes of sound but not ripeness.

•**Spätlese** (sh'PAY't-lay-zuh) wines are made from riper grapes than those used in kabinetts.

•**Auslese** (OUSE-lay-zuh) wines are from still-riper grapes. These rich wines typically have more residual sugar than either of the first two categories.

•**Beerenauslese** (bear-en-OUSE-lay-zuh) and even sweeter **trockenbeerenauslese** come from super-ripe grapes that usually have been affected by botrytis (see page 135).

•**Eiswein** (ice-vine) is an extremely rare, high-sugar, high-acid wine (see page 132) made from frozen grapes.

Mosel-Saar-Ruwer

The steep vineyards alongside the Mosel River and its tributaries the Saar and Ruwer are Riesling country par excellence, producing delicate, crisp, floral, appley wines with a steely, mineral undertone that comes from the slate soils. The especially cool Saar and Ruwer areas require warm autumn weather if they are to produce wines with the natural sugars necessary to rank them above the kabinett level (see On the Label, page 128). Wines from the Mosel-Saar-Ruwer region come in green bottles, while those from most other grape-growing areas of Germany come in brown bottles.

At the Table

The trend in Germany for the past two decades has been toward drier wines that complement today's lighter cuisines. Drier German Rieslings with strong citrus and mineral notes are perfect with raw shellfish, but they also work well with freshwater fish, chicken, and other white meats, as well as with fried foods like calamari and eggplant. With their brisk acidity, they can take on pastas made with cream-based sauces or those heavy on garlic or olive oil. Off-dry versions go beautifully with cold shellfish salads and smoked trout; or try them alongside grilled pork tenderloin served with an apple or apricot glaze.

The Bottom Line

Wines of the Mosel-Saar-Ruwer range in price from outrageous bargains in the $10 to $12 range to scarce late-harvest releases that can easily exceed $100 for a 375-milliliter bottle! For good value, look for kabinett and spätlese bottlings, which typically retail for $12 to $25.

What to Buy: Mosel-Saar-Ruwer

1994	1995	1996	1997
A-	B	B	B+

Producers and Their Wines

C. VON SCHUBERT, RUWER ★★★★ $$$$ ♥♥
Some of the most expensive wines that come out of Germany are from this producer, and they're well worth the price. From the Qualitätswein level (see On the Label, page 128) on up, these exceptional wines have good acidity as well as a strong mineral quality. **LOOK FOR:** Anything you can find.

J. J. PRUM, MIDDLE MOSEL ★★★★★ $$$ ♥♥
Consistently outstanding, vibrant Mosel Rieslings that can be difficult to taste early due to substantial CO_2 and residual sugar. Capable of very long aging. **LOOK FOR:** Wines from the Wehlener Sonnenuhr vineyard.

DR. LOOSEN, MIDDLE MOSEL ★★★ $$$$ ♥♥
Highly concentrated, tactile wines from very low yields, with higher than normal residual sugar for each ripeness category. **LOOK FOR:** Erdener Prälat Auslese; also Erdener Treppchen Kabinett, and Uerziger Würzgarten Spätlese.

KARLSMUHLE, RUWER ★★★ $$$$ ♥♥
Aromas of cinnamon, cassis, and apple blossom. Bracing acidity. **LOOK FOR:** Lorenzhöfer Mäuerchen Kabinett, Kaseler Kehrnagel, and Kaseler Nies'chen Spätlese or Auslese.

SELBACH-OSTER, MIDDLE MOSEL ★★★ $$$$ ♥♥
Strong soil flavors and velvety texture; relatively dry for their category of ripeness. **LOOK FOR:** Zeltinger Sonnenuhr.

Ready, Set, Drink: German Riesling

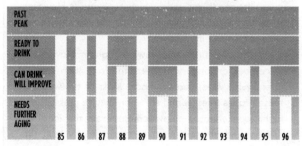

KARTHAUSERHOF, RUWER ★★★ $$–$$$$ ♥♥
Light-bodied but vibrant and intense wines, they have an earthy quality that comes from mineral- and iron-rich vineyards. **LOOK FOR:** Anything you can find.

REINHOLD HAART, MIDDLE MOSEL   ★★★ $$ – $$$$ ❢❢

Consistently excellent, large-scaled wines whose opulence often hides high acidity. **LOOK FOR:** Tropical-fruity wines from the Piesporter Goldtröpfchen.

SCHLOSS LIESER, MIDDLE MOSEL   ★★★ $$ – $$$$ ❢❢

Beautifully balanced wines with the acidity and concentration needed for long aging. Particularly good value. **LOOK FOR:** Schloss Lieser basic Riesling, kabinett, and spätlese; vineyard-designated auslese bottlings.

ADDITIONAL TOP-NOTCH POSSIBILITIES

Joh. Jos. Christoffel (Uerziger Würzgarten), *Clüsserath-Weiler* (Trittenheim Apotheke Spätlese and Auslese), *Fritz Haag* (anything from the Brauneberger Juffer vineyard), *Willi Haag* (relatively reasonably priced Brauneberger Juffer Auslese), *Heribert Kerpen* (Wehlener Sonnenuhr), *von Hövel* (Oberemmeler Hütte), *Merkelbach* (Erdener Treppchen or Uerziger Würzgarten; prices are quite reasonable), *Egon Müller Scharzfof* (look for auslese level or above, but prices can be very high), *Willi Schaefer* (Graacher Domprobst and Himmelreich), and *Zilliken* (Saarburger Rausch)

The Incredible Eiswein

Growers who gamble by leaving grapes on the vine in hopes that *Botrytis cinerea* (noble rot, see the box on page 135) will appear don't always win. Botrytis is finicky about the conditions under which it will attack. However, these unpicked bunches may yield the rarest German wine of all: eiswein.

If temperatures drop low enough in November, December, or January to freeze the fruit, then eiswein (literally ice wine) can be made. Most of the water in these grapes freezes, and so, when they're pressed, the highly concentrated pulp separates from the ice. The picking and pressing must be done quickly, and the process is extremely labor intensive. At least as sweet as and even higher in acidity than beerenausleses (see On the Label, page 128), eisweins are often frightfully expensive. They can age for decades.

Other German Wine Regions

The warmer and dryer Rheingau region yields somewhat fuller wines than those of the Mosel and is its chief rival for international fame. Among other top German regions represented in the U.S. market are the Rheinhessen (whose wines offer citric, floral, and smoky notes, and are a bit more overtly fruity than those of the Rheingau), the Nahe (which produces wines with elements of red and black fruits and generally firm acidity), and the Pfalz (the wines of which are typically full-bodied, earthy, and pungently spicy).

At the Table

The generally softer citrus flavors (orange, tangerine) and the slightly lower acidity of these wines enable them to complement Southeast Asian dishes featuring lemongrass, cilantro, ginger, and chiles, as well as Indian dishes flavored by cardamom, cumin, or *garam masala*. Try a wine from one of these regions as an accompaniment to soft-shell crabs with lime-and-cilantro salsa, sautéed scallops with Thai green curry, or grilled sesame chicken satays with coriander dipping sauce. In Germany, spätlese and auslese wines are frequently paired with duck, goose, and even venison, and no German wines are more effective in this role than the slightly earthy and smoky versions from the Pfalz.

The Bottom Line

German Rieslings from other regions can often be a couple of dollars cheaper than wines of similar quality and ripeness level from the Mosel-Saar-Ruwer. Bottles from less-known vineyards in the Pfalz and Nahe can be particularly good values.

What to Buy: Wines from Other German Regions

1994	1995	1996	1997
A-/B+	B	B-	B+

Producers and Their Wines

GUNDERLOCH, RHEINHESSEN ★★★★ $$$ ♛♛
Maker of extremely fresh and reserved but rich and concentrated wines that take time to show their best. **LOOK FOR:** Anything you can find.

KOEHLER-RUPRECHT, PFALZ ★★★★ $$$ ♛♛
Powerful but refined wines that show typical Pfalz aromas of ginger, cinnamon, and pineapple. **LOOK FOR:** Kallstadter Saumagen.

MULLER-CATOIR, PFALZ ★★★★ $$ – $$$$ ♛♛
Superconcentrated, vivid, often expensive wines from Riesling, Rieslaner, Scheurebe, and Muscat. Made from late-picked, minimally handled grapes. **LOOK FOR:** Anything you can find.

BASSERMANN-JORDAN, PFALZ ★★★ $$$ ♛♛
Big, mouth-filling, long-lived wines, with different labels used for the estate's dry and fruity (i.e., slightly to moderately sweet) wines. Quality on the rise since 1996. **LOOK FOR:** Estate Riesling (for value); single-vineyard kabinett and spätlese.

KUNSTLER, RHEINGAU ★★★ $$$ ♛♛
One of the great producers of trocken Rieslings; also makes fruitier-styled, slightly sweet estate kabinett and spätlese. **LOOK FOR:** Anything you can find.

JOHANNISHOF (H. H. ESER), RHEINGAU ★★★ $ – $$$$ ♛♛
Restrained, minerally, full-bodied wines, sometimes austere in their youth. **LOOK FOR:** Johannisberger Goldatzel and Hölle; Winkeler Jesuitengarten.

FREIHERR HEYL ZU HERRNSHEIM, RHEINHESSEN ★★★ $ – $$$ ♛♛
Best known for dry and off-dry wines from the finest vineyards of Nierstein. Brudersberg tends to be among the most flamboyant wines from the Rheinhessen. **LOOK FOR:** Pettenthal Spätlese, Oelberg Spätlese, and Auslese.

JOSEF LEITZ, RHEINGAU ★★★ $ – $$$ ♛♛
Extremely aromatic, muscular wines, aged in barrel and thus more vinous (see Glossary page 223) as opposed to simply fruity. **LOOK FOR:** Anything you can find.

BURKLIN-WOLF, PFALZ ★★ $$$ ♛♛
Increasingly rich, rather full-bodied, relatively dry wines, considerably improved since 1994. **LOOK FOR:** Rieslings from Ruppertsberg and Wachenheim, especially trocken bottlings.

ADDITIONAL TOP-NOTCH POSSIBILITIES

Josef Biffar (anything you can find), *von Buhl* (any wines from Forst), *Hermann Dönnhoff* (anything you can find), *Emrich-Schönleber* (Monzinger Frühlingspätzchen and Halenberg Spätlese and Auslese, often bottled as trocken or halbtrocken), *Fuhrmann-Eymael* (Riesling and Scheurebe spätlese or above), *Krüger-Rumpf* (spätlese bottlings at excellent prices), *Toni Jost* (Rieslings from the Bacharacher Hahn vineyard), *Lingenfelder* (Rieslings and Scheurebes, but avoid 1995), *Walter Strub* (Niersteiner Paterberg, Hipping, and Oeberg are best and generally very good value), *Robert Weil* (rare, pricey noble sweet wines are best), and *Werlé* (Forster Jesuitengarten, Forster Pechstein, and Forster Kirchenstück)

The Noble Rot

Botrytis cinerea (bo-TRIE-tiss sin-eh-RAY-ah), or noble rot, is a mold that develops under the right climactic conditions (alternating humidity and dry heat), turning grape skins purplish gray and shrivelling them. While the chemical action of this fungus is still something of a mystery, botrytis has the beneficial effect of concentrating sugars and acids and increasing glycerin as the grape dehydrates. Certain grape varieties—notably Sémillon, Riesling, and Chenin Blanc, and to a lesser extent, Sauvignon Blanc—are especially prone to noble rot. Botrytis wines are generally very sweet and sumptuous in texture, with exotic aromas and flavors of apricot, marmalade, pineapple, honey, and licorice and an uncanny persistence on the palate.

CALIFORNIA

THESE ARE BOOM TIMES FOR THE CALIFORNIA WINE industry. Wine quality—and prices—have never been higher, demand is stronger than ever, and the state has had a succession of good vintages through the 1990s. Happily for consumers, a combination of forces should put a brake on skyrocketing prices, at least temporarily: Vineyards that had to be replanted due to an epidemic of phylloxera (a vine-killing root louse) are coming back into production, massive plantings in new areas are now beginning to bear fruit, and California's 1997 crop is its largest on record. Though these factors are unlikely to result in actual price declines for California's most coveted limited bottlings, the circumstances will probably increase the availability of moderately priced wine over the coming year.

Grapes & Styles

California's world-class wines include complex Chardonnays from the cooler spots in Sonoma and Santa Barbara counties; full-flavored, strongly oaked Cabernet Sauvignons from Napa Valley; and sappy, berry-scented Zinfandels from pockets of old vines all over the state. Bracing Sauvignon Blancs and the popular Merlots are important to the state's vintners as well. In addition, winemakers are branching out to produce excellent wines from Rhône Valley varieties like Syrah and Viognier, fruit-driven yet refined Pinot Noirs from Sonoma County, and varietal bottlings from the Tuscan grape Sangiovese.

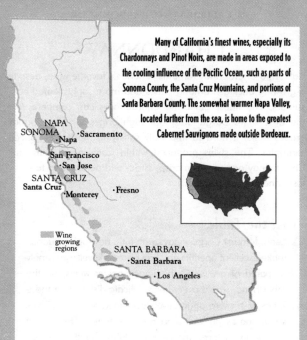

Many of California's finest wines, especially its Chardonnays and Pinot Noirs, are made in areas exposed to the cooling influence of the Pacific Ocean, such as parts of Sonoma County, the Santa Cruz Mountains, and portions of Santa Barbara County. The somewhat warmer Napa Valley, located farther from the sea, is home to the greatest Cabernet Sauvignons made outside Bordeaux.

On the Label

Like most wines that are produced outside of Europe, California's are typically labeled by grape variety (such as Chardonnay or Zinfandel) rather than by narrowly defined geographic area, or appellation. According to law, California's varietal bottlings must contain at least 75 percent of the named grape, and many of the best varietal wines contain more, all the way up to 100 percent.

Some wineries escape the confines of the 75 percent rule by giving their wines fanciful proprietary names, such as Opus One, and simply omitting the grape variety from the label. A term used by many producers is *Meritage*, which signifies a red or white wine produced from a blend of Bordeaux grape varieties. (Be warned that California wines with European place-names, such as Chablis or white Burgundy, have little to do with their namesakes.)

CHARDONNAY

California Chardonnay remains America's favorite wine, despite a growing backlash among critics and more sophisticated consumers. The finest California Chardonnays can compete with the best white Burgundies, but high prices for Chardonnay grapes make it hard to find truly satisfying moderately priced examples. The styles produced within California run the full Chardonnay gamut: from crisp, citric, and penetrating to oaky, lush, and tropical-fruity.

At the Table

Lean, lemony Chardonnays with little new-oak influence make excellent aperitifs and can also work well with simply prepared or raw shellfish. Bigger, oakier wines, on the other hand, would overwhelm delicate dishes; pair these wines with more aggressively seasoned foods. Grilling's smoky notes go well with the oak tones. The richest Chardonnays tame the heat of chiles: Try these wines with Thai or Southwestern fish or poultry preparations. Heavier Chardonnays can also stand up to fatty fish, such as salmon and tuna, and to creamy, butter-based sauces. The almost exotic tropical-fruit flavors (banana, pineapple, mango) shown by many California Chardonnays pair well with Indian or Far Eastern specialities, such as chutneys or coconut-flavored curries.

The Bottom Line

The best California Chardonnays are now $30 per bottle and up, and scarce at that. At the low end, wines priced less than $12 tend to be rather generic and lacking in personality; you may find something better among inexpensive Chardonnays from Australia or Chile. However, numerous California wines with concentration and character can be found in the $15 to $25 range; the best of these offer reasonable value.

What to Buy: Chardonnay

1995	1996	1997
A-	B+	B-

Chalk Hill 1996 Estate Bottled Chardonnay, ★★★ **$$$** ❣❣❣
Sonoma County Complex aromas of smoky oak, hazelnut, turmeric, and fennel. Silky rich and stylish on the palate, with exotic oak notes and smoke and truffle nuances. Finishes with a youthful brightness and very good length.

Chateau Montelena 1996, Napa Valley ★★★ **$$$** ❣❣❣
Aromas of apple, spearmint, truffle, melon, herbs, and butterscotch. Sweet and fat in the mouth, with hints of melon and vanilla. Finishes firm, with an intriguing yeasty quality.

Matanzas Creek Winery 1996, Sonoma Valley ★★★ **$$$** ❣❣❣
Knockout nose combines deep aromas of brown butter, truffle, and bacon fat with lively lime and floral notes. Thick, silky, and generous in the mouth, with a flavor of ripe pineapple. Finishes long and spicy, with a butterscotch hint.

Shafer 1996 Red Shoulder Ranch, Carneros ★★★ **$$$** ❣❣
Floral, herbal, lemon, and butterscotch aromas. Very rich and silky in the mouth, with a leesy complexity; concentrated and seamless. Lowish acidity contributes to the wine's impression of roundness. Fat, long, spicy finish.

Kendall-Jackson 1996 Camelot Vineyard, ★★★ **$$** ❣❣❣
Santa Maria Valley Aromas of dried tropical fruits, honey, and nuts. Dense and tactile; a sweeter-styled Chardonnay that has enough harmonious acidity to give shape to its thick, tropical fruit. Big, rich, and impressive.

Handley Vineyard 1996, Dry Creek Valley ★★★ **$$** ❣❣
Fresh, floral aromas of pineapple, mint, and licorice. Juicy and sharply delineated on the palate; shows a dusty, minerally quality. Really terrific fruit, without the distraction of new oak.

J. Fritz 1996 Dutton Ranch, ★★★ **$$** ❣❣
Russian River Valley Lemon-lime, quinine, and charred oak on the nose. Ripe, juicy, and very intensely flavored; creamy texture supported by a stony underpinning. Firm and long finish.

Mount Eden 1996 MacGregor Vineyard, ★★★ **$$** ❣❣
Edna Valley Lively aromas of lemon peel, fresh herbs, flowers, and spicy oak. Big, rich, sweet, and impeccably balanced, with crisp acidity framing the fruit. Icy-clean, palate-freshening finish hints at mint. Seamless and very long.

Talley 1996, Arroyo Grande Valley   ★★★ $$ ▼▼
Orange zest and mint on the nose. Bright and focused, with lovely balance and vinosity; holds its shape well. Nicely balanced for early drinking. Long, spicy, ripe-but-dry aftertaste.

Byron 1996, Santa Maria Valley   ★★ $$ ▼▼▼
Expressive buttery, nutty nose, with a whiff of candied fruit. Juicy and fairly intense, with lively acidity giving the wine a firm spine. Finishes spicy and a bit hard-edged.

Cambria 1996 Katherine's Vineyard,   ★★ $$ ▼▼▼
Santa Maria Valley Bright, spicy aroma of lemon ice. Dense, lush, and sweet in the mouth, with sound balancing acidity. Lingering, slightly sweet finishing flavor is spicy and firm.

The Hess Collection 1996, Napa Valley   ★★ $$ ▼▼▼
Minerals, talc, and soft citrus fruits on the nose. Flavors of orange pith and nectarine, plus a suggestion of tropical fruits. Supple and fairly full in the mouth. Easygoing, lingering finish.

Kendall-Jackson 1997 Vintner's Reserve,   ★★ $$ ▼▼▼
California Smoky, spicy-oak, and tropical-fruit aromas. Smooth and silky; slightly sweet flavors of orange Creamsicle, lemon, and toast. Good weight; decent balancing acidity.

Robert Mondavi 1996, Napa Valley   ★★ $$ ▼▼▼
Rather complex lemon, herbal, and smoky-oak aromas. Juicy, harmonious, and forthcoming, with good flavor intensity and light oak treatment. Offers personality and thorough ripeness. Finishes firm and persistent.

Zaca Mesa 1996 Zaca Vineyards,   ★★ $$ ▼▼▼
Santa Barbara County Orange blossom, grapefruit, and lime on the nose. Spicy and citric in the mouth, with an exotic perfume and good intensity. Juicy, clean, and lively, with firm acidity. Finishes slightly tart but persistent.

Arrowood Winery 1996, Sonoma County   ★★ $$ ▼▼
Initially reserved nose opens to show pineapple and charred-oak notes. Fat and rich, with just enough acidity to maintain its balance. A fairly powerful style of Chardonnay.

Meridian Vineyards 1997, Santa Barbara County   ★★ $ ▼▼▼
Ripe aromas of earth and truffle. Clean, assertive lemon-lime

flavors, complicated by orange peel and clove. Rather round and creamy but with refreshing acids. Persistent ripe finish.

Napa Ridge 1997 Coastal Vines, North Coast   ★★ $ ♥♥♥
Pear and apple aromas, plus oak notes of vanilla and scotch. Supple, direct flavors of honeydew and cantaloupe; the wood element is not intrusive. Finishes with juicy, tropical-fruit flavors.

Rodney Strong 1997, Sonoma County   ★★ $ ♥♥♥
Exotic aromas of peach and fig, plus a suggestion of oak spice. Clean, brisk flavors of lemon cream and banana skin. Offers an attractive restrained sweetness and a lively, firm finish.

SAUVIGNON BLANC

California Sauvignon Blancs range as widely in style as do its Chardonnays. In fact, the rich, barrel-aged types can deliver the impact of Chardonnay at a lower price. Crisper versions with mouthwatering acidity are as penetrating and food-friendly as examples from the Loire Valley. Generally, Sauvignon Blanc (also called Fumé Blanc) is best suited for drinking within a year or two following its release.

At the Table

Sauvignon Blancs with relatively little oak influence and strongly citric flavors (lemon, lime, grapefruit) are ideal as aperitifs; they also shine with shellfish (scallops, clams, oysters) or simply prepared freshwater fish. The crisp acids of these wines can cut through butter-based sauces, leaving the palate clean and refreshed. Large-scale, oaky versions of California Sauvignon Blanc are really designed as stand-ins for Chardonnay, even if the better versions manage to retain some of their notice-able Sauvignon acidity. These wines thus call for slightly lighter fare than you would choose for a Chardonnay: Roast chicken or grilled salmon would be good choices, as would a variety of Southeast Asian dishes, even fairly assertively flavored ones. Many blended wines based on Sauvignon Blanc are featured on the wine lists of Southwestern, Thai, Szechuan, and Indian restaurants.

The Bottom Line

Sauvignon Blanc is still an excellent place to look for value in California wine; relatively few wines are priced above $18. A host of bargains await you in the under-$12 range.

What to Buy: Sauvignon Blanc

1995	1996	1997
B+	B	B+

J. Rochioli 1997, Russian River Valley ★★★★ $$ ♟♟
Pungent, perfumed aromas of gooseberry and rose petal. Very concentrated flavors of ripe ruby grapefruit, white peach, and mineral dust saturate the palate. As rich as this wine is, bright acidity gives it excellent clarity of flavor.

Chalk Hill 1996 Estate Bottled ★★★ $$ ♟♟♟
Sauvignon Blanc, Sonoma County Expressive nose combines citrus oil, butterscotch, and fig. Fat, silky, and concentrated, with strong oak and lees notes of toffee, butterscotch, and spice. A mouth-filling Sauvignon with a long, spicy aftertaste.

Matanzas Creek Winery 1997, Sonoma County ★★★ $$ ♟♟♟
Complex nose combines lemon, honeydew melon, vanilla, licorice, mint, and other fresh herbs. Tactile and rich in the mouth, with pink-grapefruit and mineral flavors. Dense but vibrant. Finish is long and crisp, but not austere.

Buena Vista Carneros 1997, Carneros ★★ $ ♟♟♟
Varietally accurate aromas of grass and lime. Fresh flavors of pear and lime, plus a note of fig. Lively ripe acidity extends the fruit and keeps the persistent finish lively and refreshing.

Geyser Peak 1997, Sonoma County ★★ $ ♟♟♟
Crisp lemon-peel nose. Bright, focused flavors of lemon, melon, and fresh herbs. Offers good texture and body. Finishes fairly long and intense, with the note of lemon peel repeating.

Rodney Strong 1997 Charlotte's Home ★★ $ ♟♟♟
Estate Bottled, Northern Sonoma Ripe pear, apple, and melon aromas. Tangy and fresh, with a hint of CO_2. Juicy but ripe acidity gives the wine a pliable texture. Suggestion of clove spice. Firm and lively on the aftertaste.

Callaway 1997, Temecula ★ $ ♈♈♈
Bright, assertive aromas of grass, orange peel, and mint. Clean, fresh, and round, with gentle fruit balanced by firm acidity. Orange, tangerine, and pink-grapefruit flavors linger on the finish.

Lakespring 1996, Napa Valley ★ $ ♈♈♈
Cool minty, grassy nose, with a pronounced melon note. Soft and round in the mouth, but a note of lime skin keeps the wine firm and brisk. Ripe, gentle finish.

Van Asperen 1997, Napa Valley ★ $ ♈♈♈
Pungent, faintly grassy nose shows more exotic than citric fruit aromas. Plump and very ripe, with melon and tropical-fruit flavors. Could use more zip on the finish, but rich and broad.

CABERNET SAUVIGNON

Thanks to a string of strong vintages in the 1990s and to constantly improving winemaking, California's Cabernet Sauvignons are now the prime challengers to Bordeaux. Whereas the examples from a decade ago tended to be brooding, tannic monsters better as meal substitutes than as accompaniments to food, today's wines are suppler in texture, with stronger cassis and black-cherry fruit, and are more approachable in their youth.

At the Table
Familiarly called Cab, California's popular red wine is probably even better suited to food than wine from Bordeaux, because its more obviously ripe fruit, generally riper tannins, and lower acidity make it easier to enjoy in its youth. This wine provides a foil for assertive meat flavors and for smoke, pepper, and pungent spices that might clash with more austere Cabernet-based Bordeaux. California Cabernet with T-bone steak or leg of lamb is a traditional pairing. Intensely flavored or salty foods, such as beef stir-fried with ginger and soy sauce, can bring out the fruit that often hides behind the toasty, vanilla taste from the oak. California Cabernet also pairs well with wild mushrooms and garlicky, peppery marinades.

The Bottom Line

Prices for the best Cabernets have gone through the roof in the past few years: Literally dozens of labels have passed the $50 barrier. Some of these wines are superb, others simply over-priced. As with Chardonnay, examples costing less than $12 tend to lack concentration and varietal accuracy, but there is still a host of sound choices in the $15 to $30 range. Careful selection is essential.

What to Buy: Cabernet Sauvignon

1993	1994	1995	1996	1997
B-	A+	B	B+	B+

Joseph Phelps 1995, Napa Valley ★★★ **$$$ ♟♟♟**
Dusty black-cherry and leather aromas. Very sweet in the mouth, but fresh acidity gives it a bright, fruity quality. Good structure and depth. Finishes with firm tannins.

Robert Mondavi 1995, Oakville District ★★★ **$$$ ♟♟♟**
Aromas of plum, cherry, currant, tobacco, and roasted nuts. Large-scaled and rich, with attractive middle-palate sweetness and good balance. The substantial tannins hit the palate quite late and coat the mouth.

Shafer 1995, Stags Leap District ★★★ **$$$ ♟♟♟**
Deep, smoky aromas of plum, currant, and roasted nuts. Lush, plummy, and sweet; quite generous of texture. Finishes with suave tannins, a hint of tobacco, and very good length.

Swanson 1995 Estate, Napa Valley ★★★ **$$$ ♟♟**
Black currant and blackberry on the nose. Ripe and layered, with flavors of raspberry, black currant, and leather. Tangy acidity gives the fruit clarity and tempers the wine's sweetness. Firmly structured and suavely tannic.

Beaulieu Vineyard 1995 Rutherford, ★★ **$$ ♟♟♟**
Napa Valley Urgent red-currant and cranberry aromas. Fresh, concentrated, and firm on the palate, with black raspberry and cherry fruit complicated by notes of coffee, chocolate, tobacco, and mint. Persistent, juicy aftertaste.

Benziger 1995, Sonoma County　　　　★★ $$ ♟♟♟
Featuring aromas of berries, chocolate, and just a hint of bell pepper on the nose. A fat and textured wine with good ripeness but only moderate clarity of flavor. The tannins build on the finish.

Chateau Montelena 1996 Calistoga Cuvee,　　★★ $$ ♟♟♟
Napa Valley Briary black-fruit, chocolate, and shoe-polish aromas. Fat and layered in the mouth, with a flavor of sweet black cherries. A nice mouthful of accessible Cabernet fruit. Finishes with rather lush tannins.

Dry Creek Vineyard 1996, Sonoma County　　★★ $$ ♟♟♟
High-toned, assertive red-berry nose. Sweet, nicely focused flavors of raspberry, cassis, and blackberry, plus an overlay of clove and sandalwood from the oak. Lingering and sweet; moderately tannic finish.

Ready, Set, Drink: Cabernet Sauvignon

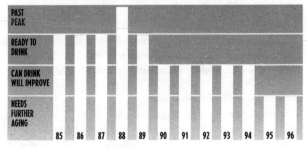

Fisher Vineyards 1995 Coach Insignia,　　　★★ $$ ♟♟♟
Napa Valley Enticing aromas include those of roasted game, plum, and gun smoke. Medium-bodied and ripe, with lively acidity; notes of eucalyptus and black cherry in the mouth. The finish is firm, but the tannins are not excessive. This is a nicely balanced wine.

Kendall-Jackson 1995 Buckeye Vineyard,　　★★ $$ ♟♟♟
Alexander Valley Cassis, black cherry, and licorice aromas. Intensely flavored but quite tightly wound at this point. The wine's firm acidity, is nicely integrated. Currently the fruit is dominated by tannic structure.

Napa Ridge 1994 Reserve, Napa Valley ★★ $$ ♥♥♥
Ripe aromas of raspberry, red currant, and exotic oak spice.
Complex cherry, cassis, mint, and vanilla-cream flavors; dusty and
floral nuances. Silky and fairly full-bodied. Finishes long and ripe.

Robert Mondavi 1995, Napa Valley ★★ $$ ♥♥♥
Currant, plum, leather, smoke, and earth aromas, along with
hints of tobacco and eucalyptus. Could use a bit more flesh and
depth of flavor but shows good spicy intensity. Finishes with
slightly drying tannins.

Rodney Strong 1995, Sonoma County ★★ $$ ♥♥♥
Tangy, fresh aromas of cherry, smoke, and tar. Bright red-berry
flavors, with spicy oak in the background. Finishes brisk and
firm, with modest, smooth tannins.

St. Francis 1996, Sonoma County ★★ $ ♥♥♥
Super-ripe aromas of red currant, tar, loam, and meat. Silky and
generous in the mouth, with red-currant flavor complicated by
a gamy nuance. Finishes with ripe, soft tannins.

Hawk Crest 1995, California ★ $ ♥♥♥
Ripe cherry and black-plum aromas have a slightly candied
quality. Juicy, supple, and round, with soft acidity and a flavor of
cherry preserves. Slightly jammy finish shows very light tannins.

Napa Ridge 1996, Central Coast ★ $ ♥♥♥
Very deep color. Roasted cherry and plum nose. Dense and lay-
ered in the mouth; flavors of plum and cassis complicated by
cedar and clove oak notes. Rather plump, owing to soft acidity.
Sweet, lightly tannic finish.

MERLOT

Merlot's popularity soared in the early 1990s as wine drinkers
suddenly discovered that this grape produced wines with lusher
textures and softer tannins than Cabernet Sauvignon.
Unflagging demand for Merlot by wine drinkers in America and
abroad has led to not only an explosion of Merlot plantings
around the world, but also a flood of thin, weedy, unsatisfying
wines in the marketplace. California's best examples offer supple,
velvety textures; aromas of cherry, plum, dark berries, and
chocolate; and smooth tannins.

At the Table

Lighter Merlots are somewhat wimpier than Cabernets: Roast chicken or beef tenderloin are good matches. Richer Merlots with chocolate and cherry/berry flavors, more texture and ripeness, and substantial tannins are perfect with fatty meats like lamb and beef, hamburger and sausages, or duck and goose. The fat brings out the vibrant fruit of these wines and softens their tannins.

The Bottom Line

Due to the number of not-yet-ready-for-prime-time wines rushed to market to capitalize on demand, Merlot bottlings are among the last places to look for value. Buying under-$15 Merlot blind is a recipe for disappointment. However, California's finest examples are, along with the best bottlings from Washington State, the most satisfying Merlot wines made outside Bordeaux.

What to Buy: Merlot

1994	1995	1996	1997
A+	B	B+	B

Shafer 1995, Napa Valley ★★★ $$$ ▾▾▾
Dusty red-currant, plum, and leather aromas. Supple, round, and a bit soft, with leather and mineral notes. Not especially vibrant but has very good texture and richness. Finishes with even, ripe tannins.

Arrowood Winery 1995, Sonoma County ★★★ $$$ ▾▾
Perfumed aromas of dark berries, plum, and smoky oak. Intense black-cherry and dark-chocolate flavors are nicely delineated. Structured, firm, and persistent.

Matanzas Creek Winery 1995, Sonoma Valley ★★★ $$$ ▾▾
Aromas of raspberry, mint, and chocolate. Lush and oaky in the mouth, with good ripeness but a firm edge of acidity. Finishes with dusty tannins and very good length.

Havens 1996, Napa Valley ★★★ $$ ▾▾
Very aromatic red-fruit nose dominated by tobacco and oak

spice. Pungent, plummy middle-palate fruit. Lovely sweetness and balance. Finishes with dusty tannins.

Ravenswood 1996 Sangiocomo Vineyard, ★★★ $$ ♥♥
Sonoma Valley Deep ruby color. Spicy aromas of dark berries and graphite. Opulent and sweet in the mouth, with strong, bright inner-mouth flavor dominated by mulberry. Long, very strong finish.

Markham 1996, Napa Valley ★★ $$ ♥♥♥
Sweet, briary aromas of berries and toasty oak; rather Zinfandel-like. Ripe and full in the mouth, with tart-edged blackberry fruit. Persistent, tangy finish features notes of sweet berry and pipe tobacco.

Rabbit Ridge 1996, North Coast ★★ $$ ♥♥
Brambly blackberry nose. Flavors of cherry, black raspberry, and cassis, plus a suggestion of maple-syrup sweetness. Fresh acidity brightens the fruit. Finishes clean and crisp, with soft, melting tannins and a hint of eucalyptus.

Beaulieu Vineyard 1995, Coastal ★★ $ ♥♥♥
Toasty aroma of blackberry. Fresh berry flavors complicated by cedar and tobacco notes. Kept fresh by sound, juicy acidity. Lingering, elegant finish, with ripe tannins hidden by fruit.

Fetzer 1997 Eagle Peak, California ★ $ ♥♥♥
Candied red-fruit nose. Fruity on the palate, with crisp acids brightening the strawberry and raspberry flavors. A soft, easy-to-drink Merlot with light tannins and a surprisingly refreshing finish.

ZINFANDEL

Like jazz, Zinfandel is an American original, as well as the only American wine imitated abroad. Even today, California produces virtually all the best examples of this spicy, full-flavored red wine. Zinfandel has gone through at least three incarnations over the past generation. As recently as the 1970s, many Zinfandels were pruney, portlike, overly alcoholic, and sometimes quite sweet wines from late-harvested grapes. When the popularity of this style plummeted, unwanted Zinfandel grapes were widely used to make an insipid, picnic-style blush wine called white Zinfandel. Since the early 1980s, though, serious (that is, red and dry) Zinfandel has staged a successful come-back. Today's Zinfandels generally fall into two categories: mid-weight, sculpted, Bordeaux-like wines with dark-berry and spice aromas and flavors; and high-alcohol (often more than 14 per-cent), outrageously rich, exotically ripe wines with aromas of citrus zest, briary black raspberry and blackberry, black pepper, and chocolate.

At the Table

Full-throttle Zinfandel, which generally packs a serious alcoholic wallop, should be paired with rich, powerful flavors: venison daube; pepper-crusted flank steak; spicy sausage and casseroles; or ripe, strong-smelling cheeses. The deeply spicy character of Zinfandel supports the use of black pepper, garlic, and fresh herbs. Charcoal-broiled meats and Zinfandel are made for each other. Zin can even stand up to sweet-spicy barbecue sauce. A medium-weight Zinfandel can fill the same role at the table as Cabernet Sauvignon. And don't forget the all-American pairing of Zinfandel and Thanksgiving turkey.

The Bottom Line

While it's hard to find excellent Zinfandel for less than $15, few bottles exceed $25. For sheer flavor per dollar, the better Zinfandels still offer very good value.

What to Buy: Zinfandel

1994	1995	1996	1997
A-	B+	B+	B

J. Fritz 1996 Old Vines, Dry Creek Valley ★★★ $$♥♥
Vibrant aromas of blackberry, orange zest, and pepper. Rich but bright in the mouth; exotic but shapely. Classic Zin flavors without excessive sweetness. Finishes with substantial dusty tannins.

Ravenswood 1996 Wood Road/Belloni, ★★★ $$♥♥
Russian River Valley Blackberry, boysenberry, and chocolate on the nose. Sweet and velvety in the mouth, but the flavors are fresh thanks to firm acidity. A strong mouthful of dark-berry flavors. Finishes very long, with dusty tannins.

Ridge 1996, Sonoma Station ★★★$$ 🍷🍷
Currants, earth, and a hint of raisiny super-ripeness on the nose. Juicy, intensely flavored, and quite tactile on the palate; the fresh curranty fruitiness comes as a surprise after the nose. Finishes bright, firmly tannic, and long.

Rosenblum Cellars 1996 Reserve, ★★★$$ 🍷🍷
Contra Costa County Perfumed aromas of blackberry and scotch. Rich, very concentrated, and vibrant, with essence-of-dark-berry flavor and strong but integrated acidity. Finishes quite firm, with strong dark-berry flavor.

Benziger 1995 Old Vines, Sonoma County ★★$$ 🍷🍷🍷
Berries and chocolate on the nose. Very sweet and ripe, but given shape and grip by firm acids. Finishes spicy and fairly long.

Dry Creek Vineyard 1996 Old Vines, ★★$$ 🍷🍷🍷
Sonoma County Cherry/berry fruitiness along with tobacco, truffle, and leather on the nose. Rather subdued cherry, dark-berry, and leather flavors are brightened by sappy acids. The slightly tough finish calls for a year or two of aging.

Robert Mondavi 1996, Napa Valley ★★$$ 🍷🍷🍷
Berries, mint, and lead-pencil aromas, plus a slight medicinal nuance. Sweet, supple, and easygoing; moderately concentrated and nicely balanced. Finishes with fine tannins and good length.

Rodney Strong 1995 Old Vines, ★★$$ 🍷🍷🍷
Northern Sonoma Spicy aromas of blackberry and cassis. Sweet and dense on the palate, with vibrant black-fruit flavors and fresh acidity. Finishes smooth and ripe, with vanillin oak.

Seghesio 1996 Old Vines, Sonoma County ★★$$ 🍷🍷🍷
Peppery aromas of blackberry, orange zest, chocolate, and spearmint. Creamy texture and compelling sweetness, enlivened by edgy acids and a strong minty nuance. Serious, slightly dry tannins.

Cline Cellars 1996 Ancient Vines, ★★$$ 🍷🍷
Contra Costa County Pungent blueberry, cassis, and spice aromas. Velvety and fruity in the mouth; sound acidity gives the wine lovely balance. Finishes with even tannins.

Rabbit Ridge 1996 Barrel Cuvée, Sonoma County ★$ 🍷🍷🍷
Sweet, jammy black-raspberry and blueberry aromas. Easygoing

flavors of boysenberry and blackberry jam; sweet and ready to drink. Very supple tannins. Has just enough acidity.

Ravenswood 1996 Vintners Blend, Sonoma County   ★ $ ♟♟♟
Briary blackberry and tar nose, with hints of nutmeg and mace. Seamless, lush berry flavors perked up by thyme and oregano. Seductive texture and sweetness. Finishes with fine tannins.

RHONE-STYLE WINES

In recent years, California has proved to be fertile ground for a host of grape varieties long associated with France's Rhône Valley. Red grapes like Syrah, Grenache, and Mourvèdre are now producing a wide range of appealing, fruit-driven wines characterized by spicy berry flavors and solid yet supple tannins. The winemakers who popularized these food-flexible wines are often referred to as California's Rhône Rangers. Viognier, an exotically perfumed white grape that makes the northern Rhône Valley wine called Condrieu, is growing rapidly in popularity.

At the Table

California's Syrah- and Mourvèdre-based wines are typically fruitier than their Rhône Valley counterparts, though they still retain the meaty, spicy qualities of the French versions. Their flavors are strong enough to complement grilled and highly seasoned red-meat dishes, especially those made with black pepper. Try these reds with grilled peppered flank steak, venison loin with blackberry or black-currant sauce, or mustard-crusted beef tenderloin. Viognier, with its super-ripe fruit notes of nectarine, peach, and apricot, pairs well with complex, exotic dishes that incorporate chiles, cilantro, garlic, or curry.

The Bottom Line

Varietal Syrah bottlings are now generally $18 or more, but the finest of them offer excellent quality/price rapport. Rhône-grape blends are often less expensive than single-variety bottlings and offer some of California's best values in red wine. Due to its scarcity, Viognier is rarely inexpensive.

RED WINES

Truchard 1996 Syrah, Carneros   ★★★ **$$$** ♥♥
Saturated ruby red. Expressive aromas of black raspberry, violet, chocolate, game, and animal fur. Sweet, sappy, and strong; dense but smooth. The black-raspberry flavor repeats in the mouth. Finishes firmly tannic and long.

Cline Cellars 1996 Mourvèdre Ancient Vines,   ★★★ **$$** ♥♥
Contra Costa County Pungent aromas of blackberry, cassis, mace, black pepper, rosemary, and mint. Silky but firm-edged in the middle palate. Really expands in the mouth and on the aftertaste. Firmly structured yet pliant. Spicy and long.

Great Gifts

- *Pol Roger 1990 Brut Chardonnay Champagne* .... page 41
- *Veuve Clicquot 1990 Vintage Réserve Champagne* .... page 41
- *J. Lassalle 1992 Special Club Brut Champagne* .... page 41
- *Billecart-Salmon NV Rosé Brut Champagne* .... page 41
- *Jean-Louis Chave 1996, Hermitage* .... page 66
- *Antinori 1995 Tignanello, IGT* .... page 96
- *Bodegas Reyes 1996 Téofilo Reyes, Ribera del Duero* .... page 108
- *Bodegas Alejandro Fernández 1996 Tinto Pesquera, Ribera del Duero* .... page 108
- *Columbia Winery 1994 Sagemoor Vineyards Cabernet Sauvingon, Columbia Valley* ..... page 170
- *Vinicola Hidalgo Napoléon Amontillado* ... page 116
- *Emilio Lustau Rare Cream Sherry Solera Superior* .... page 117
- *Dow's Twenty-Year-Old NV Tawny Port* ... page 124
- *Ferriera Dona Antonia NV Tawny Port* .... page 124
- *Graham's 1995 Malvedos Port* .... page 125
- *Dow's 1995 Quinta do Bomfin Port* .... page 125

Ridge 1995 Petite Sirah, York Creek ★★★ $$ ￼￼
Wild aromas of black raspberry, gingerbread, and raw meat.
Dense, spicy, and peppery; fresh and intensely flavored, with
firm acidity giving the middle palate a somewhat rigid character.

Simi 1996 Shiraz, Sonoma County ★★ $$ ￼￼￼
Pungent, oaky nose of red berries, clove, sandalwood, and game.
Meaty, supple, and thick, with enticing sweetness. Tarry, faintly
tart-edged finish. Made in an Australian style.

Cline Cellars 1996 Syrah, Carneros ★★ $$ ￼￼
Smoky, slightly floral aroma of dark berries, chocolate, and
pepper. Sweet, supple, and oaky in the mouth; not really expres-
sive yet but has good material and structure. Finishes with
tongue-dusting, slight dry tannins.

Edmunds St. John 1996 Syrah, California ★★ $$ ￼￼
Pepper, woodsmoke, gunpowder, and game on the nose. Ripe
and chewy in the mouth, with generous texture and firm acidity.
Pepper and game flavors call to mind a wine from southern France.

Qupé 1996 Los Olivos Cuvée, ★★ $$ ￼￼
Santa Barbara County Black cherry, tobacco, smoke, pepper, and
fur aromas. Supple, pliant; good texture and restrained sweetness.
Long, ripely tannic finish. Syrah, Mourvèdre, and Grenache blend.

Joseph Phelps 1996 Vin du Mistral Pastiche, ★★ $ ￼￼￼
Napa Valley Aromas of red currant, smoke, and tobacco. Supple
and pliant in the mouth, but the fruity cherry and red-berry fla-
vors are ripe and delineated. Finishes with ripe tannins and very
good length. A blend based on Mourvèdre and Grenache.

Bogle 1996 Petite Sirah, California ★ $ ￼￼￼
Jammy blackberry, licorice, and smoke on the nose. Fat and sweet,
with berry, bitter-cherry, and dark-chocolate flavors. Finishes with
ripe tannins. Offers impressive flavor impact for the price.

WHITE WINES

Alban Vineyards 1997 Estate Viognier, ★★★ $$$ ￼￼
Edna Valley Complex aromas including plum, litchi, smoke,
and spice. Dense and full on the palate, with spicy, well delineated flavors of peach and pear. Strong acidity is in balance with
the wine's fruit.

Qupé 1997 Roussanne, Central Coast   ★★★ **$$** ♈♈
Nuanced nose combines honeyed peach, white flowers, hay, and
spicy oak. A mouthful of honey and flowers; dry but quite rich
and textured, with enticing juicy acidity. Spicy, persistent finish
shows a smoky quality.

Rabbit Ridge 1997 Heartbreak Hill Viognier,   ★★★ **$$** ♈♈
Sonoma County Mineral-tinged nose hints at peach and pear.
Spicy, tangy flavors of white grapefruit and lemon, plus a smoky,
dusty quality. Medium-bodied but shows surprisingly brisk acids.
Suggestion of exotic fruits on the finish.

Cline Cellars 1997 Viognier, Carneros   ★★ **$$** ♈♈
Aromatic, floral nose of honeysuckle, mint, and spice. Supple
texture enlivened by citric flavors and sound acids. Finishes firm
and spicy.

Rosenblum Cellars 1997 Viognier,   ★★ **$$** ♈♈
Santa Barbara County Bright floral, minty nose complicated by
notes of orange zest and smoke. Juicy and vibrant in the mouth,
but with a dusty quality. Grows sweeter and firmer in the glass.

OTHER RED WINES

California produces some of the world's finest Pinot Noirs made
outside of Burgundy. An increasing number of wineries are offering varietal bottlings of Sangiovese, the Tuscan grape on which
Chianti is based. Among the other American reds seen on wine-
shop shelves are the Bordeaux-style Meritage blends, which may
contain Cabernet Sauvignon, Cabernet Franc, Merlot, Petit
Verdot, and/or Malbec.

The Bottom Line
California's Pinot Noirs and Meritage blends are rarely bargains,
but most Sangioveses will continue to be reasonably priced until
this varietal catches on among mainstream drinkers. Most of the
best Pinot Noirs retail for $25 or more.

Etude 1996 Pinot Noir, Carneros   ★★★ **$$$** ♈♈
Spicy aromas of raspberry, smoke, licorice, and mint, as well as
other herbs. Supple, sweet, lush, and pliant; quite stylish wine.
Sound structure covered by flesh. The long finish shows palate-
caressing ripe tannins and also a slight taste of smoked meat.

Sanford 1996 Pinot Noir, ★★★ $$ ♥♥♥
Santa Barbara County Compelling aromas of framboise, strawberry, currant, and mace. Sappy, velvety, and strong in the mouth; lush but bright. Very persistent fruit and some slightly edgy acidity on the firmly tannic finish.

Flora Springs 1996 Sangiovese, Napa Valley ★★★ $$ ♥♥
Perfumed nose of crushed raspberry, meat, pepper, and flowers. Lovely tart red-berry flavor offers excellent intensity and clarity, thanks to bright acids. Finishes firm, with light tannins.

Beringer 1995 Alluvium, Knights Valley ★★ $$ ♥♥♥
Red currant, tobacco, bitter chocolate, and grilled nuts on the nose. Fresh blackberry and smoky-oak flavors offer noteworthy intensity. Finishes quite firm, with sound acidity and tongue-dusting tannins. A Bordeaux blend.

Luna 1996 Sangiovese, Napa Valley ★★ $$ ♥♥♥
Floral, cherry-scented nose, with a hint of roasted meat. Subdued flavors of tart cherry and red currant. Rather stylish and persistent, finishing with firm but subtle tannins and a repeating floral note.

Villa Mt. Eden 1996 Pinot Noir, California ★★ $$ ♥♥♥
Smoky strawberry and cranberry aromas, along with hints of game and underbrush. Creamy and gentle in the mouth, with ripe flavors of strawberry jam and raspberry. Silky and sweet on the aftertaste.

Calera 1996 Pinot Noir, Central Coast ★★ $ ♥♥
Strawberry, gunpowder, and an earth note on the nose. Fairly rich and sweet in the mouth, with lively cherry and raspberry flavors. Finishes with dusty tannins. Will give early pleasure.

Cartlidge & Browne 1996 Pinot Noir, California ★ $ ♥♥♥
Strawberry, cinnamon, and smoky oak on the nose. Supple and spicy in the mouth, with red fruit complicated by notes of game and earth. Finishes with easy tannins and decent length. Good sweetness and texture for the price.

Laurel Glen 1996 Reds, California ★ $ ♥♥♥
Red currant, gunpowder, and a whiff of meat on the nose. Thick and supple, but with a firm acid spine. Not particularly delineated, but shows good depth of flavor. A blend of numerous red grapes, including Zinfandel and Syrah.

SPARKLING WINES

Outside of Champagne, California is the richest source of high-quality sparkling wines, though only a handful of them can be compared to true Champagne for complexity, refinement, and sheer persistence on the palate. Still, California's sparkling wines are vastly better than they were as recently as a decade ago, due in equal part to major investments by several French Champagne houses and to new vineyard plantings in cooler growing areas conducive to producing this style of wine.

At the Table

California's sparkling wines are a bit fuller-bodied and less refined than Champagne and are thus less satisfying on their own. They are also more fruit-driven and often slightly sweeter. Good with deep-fried appetizers, they also stand up to poultry preparations or fish cooked in spicy or rich sauces, especially oily fish that need the cut of strong acidity. Try chicken satays with peanut sauce, grilled squid or shrimp, or grilled snapper with ginger and lime. Drier California sparklers also work magic with bland textures that pose problems for most still wines, such as egg dishes (especially those with smoked salmon or black truffles), purees, and cream soups (mushroom, potato, onion, or lobster).

The Bottom Line

Many California sparkling wines do not merit their high price tags, but there are good examples to be found in the $15 to $25 range, particularly in nonvintage (NV) bottles.

Domaine Carneros 1992 Le Rêve, Carneros ★★★ $$$ ♟♟♟
Penetrating lemon and orange aromas. Yeasty and very fresh in the mouth, with bread-dough and lemon-rind flavors. Rather soft and gentle but given focus and grip by fresh, clean acidity.

Domaine Carneros 1993 Brut, Carneros ★★★ $$ ♟♟♟
Fine, frothy mousse. Soft, restrained flavors of orange Creamsicle and pear, plus a faint minerality. Stylish and refined. Ripe, long finish features persistent pineapple and passion-fruit notes.

Domaine Chandon NV Etoile Rosé, Carneros   ★★★ $$ ♥♥
Toast and cherry aromas. Bitter-edged cherry flavor in the mouth; rather lean at the beginning but fleshes out nicely on the back half, showing good richness and structure and finishing notes of blackberry and cherry.

Gloria Ferrer 1990 Royal Cuvée Brut, Carneros   ★★★ $$ ♥♥
Chalk, lime skin, and apple aromas. Crisp, clean, yet almost creamy. Supple but juicy finish, with hints of coconut and mango.

Domaine Chandon NV Blanc de Noirs, Carneros   ★★ $$ ♥♥♥
Aromas of red berries and orange. Round and fairly rich in the mouth, with spicy fruit and tangy acids. Mouth-filling yet nicely delineated. Persistent finish offers a flavor of sweet apple.

Domaine Chandon NV Brut Cuvée, Carneros   ★★ $$ ♥♥♥
Persistent, tiny bubbles. Bright, lemony nose. Ripe citric flavors of lime skin and orange pith. Clean, fresh, and nicely focused. Finishes with very good length.

Gloria Ferrer NV Brut, Sonoma   ★★ $$ ♥♥♥
Crisp aromas of lemon, lime, and grapefruit; then round, ripe, and surprisingly full in flavor. Finishes with flavors of apple and pear and good richness and persistence.

Iron Horse 1993 Classic Vintage Brut,   ★★ $$ ♥♥♥
Sonoma County Green Valley Lemon peel, grapefruit, and faint toast on the nose and palate. At once tangy and rich, with mouth-filling density. Finishes ripe and rather powerful.

Mumm Cuvée Napa NV Blanc de Blancs   ★★ $$ ♥♥♥
Persistent, very small bubbles. Bright, clean lemon-lime nose. Notes of grapefruit, lime oil, and toast in the mouth. Offers good cut and intensity. Lingering, fresh aftertaste.

Mumm Cuvée Napa NV Blanc de Noirs   ★★ $$ ♥♥♥
Pinkish onionskin color. Strawberry and litchi nose shows exotic hints of fruit cocktail. Rich, full, and supple in the mouth. Persistent, rather soft finish offers a flavor of Granny Smith apple.

Scharfenberger Cellars NV Pacific Echo Brut,   ★★ $$ ♥♥♥
Mendocino County Fresh, toasty aromas of lemon and lime. Begins minerally and firm, then turns fat and soft in the middle palate. Could use a bit more bite and grip, but ultimately quite satisfying.

OREGON

WITH FEW EXCEPTIONS, OREGON'S WINERIES ARE small, and their winemaking rather idiosyncratic. Virtually every year, new boutique operations spring to prominence with distinctive wines that are well worth trying.

Nearly all of Oregon's Pinot Noir, the most important red, and much of its Pinot Gris, the top white, come from the Willamette Valley, making the area the state's obvious wine capital. In this marine-influenced valley between the Pacific Ocean and the Cascade mountains, fruit ripens gently, and harvesttime rain is always a possibility.

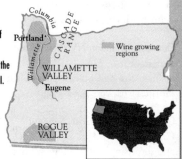

Grapes & Styles

Oregon's chief claim to vinous fame is its fruit-driven, black-cherry-scented Pinot Noirs, which are widely considered to be among the finest examples of this varietal made outside Burgundy. In recent years, Pinot Gris, an ancient white mutation of Pinot Noir that has been found to take well to Oregon's temperate climate, has been the state's fastest growing variety.

On the Label

As with most New World wines, Oregon's are labeled by variety. Other information frequently shown on the bottle, in addition to appellation, includes the vineyard designations and, sometimes, proprietary names.

PINOT NOIR

Oregon's Pinot Noirs are usually ready to drink when young, though the most interesting examples grow in complexity with four to six years of aging after release. Typically they show spicy aromas and flavors of black cherry and raspberry, medium body, and an element of toasty oak. In very ripe, low-acid years like 1994, Oregon Pinots often present jammy, slightly cooked flavors and should be consumed early before their fruit fades.

At the Table

Most Oregon Pinot Noirs have an inherent delicacy and grace that calls for lightly seasoned, simply prepared foods. Northwest consumers frequently pair them with salmon or tuna, especially from the grill. Grilled chicken and roast duck are equally suitable companions for these Pinot Noirs. Fresh cheeses are another option: The acidity of Pinot Noirs pairs well with the bright, pungent flavors of chèvre or sheep's-milk cheeses. More powerful, weightier Oregon Pinots can work well with game birds and lamb.

The Bottom Line

Oregon Pinot Noir pricing leaped upward with the popular 1994 vintage, grown in a dry year. Vintages since then have been subjected to normal Oregon rain, so that many of today's releases are overpriced. Still, the most successful wines in the $18 to $25 range offer the best affordable alternatives to Burgundy.

What to Buy: Pinot Noir

1994	1995	1996	1997
B+	C-	B-	C+

King Estate 1995, Oregon   ★★ $$ ♟♟♟

Attractive aromas of red currant, cola, tar, and mint, plus perfumed sandalwood and nutmeg nuances. Supple and easygoing, with fresh, delineated fruit and good balance. Not especially complex but pliant for the vintage.

159

Broadley Vineyards 1996 Reserve, Oregon   ★★ $$ ♈♈
Deep aromas of black raspberry, spice, earth, and pepper, plus a
whiff of bourbon. Supple and sweet in the mouth, with oaky fla-
vors of red licorice and tar. Finishes fruity and fairly long, with
firm tannins.

Foris 1996 Siskiyou Terrace, Rogue Valley   ★★ $$ ♈♈
Decadent aromas of jammy blackberry, strawberry, and earth.
Sweet and spicy in the mouth, with the slight cooked-fruit flavor
repeating. But offers silky texture and good depth of flavor, not
to mention persistence on the finish.

Oak Knoll 1995, Willamette Valley   ★★ $$ ♈♈
Burgundian aromas of strawberry, raspberry, espresso, and under-
brush. Rich, lush, and pliant in the mouth; offers impressive tex-
ture and sweetness for the vintage. Finishes with sweet, easy
tannins and lingering fruit.

Panther Creek 1996, Willamette Valley   ★★ $$ ♈♈
Pungent aromas of black raspberry and bitter chocolate. Fat,
ripe, and loaded with youthful bitter-cherry fruit; not overly
sweet but has noteworthy depth of flavor. Subtle, lingering,
firmly tannic finish hints at pepper.

Bridgeview Vineyards 1996, Oregon   ★★ $ ♈♈
Sweet aromas of cherry, cinnamon, and toasty oak. Silky, textured, and sweet, with enticing raspberry fruit. Offers attractive
fruitiness and good intensity. Finishes with light, slightly dry
tannins. Superb value.

Amity Vineyards 1996, Oregon   ★ $$ ♈♈♈
Pale brick-red. Floral, cherry-scented nose shows a faintly can-
died perfume. Decent texture and sweetness in the mouth;
pleasant but lacking in nuance. Finishes with decent fruit and a
hint of alcohol. For early drinking.

PINOT GRIS

Oregon's version of Pinot Gris is a slightly more restrained but
perhaps more refreshing rendition of the full-bodied, spicy white
wine made from the same grape in Alsace. Fruity yet dry,
Oregon Pinot Gris offers an enticing combination of citrus- and
exotic-fruit aromas and generally crisp acidity, as well as a level

of richness that can approach that of Chardonnay. Although Pinot Gris takes well to barrel fermentation and new-oak aging, the most food-flexible examples are generally made with little obvious oak influence.

At the Table

In Oregon, this particularly versatile variety is consumed alongside a range of local specialties, including shellfish, salmon, pork, and game birds. It is also a favorite as an aperitif. Pinot Gris generally has the texture and brisk acidity to work well with fish or chicken in cream or butter sauces. More refined, unoaked examples harmonize with sushi and raw oysters. Oregon Pinot Gris also complements delicate Vietnamese and Japanese fish dishes that would be overwhelmed by bigger, oakier, or more alcoholic white wines.

The Bottom Line

With most of the better examples priced around $15, Oregon Pinot Gris is one of the best values in American white wine.

What to Buy: Pinot Gris

1995	1996	1997
C	B	B-

Archery Summit 1997 Vireton, Oregon   ★★★ $$ ♥♥
Honey and tropical fruit on the rich nose. Very round and spicy on the palate; nicely defined flavors of orange peel, Granny Smith apple, and nutmeg. Long finish. A blend based on Pinot Gris.

Eyrie Vineyards 1996, Willamette Valley   ★★ $$ ♥♥
Cooler aromas of lemon, grapefruit, and melon. Assertive, spicy, and vivid in the mouth, with notes of mint, pink grapefruit, and gingerbread. Excellent flavor intensity. Firm, lingering aftertaste.

Foris 1997, Rogue Valley   ★★ $$ ♥♥
Citric and mineral aromas. Ripe and round in the mouth, with citric flavors of orange peel and lime blossom and a chalky nuance. Clean, bright, dusty finish. Good aperitif-style Pinot Gris.

WillaKenzie Estate 1997 Estate Bottled, Oregon   ★★ $$ ♈♈
Exotic aromas of honey, peach, and dried apricot. Rich and fat,
with a mouth-filling creamy texture. Just manages to hold its
alcohol. Soft and ripe on the finish.

Elk Cove 1997, Willamette Valley   ★ $$ ♈♈
Fruity nose suggests sweet, tropical fruit. Clean, rich flavor of
pink grapefruit freshened by firm acidity. Crisp finish features
subtle lemon-skin and mineral notes.

Rex Hill 1996, Willamette Valley   ★ $$ ♈♈
Ripe, toasty aromas of orange and pink grapefruit, plus a truffley
nuance. Plush and weighty, with ripe, smoky flavors of peach,
pear, and cooked apple. Undeniably rich, but just short of heavy.

OTHER WHITE WINES

Among the other standouts from Oregon are floral Rieslings and
spicy Gewürztraminers, generally in a rather delicate, dry, and
food-friendly style. The state's Chardonnays, which until recently
tended to be overly lean and acidic, are now showing more rich-
ness and fresh-fruit character as growers plant Chardonnay
clones that are better suited to Oregon's climates and soils.
Pinot Blanc is also widely successful.

The Bottom Line
The best Oregon Rieslings and Gewürztraminers, many of which
are still priced in the $10 to $12 range, offer very good value.
Chardonnays are distinctly hit-or-miss, though reasonably priced
when compared to those from California. Pinot Blanc can be
excellent value.

Cristom 1996 Chardonnay Celilo Vineyard,   ★★★ $$ ♈♈
Oregon Tropical-fruit aromas complicated by notes of chalk,
smoke, and truffle. Rich but focused flavors of ripe pear, poached
apple, and cinnamon. Assertive, nicely balanced, and long on
the palate. Finishing notes of pear and smoke.

Bethel Heights 1996 Chardonnay Reserve,   ★★ $$ ♈♈
Willamette Valley Estate Grown Reticent but rich aromas of
toast and minerals. Lively flavors of pineapple and pear, along
with assertive oak spice. Good weight in the mouth. Smoke and
mint nuances contribute complexity to the lingering finish.

WillaKenzie Estate 1997 Pinot Blanc, Oregon ★★ $$ ❦❦
Juicy, pure aromas of lemon peel and Key lime pie. Bright and
intensely flavored but quite supple, thanks to sound but harmo-
nious acidity. Plump but thoroughly dry. Firm, ripe finish offers
very good persistence.

Willamette Valley Vineyards 1996 Chardonnay, ★★ $$ ❦❦
Oregon Ripe aromas of toast, orange, and tangerine. Layered
and mouth-filling, with exotic, smoky, peach and apricot flavors
given clarity by crisp acidity. Finishes long, juicy, and ripe.

Argyle 1996 Riesling, Willamette Valley ★★ $ ❦❦
Bright, steely, varietally accurate aromas of minerals and grapefruit.
Crisp, sharply focused, and quite dry, with a flavor of lemonade.
Finishes firm and persistent, with a suggestion of white flowers.

Bethel Heights 1997 Pinot Blanc, Willamette Valley ★ $$ ❦❦
Estate Grown Focused aromas of lemon and minerals. Bright
and fresh; showing a bit of CO_2 spritz. Vivid and crisp, almost
like a Muscadet. Flavors of grapefruit and minerals carry through
to the finish, which also hints at honey.

Ken Wright Cellars 1997 Pinot Blanc, ★ $$ ❦❦
Willamette Valley Rich, honeyed aromas of pineapple and
spiced apple. Round but reasonably juicy in the mouth, with
exotic fruit flavors and modest acid structure. Finishes rather
soft, with a note of licorice.

Find Your Match

When matching wine with food, the style of the wine is
often the most important consideration. Oregon Pinot
Noir, for instance, falls into the style classification medium-
bodied red. Wines from this group are perfect with
salmon and pork, roasted chicken and game birds.
When you're looking for a particular style, from light, dry
white to full-bodied red, check our Wine-Style Finder on
pages 204 through 206.

WASHINGTON STATE

WHILE OREGON WAS THE FIRST STATE AFTER California to be taken seriously by American wine lovers familiar with European wines, today it is Washington that provides a broader range of high-quality bottles. Small wineries abound, but three large ones—Chateau Ste. Michelle, Columbia Crest, and Hogue—make nearly 50 percent of the state's wine.

Most of Washington's wine grapes are grown in the irrigated high desert of the Columbia and Yakima river valleys, east of the Cascade mountains. Although daytime temperatures can be hot, cool September nights allow the grapes to retain sound acidity, resulting in wines with strong varietal character and flavor intensity.

Seattle

COLUMBIA VALLEY

Yakima

YAKIMA VALLEY

WALLA WALLA VALLEY

Walla Walla

Columbia

Snake

CASCADE RANGE

Wine growing regions

Grapes & Styles

Washington State excels in two very different categories: inexpensive, crisp white wines, particularly from Semillon, Sauvignon Blanc, and Riesling grapes; and generally pricier Cabernets and Merlots, which frequently combine the explosive fruit of California reds and the suaver texture of Bordeaux.

On the Label

Washington bottles feature the varietal rather than the place the wine was made, as is common in Europe.

SEMILLON and SAUVIGNON BLANC

The two grapes Semillon and Sauvignon are the mainstay white varieties of Bordeaux, where they produce both sweet and dry wines. In Washington State, the wines from these varieties are normally dry. The Semillons range from lemony and minerally to rich and honeyed, often with notes of fig and melon, but they usually retain a firm citric spine. Sauvignon Blancs are generally crisp, light, and penetrating. To flesh out Sauvignon, some Semillon is often added, while Sauvignon can be used to freshen Semillon.

At the Table

With its generally vibrant fruity acidity, Semillon offers the perfect foil for oily fish, especially salmon and tuna. An ideal match is Washington State Semillon and smoked salmon, and most other smoked fish will work well, too. Semillon with raw oysters or crab is another favorite local combo. Sauvignon Blanc is similarly served with a wide range of shellfish; it has the cut to cleanse the palate of rich sauces like mayonnaise and hollandaise. Examples with a strong herbal component can stand up to such difficult vegetables as artichokes and asparagus, as well as to tangy salad greens. Spicier versions go well with Thai flavors like coconut, lime, lemongrass, and fish sauce, and Southwestern dishes flavored with cilantro or lime.

The Bottom Line

Washington Semillon and Sauvignon Blanc are among the best sources of fresh, inexpensive, food-friendly white wines.

What to Buy: Semillon & Sauvignon Blanc

1995	1996	1997
C+	B-	B-

DeLille Cellars 1996 Chaleur Estate Blanc,   ★★ $$ ♟♟
Columbia Valley Extravagant aromas of pineapple, grapefruit, fig, and clove oil. Tactile, silky, and dry, with reticent fig and

mineral flavors. The spice and citrus-skin flavors build impressively on the finish. A blend of Sauvignon Blanc and Semillon.

L'Ecole No. 41 1996 Barrel Fermented Semillon, ★★ $$ 🍷🍷
Washington State Aromas and flavors of oak spice, fig, and lemon. Silky on the palate, with strong framing acidity and restrained ripeness. Finishes firm, with a note of resiny oak.

Columbia Crest 1997 Sauvignon Blanc, ★ $ 🍷🍷🍷
Columbia Valley Aromas of lemon, melon, spice, and licorice. Supple and bright, with creamy flavors of citrus skin and fennel. Lemony acidity keeps the aftertaste firm and brisk.

Hogue 1997 Fumé Blanc, Columbia Valley ★ $ 🍷🍷🍷
Aromas of grapefruit, lemon, peach, and fresh herbs. Tangy grapefruit flavor offers a musky complexity, but turns a bit tropical and soft on the finish, with some alcohol showing.

Chateau Ste. Michelle 1996 Sauvignon Blanc ★ $ 🍷🍷
Horse Heaven Vineyard, Columbia Valley Oak-influenced aromas of candied lemon peel and clove. Supple, rich lemon and smoke flavors are firmed by slightly tart acidity.

Hogue 1996 Semillon, Columbia Valley ★ $ 🍷🍷
Aromas of honey, pear, and spice. Dry, spicy, intense flavors of lemon, tangerine, and melon. Supple in the middle palate, but crisp on the aftertaste, with good persistence.

CHARDONNAY

Washington State's Chardonnays fall into two categories: briskly fruity, mostly inexpensive wines made, as a rule, with little noticeable oak; and altogether richer—and generally pricier—examples with toasted-nut and spice aromas and buttery texture.

At the Table

Serve Washington States's lighter Chardonnays as aperitifs or alongside simple fish dishes. The new-wave, oakier versions can stand up to grilled fish and spicy fare. Either style works with cream sauces, thanks to the generally sound underlying acidity of the wines.

The Bottom Line

Prices vary widely, but there are bargains to be found. Values are scarcer among the richer, barrel-fermented Chardonnays, which too often are oaky California wanna-bes.

What to Buy: Chardonnay

1995	1996	1997
C+	B	B-

Chateau Ste. Michelle 1996 Cold Creek Vineyard, ★★ $$ ❦❦❦
Columbia Valley Reticent but nuanced aromas of smoke, melon, and pineapple. Offers good texture and concentration, but is youthfully unevolved today. Acids are harmonious and ripe. Builds nicely on the subtle, juicy aftertaste.

Caterina 1997, Columbia Valley ★★ $$ ❦❦
Dusty aromas of talc, lemon pith, and clove. Rich, layered, and spicy, with exotic notes of banana oil and litchi. Powerful, slightly alcoholic finish. A bit like Gewürztraminer in its fat, silky texture.

L'Ecole No. 41 1996, Washington State ★★ $$ ❦❦
Extroverted, sweet nose combines dried apricot, honey, and licorice. Large-scaled and layered in the mouth; offers almost roasted flavors of peach and creamed corn. Finishes very rich but with a slight dry edge.

Columbia Winery 1996 Woodburne Cuvée, ★ $ ❦❦❦
Columbia Valley Oak-dominated aromas of vanilla, resin, and spice. Round, supple, and oaky in the mouth, with just enough melon and peach fruit to support the wood notes. Ripe finish of modest length.

Hogue 1996 Chardonnay, Columbia Valley ★ $ ❦❦❦
Fruit cocktail, honey, guava, and a roasted note on the nose. Fat and supple in the mouth, with good texture and moderate flavor intensity. Some CO_2 keeps it fresh. Slightly acidic finish.

Washington Hills 1997, Columbia Valley ★ $ ❦❦❦
Lemon, melon, fresh herbs, and a minerally edge on the nose; no obvious oak showing. Round, decently concentrated, and ripe, with citrus-skin and fresh-herb notes giving the finish good bite.

OTHER WHITE WINES

Washington State's Rieslings are ripe, fruity, and crisp, with flavors of citrus, peach, and apricot. They are among the best-balanced examples of this varietal made outside Europe: Even those with noticeable residual sugar generally have enough piquant acidity to equalize their sweetness. Like Washington's Rieslings, the state's highly aromatic Chenin Blancs and Gewürztraminers are often slightly sweet, but they are kept fresh by sound acidity.

The Bottom Line
Washington State's other whites are some of the world's better values for fresh, varietally accurate white wine.

Columbia Crest 1997 Johannisberg Riesling, ★★ $ ♥♥♥
Columbia Valley Shy nose suggests mint and orange peel. Juicy, minty, and intensely flavored; fresh and firm, with strong balancing acidity. Suggestion of lemonade. In a lively, fairly dry style; finishes with good length and grip.

Hogue 1997 Late Harvest White Riesling, ★★ $ ♥♥♥
Columbia Valley Floral, fruit-salad aromas. Strong, juicy flavors of canteloupe, peach, spice, and honey. Quite sweet but with enough ripe acidity for balance. Not especially complex but an impressive mouthful of fruit for the price.

Columbia Winery 1997 Cellarmaster's Reserve ★ $ ♥♥♥
Riesling, Columbia Valley Pungent grapefruit and pineapple aromas complicated by apricot and floral nuances. Rich and fairly sweet but supported by ripe acids. A satisfying if unsubtle Riesling, finishing with sweet pineapple and honey flavor.

Hogue 1996 Semillon-Chardonnay, Columbia Valley ★ $ ♥♥♥
Lemon, honey, and hints of tropical fruits on the nose. Good texture in the mouth; flavors of peach, honey, and cooked pear. A bit lean on the finish.

Covey Run 1997 Chenin Blanc, Columbia Valley ★ $ ♥♥
Subdued aromas of honeydew melon, apricot, and quinine. Slightly sweet, floral flavors of peach, orange, and honeysuckle; round and rather soft but boasts very good intensity. Perfect with spicy foods.

Covey Run 1997 Dry Riesling, Washington State ★ $ ♥♥
Precise aromas of lime, fresh herbs, rose petal, licorice, and

spice. Ripe honeysuckle flavor is framed and extended by bright acidity. Finishes with an urgent floral quality.

Covey Run 1997 Gewürztraminer, Columbia Valley ★ $ ❢❢
Deep aromas of smoke, litchi, honeysuckle, and earth. A medium-weight, crisply fruity wine with slight sweetness balanced by sound acids. Slightly skinny on the finish.

Kiona 1997 Dry White Riesling, Columbia Valley ★ $ ❢❢
Floral, minty aromas of pear blossom and peach. Mouth-filling and quite ripe, with thick fruit framed by a ripely citric character. Gewürztraminer-like notes of litchi and rose petal. Finishes ripe and persistent.

Washington Hills 1997 Dry Chenin Blanc, ★ $ ❢❢
Columbia Valley Pale color. Delicate aromas of honey, lime, and parsley. Strong acid spine buffered by fleshy, lemony fruit. Not especially complex, but offers plenty of flavor intensity and structure, and a ripe, lingering finish.

CABERNET SAUVIGNON and MERLOT

Washington State Cabernet Sauvignons and Merlots are among America's most distinctive reds. With their sharply defined, sappy dark-berry flavors and dense textures, they fall midway between California and Bordeaux in style. Because of their strong fruitiness and fleshy feel on the palate, they are typically delicious when young, but they also have the acid structure to age gracefully for a decade or more.

At the Table
With their vibrant, ripe fruit, Washington State's Cabernets and Merlots call for meat that is sweet and juicy (beef ribs, oxtail, sausages, spareribs, lamb) or that is prepared with ingredients that confer sweetness. Try these wines with braised rabbit with a touch of balsamic vinegar, braised lamb shanks with root vegetables, or beef tenderloin with caramelized onions. Note that black pepper will help to bring out the fruit in these wines.

The Bottom Line

Prices for Washington State's top reds vary widely, with prices for scarce boutique wines often more a function of supply and demand than quality. But numerous Cabernets and Merlots from high-volume producers offer sound value.

What to Buy: Cabernet Sauvignon & Merlot

1994	1995	1996	1997
A	B+	B-	B

Columbia Winery 1994 Sagemoor Vineyards ★★★★ $$ ❢❢❢
Cabernet Sauvignon, Columbia Valley Complex aromas of black currant, roasted coffee, and smoky oak. Silky, lush, and very deep; stuffed with concentrated, sweet fruit. Already approachable despite tangy acids and solid tannic structure. Really carries on the finish.

Columbia Winery 1994 Cabernet Sauvignon ★★★ $$ ❢❢❢
Otis Vineyard, Yakima Valley Brooding smoke, dark-berry, and tobacco aromas. Very concentrated, but today the sweet fruit is dominated by the wine's taut structure. Finishes very long, with explosive blackberry, licorice, and espresso-bean flavor and dusty tannins.

Columbia Winery 1994 Cabernet Sauvignon ★★★ $$ ❢❢❢
Red Willow Vineyard, Yakima Valley Exotic aromas include those of iris, peach, and blackberry syrup. Juicy and silky but very unevolved, with strong acids and tannins. Intense flavor of red licorice. The singular peach and apricot character repeats on the finish.

Canoe Ridge 1996 Merlot, Columbia Valley ★★★ $$ ❢❢
Expressive nose of briary red currant, underbrush, and tobacco. Sweet, spicy, and concentrated, with sappy red-berry, leather, and sandalwood flavors. Dryish and sophisticated. Firm tannins give the wine good grip.

Chateau Ste. Michelle 1995 Cabernet Sauvignon ★★ $$ ❢❢❢
Horse Heaven Vineyard, Columbia Valley Ruby red. Brooding cassis, raspberry, mineral, and mocha aromas. Bright and delineated, with tart berry notes and a subtle sweetness. Youthful and structured to age. Dusty, ripe tannins are in balance with the fruit.

Chateau Ste. Michelle 1995 Merlot, Columbia Valley ★★ $$ 🍷🍷🍷 Bright aromas of cassis, mocha, mint, and smoky oak. Pliant and ripe in the mouth; nicely balanced and soundly structured. Berry and oak flavors offer attractive sweetness. Finishes with palate-coating, even tannins.

Columbia Crest 1995 Estate Cabernet Sauvignon, Columbia Valley ★★ $$ 🍷🍷🍷 Bright, nuanced nose combines cassis, raspberry, smoke, tar, and tobacco leaf. Silky and concentrated; harmonious, ripe acids give clarity to the pungent red-berry flavor. Finishes with fine tannins and notes of red raspberry and toast.

Columbia Crest 1995 Estate Merlot, Columbia Valley ★★ $$ 🍷🍷🍷 Dark berries, licorice, toast, and a whiff of scotch on the nose. Silky and fat in the mouth, with tar and nutty-oak elements complementing the red-currant and raspberry flavors. An easygoing Merlot with a lush, oaky finish.

Covey Run 1995 Cabernet Sauvignon Whiskey Canyon Vineyard, Yakima Valley ★★ $$ 🍷🍷 Bright black-currant and coffee aromas. Supple, intense flavors of bitter cherry and chocolate, with a strong component of vanillin oak. Rather tannic finish, but the tannins are ripe and even.

L'Ecole No. 41 1997 Cabernet Sauvignon, Columbia Valley ★★ $$ 🍷🍷 Smoky, slightly roasted aromas of black raspberry, currant, mint, and mocha. Lush, concentrated currant and game flavors are given shape by slightly edgy acidity. Finishes with firm tannins and good length.

Kiona 1996 Merlot, Columbia Valley ★★ $$ 🍷🍷
Raspberry, cinnamon, and tobacco on the nose. Supple but insinuating in the mouth, with attractive, claretlike flavors of red currant, tobacco, and oak spice. Shapely, firm, and fresh. Finishes with dusty, even tannins.

Hogue 1995 Barrel Select Merlot, Columbia Valley ★ $ 🍷🍷🍷
Red currant, woodsmoke, tobacco and a meaty nuance on the nose. Supple, rather soft red-currant and tobacco flavors offer good concentration and intensity. The smoke and tobacco notes repeat on the ripe finish.

Hedges 1996 Cabernet-Merlot, Washington State ★ $ 🍷🍷
Flamboyant aromas of raw meat, crushed berries, and exotic

wood spices. Bright dark-berry flavor offers modest complexity but impressive intensity for the price. Finishes with tongue-dusting, even tannins and a note of espresso.

OTHER RED WINES

Lemberger is an obscure Washington State red grape whose exuberant berry and spice flavors can often call to mind a lighter California Zinfandel. Among international varieties showing promise in Washington are Rhône Valley grapes, like Syrah and Grenache, and Cabernet Franc. In Bordeaux, Cabernet Franc is blended with Cabernet Sauvignon or Merlot, but in Washington State the grape appears capable of making intensely fruity, complete wine on its own.

The Bottom Line
Since these wines are not as popular as the state's Merlots and Cabernet Sauvignons, they are often more reasonably priced.

Chateau Ste. Michelle 1995 Cabernet Franc ★★ $$ ♟♟♟
Cold Creek Vineyard, Columbia Valley Cherry, espresso, smoke, and loam on the nose. A supple midweight showing restrained sweetness and an intriguing iron and smoke character on the back half. Finishes with a dusty, earthy quality and slightly dry tannins.

Chateau Ste. Michelle 1995 Syrah, ★★ $$ ♟♟♟
Columbia Valley Dark ruby red. Varietally accurate aromas of black raspberry, gunflint, and smoked meat, with an overlay of spicy oak. Juicy dark-berry flavors offer modest flesh but very good intensity. More acidity than tannin on the finish.

Columbia Crest 1996 Syrah Reserve, ★★ $$ ♟♟♟
Columbia Valley Deep red ruby. Aromas of sappy black raspberry, woodsmoke, and cocoa powder. Sweet and lush in the mouth, with a pleasing balance of red-fruit flavors, sweet oak, and ripe acidity. Tannins are soft and ripe.

Columbia Winery 1995 Cabernet Franc ★★ $$ ♟♟♟
Red Willow Vineyard, Yakima Valley Exotic aromas of sandalwood, cinnamon, blackberry, and stone fruits. Rich and concentrated, with a creamy red-berry sweetness encased in a firm spine of acidity. Quite penetrating on the finish. Needs bottle aging.

Covey Run 1997 Lemberger, Columbia Valley ★ $ ♟ ♟
Aromatic nose combines black raspberry, grilled nuts, meat, and dill. Floral, fruity, and bright; a juicy, light wine with sweetish fruit, built for immediate consumption.

Our 15 Top Picks Under $12

WHITE WINES

RED WINES

SOUTH AFRICA

MOST OF THE WINE SHIPPED TO THE UNITED STATES after the lifting of trade sanctions on imports from South Africa in 1991 was strictly mediocre. However, South African wine is improving dramatically, as a new generation of progressive winemakers learns what it takes to compete internationally. Giant co-ops still dominate, but virtually all of the more distinctive bottles shipped to America come from small estates, and the number of these is growing rapidly.

South Africa's wine-producing areas are located in the southwestern tip of the country, around Cape Town. In recent years, the classic grape varieties, such as Sauvignon Blanc, have often been planted in cooler spots that benefit from sea breezes off the Atlantic and Indian Oceans.

Wine growing regions

ROBERTSON
PAARL · Franschhoek
Cape Town STELLENBOSCH

Grapes & Styles
Reds, including Cabernet, Merlot, Pinot, Shiraz, and Pinotage, are more important than whites in South Africa, though all of today's better wines show fresh, concentrated fruit flavors and accurate varietal character.

On the Label
South African wines are labeled according to the variety of grape, although proprietary names may be used for blends.

RED WINES

In style, South Africa's reds show more of the restraint and slightly rustic soil tones of French wine than the explosive fruit flavors that characterize so much New World wine.

At the Table

Older-style Pinotage, with its faintly dry edge, goes well with roast chicken, beef stew, and game birds; in South Africa, it is frequently paired with barbecued sausage. Softer, fruitier examples are very good with grilled salmon and tuna. South Africa's lightly peppery Shirazes are fine with steak and lamb; or try them with turkey or hamburgers. Cabernet Sauvignon is generally firm and juicy enough to be served with fattier meat dishes such as grilled baby back ribs. Lighter examples pair well with simply prepared chicken and pork.

The Bottom Line

Even though South Africa's reds are climbing in price, the best bottles generally possess the character to justify their prices.

What to Buy: Red Wines

1995	1996	1997
A-	B	A-

Backsberg 1996 Shiraz, Paarl ★★★ $$ ♥♥
Raspberry, woodsmoke, and roasted meat on the nose. Intensely flavored and almost sweet; a tangy mulberry flavor is complicated by spicy and herbal nuances. Finishes tannic but ripe.

Saxenburg 1995 Cabernet Sauvignon, ★★★ $$ ♥♥
Stellenbosch Spicy cassis, black-cherry, and truffle aromas. Full-bodied and fruity, with cherry and cassis flavor complicated by a woodsmoke note. Finishes with substantial soft tannins.

Saxenburg 1996 Pinotage, Stellenbosch ★★★ $$ ♥♥
Ripe-plum and toast aromas are quite Merlot-like. Fat, sweet, and mouth-filling, with a terrific core of smoky fruit and excellent flavor intensity. Impressively long and suave on the finish.

Backsberg 1996 Cabernet Sauvignon, Paarl   ★★ $$ ♟♟♟
Super-ripe aromas of cassis, black cherry, and maple syrup. Rich
and mouth-filling, with very ripe cassis, chocolate, and mocha
flavors. Ripeness just short of raisiny.

Backsberg 1995 Pinotage, Paarl   ★★ $ ♟♟♟
Red currant, smoke, and tobacco on the nose. Fruity, nicely
delineated, and fairly concentrated on the palate; intriguing
notes of iron and mocha. Lovely sweet fruit carries through to
the ripe, subtle, lightly tannic finish.

Beyerskloof 1997 Pinotage, Stellenbosch   ★★ $ ♟♟♟
Aromas of crushed berries, licorice, and mocha. Sweet, supple,
and fresh, with dark-berry and spice flavors complicated by a hint
of iron. Finishes with fine, dusty tannins and very good length.

Swartland 1997 Pinotage, Swartland   ★★ $ ♟♟
Tart black-cherry and mint nose, plus musky and candied
nuances. Bright red-fruit flavors of red currant and cranberry,
complicated by a tobacco note. Sweet, supple, and fruity.

Kanonkop 1996 Kadette, Stellenbosch   ★ $ ♟♟♟
Berry, wood-smoke, and rose-petal aromas. Red berries, leather,
mocha, and a floral note in the mouth. A dryer-styled yet fresh and
reasonably fruity blend of Cabernet and Merlot. For early drinking.

WHITE WINES

Chenin Blanc is widely planted. Riesling is popular, too, and
Chardonnay and Sauvignon Blanc have surged in recent years.

At the Table

Dry and off-dry Chenin Blanc (called Steen in South
Africa) are local choices with lobster, fish salads, and
vegetable pastas. Riesling goes well with sushi and
matches spicy fare such as curried fish. Sauvignon
Blanc, too, stands up to spices and is also fine with sim-
ply prepared (or raw) shellfish. Richer Chardonnays go
with roasted chicken, fish steaks, and butter-based
sauces, but less concentrated versions pair better with
river fish and light poultry dishes.

The Bottom Line

Few bottles are priced above $15, and many are lower.

What to Buy: White Wines

1995	1996	1997
B-	B-	B+

Mulderbosch 1997 Sauvignon Blanc, ★★★ $$ ♟♟
Stellenbosch Vibrant aromas of smoke, gooseberry, quinine, citrus oil, and lime skin. Citric flavors are penetrating and pristine, but also remarkably rich and supple. Very long, tactile aftertaste.

Thelema 1996 Chardonnay, Stellenbosch ★★★ $$ ♟♟
Enticing aromas of smoke, oak spice, and buttered toast. Full and oaky on the palate, with a ripe lemon-cream flavor and excellent density. Lovely texture and depth.

Boschendal 1996 Chardonnay Reserve, Paarl ★★ $$ ♟♟
Lemon, honeydew melon, smoke, and vanilla on the nose. Rich, supple, and fairly full in the mouth; spicy and firm, with subtle oak treatment. Finishes spicy and firm.

Brampton 1997 Chardonnay, Stellenbosch ★★ $$ ♟♟
Aromas of grapefruit, lemon cream pie, fresh herbs, and spicy oak. Fresh, bright, and intense in the mouth, with perfumed flavors of orange and tangerine. Vibrant and firm on the aftertaste.

De Wetshof 1997 Lesca Chardonnay, Robertson ★★ $ ♟♟
Floral, spicy nose, with hints of caraway seed and grapefruit. Dense and layered on the palate; flavors of soft citrus fruits give shape to this very ripe, full Chardonnay. Good lingering aftertaste.

Saxenburg 1997 Sauvignon Blanc, Stellenbosch ★★ $ ♟♟
Perfumed, assertive grassy minerally aromas, with floral and gooseberry nuances. Lively, lightly herbaceous Sauvignon character; offers good weight and texture in the mouth. Supple and ripe.

KWV 1997 Steen, Western Cape ★ $ ♟♟♟
Lemon, guava, and melon aromas. Supple on the palate, with slight residual sugar giving the wine a creamy fullness. Finishes brisk and firm, with some acidity showing.

AUSTRALIA

SMALL CROPS IN A COUPLE OF RECENT VINTAGES
drove up prices of Australian wine in the mid-
1990s, but tariffs have stabilized, and this country
remains a rich source of easygoing wines, both red
and white, at bargain rates.

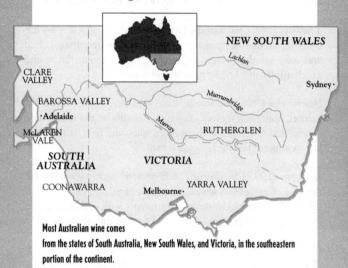

Most Australian wine comes
from the states of South Australia, New South Wales, and Victoria, in the southeastern
portion of the continent.

Grapes & Styles
Australian wines tend to be more immediately
accessible, more obviously fruity, and perhaps less
complex than their Old World counterparts.

On the Label
Like most New World wines, Australia's bottles are
usually labeled by variety, such as Chardonnay,
Shiraz (Syrah), or Cabernet Sauvignon. The general
appellation South Eastern Australia covers all the
major wine regions except Western Australia.

CHARDONNAY

While Australia has long been known for plump, oaky Chardonnays with bold flavors of tropical fruit, the trend in recent years has been toward crisper, more refined wines made from grapes grown in cooler areas or produced with less new oak. Nevertheless, the overwhelming majority of Australian Chardonnays are best consumed within three years of the vintage.

At the Table

More restrained Australian Chardonnays marry well with simply grilled lean fish like sole, flounder, and trout. But larger-scaled examples, with their oak notes of toast, vanilla, and butterscotch, and their ripeness that verges on sweetness, should be matched with richer foods: grilled tuna, for instance, or duck with fruit glaze. Spicy or salty dishes, featuring chile, ginger, or garlic, also pair nicely, as the exotic, tropical-fruit character of bolder Australian Chardonnays can soften the blow of aggressive spicing.

The Bottom Line

Australia's under-$15 Chardonnays are generally far more satisfying than cheap examples from California. Its more expensive limited-production items still cost significantly less than California's boutique Chardonnays.

What to Buy: Chardonnay

1995	1996	1997
B+	A-	B

Penfolds 1996 Trial Bin, Adelaide Hills ★★★ $$ ♟♟
Complex aromas of minerals, clove, smoke, and nectarine. Intensely flavored and harmonious; fresh flavors of lemon, pear, and minerals. Fascinating and distinctive.

Lindemans 1997, Padthaway ★★ $$ ♟♟♟
Very ripe aromas of dried stone fruits and charred oak. Big, full, and rich; fairly concentrated melon and spice flavors are given freshness by sound acidity. Honeyed aftertaste.

D'Arenberg 1997 The Olive Grove, McLaren Vale ★★ $$??
Dried fruits, pineapple, lime, butterscotch, and oak-spice aromas.
Dense and rather rich in the mouth, with limey acidity giving the
wine firm shape. Will need some time for the oakiness to soften.

Did Columbus Discover
the New World?

In wine parlance, *New World* encompasses not only
North and South America but every place that's not in
Europe, which is the Old World. Bottles from Australia,
the Americas, and South Africa all get the moniker *New
World wine*.

Green Point 1996, Yarra Valley ★★ $$??
Spicy, honeyed nose. Fat and oaky, with very ripe pineapple
flavor complicated by spice, honey, and peach notes. The wine
is generous and pliant.

Hugo Estate 1997 Unwooded, McLaren Vale ★★ $$??
Lemon, grapefruit, spice, and tropical fruit on the nose. Sweet
and peachy in the mouth; firm acidity gives the wine a refreshing
quality. Good intensity of pure fruit flavor. Fresh, lingering finish.

Wolf Blass 1996 President's Selection, McLaren Vale ★★ $$??
Aromatic nose combines citrus zest, white flowers, fresh herbs,
and a hint of oyster shell. Fairly intensely flavored and minerally,
with good density and a restrained sweetness. Fat and juicy.

Mitchelton 1997 Thomas Mitchell, South Eastern ★★ $???
Pineapple, melon, and fresh-herb aromas, complicated by a honeyed note. Intensely flavored and lemony, with nicely integrated
ripe acidity and supple texture. Herbal and piney nuances are
evident on the finish.

Penfolds 1997 Koonunga Hill, South ★★ $???
Australian fruit cocktail of peach and apricot, with a spicy note.
Surprising fruit intensity for a wine in this price range; nicely
integrated acidity gives clarity to the peach and orange-peel
flavors. Balanced and firm.

Rosemount 1997 Diamond Label,   ★★ $ ♟♟♟
South Eastern Australia Expressive aromas of orange, cantaloupe, tarragon, and earth. Slightly spritzy and juicy in the mouth, with good fruit intensity and a creamy orange-sorbet quality. The finish is quite dry but refreshing and persistent.

Wynns Coonawarra Estate 1997, Coonawarra   ★★ $ ♟♟
Apricot, apple, and smoke on the nose, plus a faintly gamy nuance. Medium-bodied, fairly intensely flavored, and shapely, with spicy pear and apple flavors and brisk acidity.

OTHER DRY WHITE WINES

Two other top whites from Australia are soft, lemon-limey, and sometimes off-dry Riesling and Semillon, the latter ranging from crisp and citric to rich and long-lived. Semillon blended with Chardonnay is one of Australia's most popular white wines.

The Bottom Line
Australia's Rieslings and Semillons, as well as its Marsannes and Sauvignon Blancs, are generally very good value.

Leeuwin 1997 Riesling, Margaret River   ★★★ $$ ♟♟
Musky aromas of pineapple and stone. Fat but quite dry, with a stony/minerally quality and strongly citric flavors giving the wine a penetrating quality. Finishes firm and long.

Penfolds 1996 Semillon, Adelaide Hills   ★★★ $$ ♟♟
Expressive aromas of butterscotch, grilled nuts, honey, lemon, and grapefruit. Lush, velvety, and quite rich, with a seamless texture, a nutty complexity, and plenty of soft-citrus fruits to support the oak.

Peter Lehmann 1997 Semillon, Barossa   ★★★ $$ ♟♟
Aromas of clove oil, oak spice, and fennel seed. Concentrated and complex; lively flavors of clove, licorice, melon, lemon, and mint are brightened by fresh acidity. Lovely, violety inner-mouth perfume.

Lindemans 1997 Bin 95 Sauvignon Blanc,   ★ $ ♟♟♟
South Eastern Australia Grassy, lemony nose, with a ripe hint of apricot. Similar grassy and citric flavors on the palate; a bit hard-edged, but finishes with a lemony briskness.

Penfolds 1997 Koonunga Hill Semillon/Chardonnay, ★ $ 🍷🍷🍷
South Australia Ripe peach, honey, and smoke aromas. Round
and rather simple, with modest texture and complexity. Soft,
ripe citrus flavors.

Salisbury 1997 Sauvignon Blanc, Victoria ★ $ 🍷🍷
Ripe aromas of honey, smoke, and fresh herbs. Soft, ripe, and
easygoing on the palate, but fresh and not overly sweet.
Moderately concentrated and rather attractive. Good dry finish.

Taltarni 1997 Sauvignon Blanc, Victoria ★ $ 🍷🍷
Lemon, grapefruit, gooseberry, and mint aromas with similar
flavors. Bright, focused, and penetrating; acidity is brisk but not
hard. Finishes firm and persistent. A very refreshing Sauvignon.

SHIRAZ

Australia's most important red variety, Shiraz, is the same grape as
the northern Rhône Valley's Syrah. But most Australian examples
offer a more direct fruitiness, a less serious structure, and earlier
drinkability. Think of Shiraz as Australia's Merlot, only more
assertively flavored: a medium-to-full-bodied wine with forthright,
spicy black-cherry and berry flavors and generally lusher texture
and suppler tannins than the local Cabernet Sauvignon.

At the Table
Although the smoky, spicy, peppery nature of this wine
generally demands boldly flavored food, Shiraz is remarkably versatile at the table. Shiraz works well with a wide
range of red-meat and game dishes, especially those
grilled over wood. Its sweet fruit flavors were made for
roast lamb. Roast turkey, duck confit, barbecued spareribs,
and hamburgers also harmonize with Shiraz. The greatest
mature examples are ideal accompaniments to venison,
as well as to hard, sharp cheeses such as cheddar.

The Bottom Line
The overwhelming majority of Australian Shirazes are priced in
the $10 to $20 range, offering superb value.

What to Buy: Shiraz

1994	1995	1996	1997
A-	B	B+	B+

Rosemount 1995 Balmoral, McLaren Vale ★★★ $$$ ♟♟

Flamboyant aromas of black raspberry, graphite, smoked meat, cola, and maple syrup. Thick, concentrated, and creamy; sappy and deeply spicy. Structured to age but already pliant and enjoyable. Worth the price premium.

Coriole 1996, McLaren Vale ★★★ $$ ♟♟

Aromas of black and red raspberry, cinnamon, and smoky oak. Rather densely packed but intensely flavored, bright, and delineated. Spicy dark-berry flavor and a hint of bourbon. Finishes spicy and firmly tannic.

Richard Hamilton 1996 Old Vines, ★★★ $$ ♟♟

McLaren Vale Sappy blackberry, game, and sweet oak aromas. Thick, sweet, rich, and strong in extract. Pepper and game notes add complexity to the strong berry fruit. High-toned and very expressive; generously textured, long, and very ripe.

Penfolds 1995 Bin 128, Coonawarra ★★ $$ ♟♟♟

Black raspberry, coffee, and chocolate on the nose; shows framboise and fresh herbal notes with aeration. Juicy, spicy, and supple, with enticing inner-mouth perfume and a mineral nuance. Finishes bright and firm, with fine tannins.

Hugo Estate 1996, McLaren Vale ★★ $$ ♟♟

Black raspberry, black cherry, smoke, and cocoa powder aromas. Supple and fat, with lovely depth of berry fruit. But a slight green edge to the flavors carries through to the finish.

Bowen 1995, Coonawarra ★★ $ ♟♟

Red-currant, truffle, game, and woodsmoke aromas. Sweet and truffley in the mouth, with good intensity; slightly elevated acidity gives the wine a faint hard edge. But offers good fruit and freshness.

Deakin Estate 1997, Victoria ★★ $ ♟♟

Expressive aromas of blackberry, smoked meat, root beer, and cola. Sweet, lush, and pliant in the mouth; fairly deep flavors of red currant, pepper, leather, and meat. A distinctly gentle style. Finishes smoky and persistent.

Peter Lehmann 1996, Barossa ★ **$$** ♟♟

Black raspberry, chocolate, and eucalyptus on the nose. Sweet and rather silky, but currently dominated by menthol and clove notes. Finish is somewhat oaky, but has sweet tannins.

CABERNET SAUVIGNON

Australia's Cabernet Sauvignon typically offers generous cassis and sweet oak flavors, as well as early drinkability, even if the best are increasingly being made to age. As with Shiraz, some of Australia's higher-priced Cabernets rank among the world's finest examples of this varietal.

At the Table

Serve Australian Cabernet as you would a Cab from California—alongside red-meat dishes with the sweetness to bring out the wine's ripe fruit. Attention carnivores: This wine is also suitable to accompany beef kidney and heart. Like Australian Shiraz, it goes well with hard, sharp cheeses. Keep in mind that many Australian Cabernets are made in a substantial percentage of American oak, which can yield a pungently tarry, scotchlike character that is sure to overwhelm subtler foods.

The Bottom Line

Australian Cabernets are generally far less expensive than their California equivalents, with many excellent values still to be found in the $12 to $20 price range.

What to Buy: Cabernet Sauvignon

1994	1995	1996	1997
A-	B-	B+	B+

Katnook 1994, Coonawarra ★★★ **$$$** ♟♟

Cassis, chocolate, eucalyptus, and smoky oak on the nose. Silky on the palate, with a juicy quality and a lovely core of spicy dark-berry and licorice flavor. Oak is nicely integrated. Finishes subtly and persistently, with ripe tannins.

Lindemans 1994 Pyrus, Coonawarra ★★★ $$$ ♥♥
Plum, smoky oak, and celery-seed aromas. Juicy black-currant and mineral flavors complicated by a hint of tobacco. Good concentration and structure. Acids are slightly elevated but give the fruit excellent clarity.

Vasse Felix 1996, Western Australia ★★★ $$ ♥♥
Vibrant, nuanced nose combines a panoply of aromas: cassis, black cherry, game, tobacco leaf, leather, chocolate, and toasty oak. The wine is dense but pliant in the mouth, with juicy, sweet black-currant and mineral flavors. The finish includes both fruit and spicy oak.

Rosemount 1995 Traditional, McLaren Vale ★★ $$ ♥♥
Aromas of dark berries, mocha, smoky oak, and fennel seed. Supple and sweet in the mouth; really fat with berry fruit. Slightly high-toned and oaky. Hints of menthol and bourbon. Finishes with chewy tannins.

Rosemount 1996 Diamond Label, South Australia ★ $ ♥♥♥
Aromas of dark berries and smoky oak. Rather simple dark-berry flavor, but juicy and fairly intensely flavored, with a touch of sweetness. Not especially textured or deep, but nicely made. Cherry flavor on the finish.

OTHER RED WINES

Cabernet/Shiraz is a classic Australian blend, with the former grape contributing structure and refinement, the latter rich and spicy fruit. Rhône Valley grapes like Grenache and Mourvèdre are also increasingly turning up in lush, fruit-driven reds meant for immediate consumption.

The Bottom Line
The better examples of Australian red blends costing around $15 are among the world's best deals for flavor intensity.

Lindemans 1994 Limestone Ridge, Coonawarra ★★★ $$$ ♥♥
Bright ruby. Enticing aromas of plum, raspberry, tobacco, lead pencil, and nutty oak. Rich, sweet, and powerful, with a mineral underpinning contributing to the impression of brightness. A Shiraz/Cabernet blend.

Penfolds 1994 St. Henri Shiraz/Cabernet, ★★★ $$ ♟♟
South Australia Portlike aromas of raspberry, coffee, chocolate, game, and woodsmoke. Sweet, fleshy, very ripe flavors of black raspberry and minerals; smooth and intensely flavored. Finishes long and juicy, with chewy tannins.

Coriole 1996 Redstone, McLaren Vale ★★ $$ ♟♟
Dark berries, game, leather, clove, and peat on the nose. Lush and sweet; rustic notes of leather and cigar ash give the wine personality without overwhelming the fruit. Shiraz, Cabernet Sauvignon, and Grenache.

D'Arenberg 1996 d'Arry's Original ★★ $$ ♟♟
Shiraz/Grenache, McLaren Vale Very fruity aromas of dark cherry, spices, and herbs. Fruity, smooth, and harmonious, with complicating mineral and cedar notes. Nicely structured, with firm acidity and chewy tannins hitting the palate late.

Hot Wines

In reference to wines, *hot* has nothing to do with temperature but rather with the fiery sensation from alcohol content that's all too obviously high. For new understanding of the likes of *lean* and *plump, tough* and *soft, firm* and *flabby,* see our Glossary, pages 219 through 223.

Tim Adams 1996 The Fergus Grenache, ★★ $$ ♟♟
Clare Valley Eucalyptus, pine oil, chocolate, and pungent oak spice on the nose. Strong raspberry and mint fruit; fat and fresh, but could use a bit more shape. Ripe and pliant on the finish.

Penfolds 1996 Koonunga Hill Shiraz/Cabernet ★ $ ♟♟♟
Sauvignon, South Australia Raspberry and a whiff of smoked-meat aromas. Juicy and fruity on the palate, with bright dark-berry flavor. Firm, moderately tannic finish. For early drinking.

Rosemount 1997 Grenache/Shiraz, ★ $ ♟♟♟
South Eastern Australia Cherry, plum, rhubarb, tar, and a note of stewed fruit on the nose. Sweet, thick, raspberry-flavored fruit shows a faint cooked quality. Soft and peppery on the finish.

SWEET and FORTIFIED WINES

So-called stickies (wines with substantial residual sugar) have long been an Australian specialty. Often based on the Sauternes grapes Semillon and Sauvignon Blanc, they're generally ready to drink upon release, as are Australia's port-style fortified wines.

At the Table

Sauternes-style wines are perfectly matched with fruit tarts (apple, pear, peach, apricot), as well as with buttery, nutty desserts like crème brûlée, almond tart, and pecan pie—or with just plain almond biscuits. These sweet, luscious wines also pair magically with salty, acidic blue cheeses like Roquefort. A particularly decadent combination is Sauternes-style sweet wine and foie gras. Australia's mellow port-style fortified wines are best sipped by themselves or served with Stilton and a dish of nuts.

The Bottom Line

Compared to Sauternes and ports, the inexpensive Australian versions number among the world's great buys in sweet wines.

Chambers Rosewood Vineyards NV Muscat, ★★★ $$ ❢❢
Rutherglen *(half bottle)* Aromas of orange peel, quince, and spices. Smooth and viscous in the mouth, but bright acids and spicy, citric notes give it good clarity and freshness.

Peter Lehmann 1997 Botrytis Semillon Sauternes, ★ $$ ❢❢
Barossa Valley *(half bottle)* Candied apple, peach syrup, and mandarin orange on the nose. Moderately sweet with pineapple and peach flavors. Slightly medicinal; strong acidity.

Lindemans NV Macquarie Tawny Port, ★★ $ ❢❢
Barossa Valley Nuts, orange-peel, and clove aromas. Supple, sweet, and velvety in the mouth; the orange-peel edge keeps the nutty flavor bright. Finishing notes of walnut and maple syrup.

Penfolds NV Club Port Reserve, South Australia ★ $ ❢❢
Nuts, caramel, and smoke aromas. Mellow, smooth, and moderately sweet, with flavors of caramel, almond, and orange peel. Finishes with a note of vanilla and a citric edge.

NEW ZEALAND

NEW ZEALAND'S OCEAN-COOLED CLIMATE PRODUCES white wines with accurate varietal character, excellent flavor intensity, and brisk acidity. However, the same weather does not favor its typical reds, and when, in particularly warm years, they *are* good, they're too expensive to be of much interest in most export markets.

New Zealand grows the world's most southerly grapes. Its maritime climate brings moderate temperatures and the threat of harvesttime rains. Particularly bracing wines, especially Sauvignon Blancs, are made in Marlborough, at the northern edge of New Zealand's South Island.

Auckland

GISBORNE

NORTH ISLAND

HAWKE'S BAY

■ Wine growing regions

Wellington

MARLBOROUGH

SOUTH ISLAND

Christchurch

Grapes & Styles

In recent years, Chardonnay and Sauvignon Blanc have largely replaced the undistinguished Müller-Thurgau as the most important New Zealand white grapes. White wine definitely rules in New Zealand. Among the country's reds, Pinot Noir shows the greatest promise.

On the Label

New Zealand's wines are labeled by variety. Most of the best examples come from the Marlborough, Hawke's Bay, and Gisborne appellations.

SAUVIGNON BLANC

New Zealand's most distinctive white wine is its citric, grassy, herbal, unoaked Sauvignon Blanc, as sharply focused and penetrating as Sauvignon Blanc from France's Loire Valley.

At the Table

Flavorful and versatile, this wine is perfect with fresh shellfish, especially raw oysters or clams. Its pungent grassy-herbal character makes it a good choice for any dish that incorporates goat cheese, and few wines fare as well with fresh asparagus and artichokes. New Zealand Sauvignon Blanc also pairs well with vegetable antipasti, light pasta dishes, boiled shellfish, smoked trout, and river fish.

The Bottom Line

The top bottles in the $12 to $20 range are good value, comparing favorably with the finest Sauvignon Blancs worldwide.

What to Buy: Sauvignon Blanc

1995	1996	1997
C	A-	B

Cloudy Bay 1997, Marlborough   ★★★ $$ ♈♈♈
Aromas of gooseberry, grapefruit, lime, and truffle. Bright, racy, and assertive, with razor-sharp citric flavors and strong acidity. Finishes extremely firm, with an almost saline quality and a note of lime.

Brancott 1997 Reserve, Marlborough   ★★ $$ ♈♈♈
Bright gooseberry, pear, and mint aromas. Supple and dense, with spicy citric, juniper, and hay notes. Lively acidity intensifies the rich fruit. Firm aftertaste hints at citrus fruit and mint.

Villa Maria 1997 Private Bin, Marlborough   ★★ $$ ♈♈♈
Highly aromatic nose combines herbs, honey, and spices. Full, slightly sweet, and rich, with perfumed flavors of grapefruit, mint, and spices. Offers a layered texture and excellent length.

Stoneleigh 1997, Marlborough   ★★ $ ♈♈♈
Complex grassy and spicy nose shows a slightly candied quality and

a note of smoke. Soft and easygoing on the palate, with a faintly herbaceous quality and moderate concentration. Spicy finish.

Matua Valley 1997, Hawke's Bay ★ $ ♟♟
Aromas of creamed corn, earth, and tropical fruits. Fat and full; spicy flavors of pineapple and grapefruit. Soft, ripe aftertaste.

CHARDONNAY

New Zealand's Chardonnays range in style from lean, citric, Sauvignon Blanc–like wines to richer, more textured examples made primarily in new-oak barrels.

At the Table
The crispness and intensity of New Zealand fruit should show through in all but the country's oakiest renditions of Chardonnay, so select foods that emphasize freshness and brightness rather than richness. Unoaked versions can be used almost like Sauvignon Blanc due to their assertively citric, herbal character. Pair oakier examples with chicken and fish in cream sauces and with pork or veal. More vibrant Asian dishes, especially those of Vietnam and Thailand, generally work well with these Chardonnays.

The Bottom Line
Good but not compelling value in the $12 to $20 range.

What to Buy: Chardonnay

1995	1996	1997
C+	A-	B

Brancott 1997 Reserve, Gisborne ★★ $$ ♟♟♟
Oak-dominated aromas of spice, resin, butter, and vanilla. Lush and silky in the mouth, with tropical-fruit flavors supported by lively, harmonious acids. Oak-spicy aftertaste.

Villa Maria 1997 Private Bin, Gisborne ★★ $$ ♟♟♟
Aromas of pear and spice, with a floral nuance. Honeyed, spicy flavors of peach and pear. Brisk acidity.

Grove Mill 1996, Marlborough   ★★ $$ ♥♥
Sweet aromas of pineapple, honey, and oak spice. Fat and fruity
in the mouth, with lovely layered texture; the pineapple and
spice notes repeat on the palate. Finishes firm and bright.

Te Kairanga 1996, Martinborough   ★★ $$ ♥♥
Super-ripe honey, creamed-corn, and smoke aromas. Supple,
intensely flavored, and quite full, with a spicy, leesy complexity
and ripeness verging on sweet. Finishes ripe and very long.

Babich 1997, Gisborne   ★★ $ ♥♥♥
Lemon, pineapple, and minerals on the nose. Dense, spicy, and
fruit-driven, with harmonious acidity giving the wine good
backbone. Finishes with a minerally firmness and very good length.

Matua Valley 1997, Eastern Bays   ★★ $ ♥♥
Smoke, honey, and suggestions of apricot and guava on the nose.
Full and ripe in the mouth, with lively pineapple fruit deepened
by smoke and honey notes. Honeyed but firm on the ripe finish.

OTHER WHITE WINES

New Zealand produces crisp, satisfying Rieslings with excellent
fruit intensity and soil character. Some good Gewürztraminers
and Pinot Gris can also be found in the marketplace.

The Bottom Line
Though not bargains, Rieslings are fairly priced for their quality.

Allan Scott 1997 Riesling, Marlborough   ★★ $$ ♥♥
Complex nose combines fresh herbs, honey, mint, orange peel,
and a stony nuance. Dry, minerally, and intensely flavored, with
an intriguing floral character. Very firm, lingering finish.

De Redcliffe 1996 Dry Riesling, Marlborough   ★★ $ ♥♥
Apple, grapefruit, minerals, and a petrolly note. Dry and stony
in the mouth; offers a supple texture despite possessing firm,
penetrating pineapple flavor. Quite dry and brisk on the finish.

Grove Mill 1997 Pinot Gris, Marlborough   ★ $$ ♥♥
Ripe peach and licorice aromas, with a smoky, buttery richness.
Slightly sweet peach and earth flavors are soft and supple, with just
enough acidity to maintain freshness. A fruit bomb of a Pinot Gris.

CHILE

NO ONE CAN COMPLAIN ABOUT THE SINGLE-DIGIT prices of Chilean exports, and most of the wines are soundly made, even though few have the personality and intensity of flavor to merit more than two stars.

Nestled between the Andes mountains and the Pacific Ocean, the Chilean wine region enjoys sunny weather during the growing season. Thus, rapidly improving viticultural techniques and winemaking skills have been far more important to wine quality in recent years than vintage variation.

Grapes & Styles

The production of export-grade Cabernet Sauvignon and Merlot varietals has a long history in Chile. Recently, the popular whites Chardonnay and Sauvignon Blanc have joined the ranks of these reds. All four varietals tend to be lighter wines than they are when made in other parts of the world because of the large crops that result from the endless supply of melting snow from the Andes. (The smaller the vine yield, the more intense the resulting wines.)

On the Label

As with most other wines from the Americas, the grape variety is indicated on the labels of Chilean bottles.

Wine growing regions

CASABLANCA VALLEY
•Casablanca
Santiago

MAIPO VALLEY •Maipo

RAPEL VALLEY

COLCHAGUA VALLEY
Lontué

ANDES MOUNTAIN RANGE

RED WINES

Cabernet remains Chile's most important red and generally offers more personality than Merlot from recently planted vines.

At the Table

Chile's light, crisp reds suit lighter foods—like chicken and pork—better than do the Cabernets and Merlots from France, America, and Australia. The most concentrated Cabernets can stand up to game birds and steak.

The Bottom Line

Chile is *the* source for good reds that sell for less than $10.

What to Buy: Red Wines

1995	1996	1997
B+	B+	A-

Casa Lapostolle 1996 Merlot Cuvée Alexandre, ★★★**$$** ♟♟
Rapel Valley Black-ruby color. Brooding, intense cherry and tobacco nose. Very ripe, thick, and intense, with urgent, tarry flavors of cassis and blackberry. Fine but substantial tannins are buried by explosive black-fruit flavor.

Stonelake 1996 Cabernet Sauvignon, Lontué ★★★**$$** ♟♟
Dusty aromas of cherry and tobacco. Rich and firm on the palate, with a kick of bright cherry fruit. Finishes with tongue-dusting tannins and notes of tobacco and espresso.

Santa Rita 1996 Cabernet Sauvignon ★★**$$** ♟♟♟
Medella Real, Maipo Valley Dark ruby. Cherry/berry, vanilla, and oak spice on the nose. Exotic spices and coconut on the palate, along with jammy cherry fruit. Long, strong finishing flavors are complemented by nicely integrated tannins.

Carmen 1996 Cabernet Sauvignon Reserva ★★**$$** ♟♟
Grande Vidure, Maipo Valley Rich cherry-scented nose offers a whiff of spicy, vanillin oak. Intense, ripe cherry and cassis flavors, complicated by a hint of fresh, dusty herbs. Long, supple, softly tannic finish features a kick of oak spice.

Caliterra 1995 Cabernet Sauvignon Reserva,   ★★ $ ♟♟♟
Valle Central Ruby red. Blackberry, raspberry, strawberry, and a minty nuance on the nose. Supple, smooth, and concentrated, with a layered texture and notes of berries, bitter chocolate, and herbs. Good richness and volume in the mouth.

Casa Lapostolle 1996 Cabernet Sauvignon,   ★★ $ ♟♟♟
Rapel Valley Jammy blackberry and cassis aromas, with hints of vanillin oak and clove. Nicely concentrated black-fruit flavors on the palate; almost velvety in texture. Finishes with ripe, smooth tannins and a note of blackberry compote.

Casa Lapostolle 1996 Merlot, Rapel Valley   ★★ $ ♟♟♟
Rich black-raspberry and dark-chocolate aromas. Round and creamy in the mouth, with blackberry and tobacco notes. Very Bordeaux-like, with firm, slightly dry tannins framing the fruit.

Cousiño-Macul 1995 Cabernet Sauvignon   ★★ $ ♟♟♟
Antiguas Reservas, Maipo Valley Tangy cherry, spice, and mint on the nose. Suave, claretlike texture; flavors of cherry, tobacco, and mint. Firm but harmonious acidity. Gentle tannins give shape to the smoky red fruit. Long, clean finish.

Undurraga 1997 Cabernet Sauvignon,   ★★ $ ♟♟♟
Colchagua Valley Fresh berry nose complicated by notes of tar and herbs. Flavors of black raspberry, cassis, and blackberry on the palate. Long, crisp, lightly tannic aftertaste.

WHITE WINES

Chile's Chardonnays are generally lean in style, with notes of citrus, apple, and pear, but an increasing use of oak means richer, spicier wines. Sauvignon Blancs are aromatic and lively.

At the Table
The light Chilean Chardonnays make excellent aperitifs and pair well with simple fish dishes or vegetable stir-fries. Creamier, riper examples demand richer foods or even dishes that incorporate exotic fruits (chicken with pineapple, Indian dishes with mango chutney). Sauvignon Blancs go especially well with shellfish.

The Bottom Line
Chile's whites rank among the best buys on the market today.

What to Buy: White Wines

1995	1996	1997
B-	A-	B+

Carmen 1996 Chardonnay Reserva, Maipo Valley ★★ $$ ♟♟
Dusty, minerally nose hints at orange and oak spice. Juicy fruit-cocktail flavors are supported by sound acidity. Clean, vibrant finish features apple, pear, and lime notes.

Casa Lapostolle 1996 Chardonnay Cuvée ★★ $$ ♟♟
Alexandre, Casablanca Valley Assertively oaky aromas of cinnamon, clove, and honey, plus exotic melon and pineapple. A wave of buttery tropical fruit in the mouth; thickly textured and creamy. Finishes quite long, with notes of toffee and cappuccino.

Undurraga 1997 Chardonnay, Colchagua Valley ★★ $ ♟♟♟
Exotic melon and peach nose. Clean and brisk in the mouth, with flamboyant cantaloupe and pineapple flavors enlivened by bright acidity. Finishes with a dusty, tactile quality.

Caliterra 1997 Chardonnay, Valle Central ★ $ ♟♟♟
Tangerine and orange sorbet on the nose. Supple, juicy, and shapely in the mouth, with dusty, ripe citric flavors and good texture. The ripe orange note repeats on the firm finish.

Carmen 1997 Sauvignon Blanc, Valle Central ★ $ ♟♟♟
Dusty lime and lemon-drop nose. Round and ripe, with lime, pear, and quince flavors and a suggestion of minerals. Snappy acids give the finish a crisp, clean quality.

Luis Felipe Edwards 1997 Chardonnay, ★ $ ♟♟♟
Colchagua Valley Brisk aromas of lime cream, banana, and pear. Clean, appley, and refreshing in the mouth; flavors are nicely focused. A lively Chardonnay, with a bracing hint of quinine.

Walnut Crest 1997 Sauvignon Blanc, ★ $ ♟♟♟
Mulchen Valley Pungent grassy nose. Lemon, grapefruit, and quince flavors, plus a hint of pear skin. Bright acidity gives the wine sound structure. Finishes rather long and spicy, with a hint of nutmeg.

ARGENTINA

ARGENTINA'S WINES TEND TO BE A BIT MORE rustic than their counterparts from nearby Chile, but the reds can also be more concentrated and distinctive. The country's wine industry has been radically modernized in recent years, and many wineries have benefited from the experience of consulting winemakers from Europe and California.

Mendoza, the most important Argentine wine region, is much hotter than the grape-growing areas in nearby Chile. Planting vines at high altitudes partly mitigates the effects of the heat, but irrigation is necessary in this semidesert climate. Harvesttime rain is a rarity—or was, until the dismal El Niño year of 1998.

Wine growing region

Mendoza·

MENDOZA

ANDES MOUNTAIN RANGE

Grapes & Styles

Cabernet Sauvignon is becoming increasingly popular in Argentina. But Malbec—a grape that was once important in Bordeaux and that is still the backbone for the burly "black wine" of Cahors in southwestern France—has traditionally been Argentina's most widely planted red. Malbec produces dense, sometimes coarse wines with noteworthy depth of fruit.

On the Label

For most New World winemakers, the grape variety is the most important information on the bottle, and Argentina is no exception.

RED WINES

Argentina is the world's fifth-largest wine producer, but until recently, its rather rustic wines offered little interest to export markets. Its red wines far outshine its whites: Today's better reds, generally made from Cabernet or Malbec, show super-ripe currant, black-cherry, chocolate, and spice flavors and aromas, along with substantial body and concentration.

At the Table

Many Cabernets and Malbecs from Argentina finish with slightly dry, dusty tannins, so these wines call for fattier foods that can soften the tannins and bring out the fruit flavors. Beef is a better match than lamb, and preparations that include olive oil or butter are good bets. Braised meats often have a juicy quality that helps to ameliorate red-wine tannins. Try these wines alongside pot roast with root vegetables, braised short ribs, or braised oxtails. The fruity, new-wave Argentine reds, especially Merlots, can be served with lamb or sausage, or with dried cured meats like prosciutto or bresaola.

The Bottom Line

Argentina's red wines are generally a few dollars more than their Chilean counterparts, but the best examples costing about $15 offer very good value.

What to Buy: Red Wines

1995	1996	1997
A-	A	B

Catena 1995 Lunlunta Vineyards Malbec, ★★★ **$$** 🍷🍷
Mendoza Deep, dark ruby. Briary aroma of black cherry, plum, and tobacco. Plummy, round, and ripe, with excellent weight in the mouth and an intriguing floral note. Very long finish features substantial but supple tannins and ripe-cherry flavor.

Weinert 1995 Merlot, Mendoza ★★★ **$$** 🍷🍷
Explosively sweet red-fruit and new-oak aromas. Very ripe,

197

velvety, and full-bodied, with flavors of fresh cherry and bitter chocolate. The finish is quite long, with gentle tannins and super-ripe red fruit.

Weinert 1994 Cabernet Sauvignon, Mendoza ★★ $$ 🍷🍷
Has spicy aromas of clove, mace, and pepper. Concentrated and soundly structured, with a cassis flavor complicated by notes of black pepper and pipe tobacco. Finishes long and intense, with soft tannins and bitter-cherry and tobacco notes.

Alamos Ridge 1996 Cabernet Sauvignon, Mendoza ★ $ 🍷🍷🍷
Assertive red-cherry and cassis aromas, with nuances of mint and other fresh herbs. Leathery, briary bitter-cherry and leather flavors. Firmly structured. Persistent, vibrant aftertaste.

Alamos Ridge 1996 Malbec, Mendoza ★ $ 🍷🍷🍷
Clean, brisk, raspberry-scented nose. Firm and bright on the palate, with moderate richness and nicely defined flavors of red currant and white pepper. The red-berry character carries through to the lightly tannic, fresh finish.

Trapiche 1996 Oak Cask Malbec, Mendoza ★ $ 🍷🍷🍷
Vibrant red-raspberry aroma. Fresh and crisp, with lively acidity and hints of red currant and cranberry. Quite light on its feet. Finishes bright, persistent, and briskly tannic, with a repeating note of cranberry.

Trumpeter 1995 Cabernet Sauvignon, Maipu ★ $ 🍷🍷🍷
Fresh red-berry nose. Crisp, crunchy black-cherry flavors. A medium-bodied, rather stylish wine with good ripeness and flavor definition. Persistent finish hints at blackberry.

Trumpeter 1996 Malbec, Vistalba ★ $ 🍷🍷🍷
Bright ruby with purple highlights. Juicy aromas of red currant and raspberry jam. Bright and crisp, with urgent red-berry flavors and juicy acidity. Clean, lingering finish features delicate tannins and a note of tart cherry.

Trapiche 1996 Syrah, Maipu-Mendoza ★ $ 🍷🍷
Dark ruby color. Ripe berry, black-pepper, and spice aromas. Plump and juicy on the palate, with flavors of raspberry and pepper. Finishes long and smooth, with supple tannins and sweet blackberry fruit.

WHITE WINES

White wines from Argentina used to be thin, overly oxidized, and lacking in fruit aromas and flavors. Then Argentina's wineries began to focus their attention on export markets and invest in the equipment needed to control the temperature of fermentation. Today, altogether fresher wines are produced from internationally favored varieties like Chardonnay, Sauvignon Blanc, and Sémillon.

At the Table

Most Argentine Chardonnays in export markets are relatively uncomplicated and fruit driven and best suited to lighter, fresher dishes. Try them with hot-weather fare: chicken and seafood salads, tabbouleh salad with mint, and chicken or turkey sandwiches. The majority of the white wines are good bets with shellfish, salmon, and tuna.

The Bottom Line

The quality of white wines from Argentina is still very uneven, but the best examples are good value.

What to Buy: White Wines

1995	1996	1997
B-	B+	B-

Catena 1996 Agrelo Chardonnay, Mendoza ★★★ $$ ♈♈
Very ripe aromas of pineapple, butter, and oak spice. Impressively rich in the mouth, with crisp acidity buttressing exotic nectarine and plum flavors. A medium-weight, classy Chardonnay with a fresh, very long aftertaste.

Alamos Ridge 1996 Chardonnay, Mendoza ★ $ ♈♈♈
Lemon-cream aroma shows a buttery, leesy complexity. Stony and crisp, with sharply focused lime and mineral flavors, along with hints of citrus skin and quinine. Lingering, refreshing aftertaste.

Trumpeter 1996 Chardonnay, Tupungato ★ $ ♈♈♈
Buttery and tropical fruit aromas. Rich, ripe, and round; flavors of banana and mango. Quite creamy on the palate. Rather long, fresh finish hints at pineapple and ripe pear.

Widely Available Wines Under $15

Many wines that may not be as special as those suggested in the body of this guide are nevertheless worthy values and are exceptionally easy to find. We recommend all of the following possibilities.

France

WHITE WINES FROM ALSACE
- Albert Mann Pinot Auxerrois Vieilles Vignes
- Hugel Gentil
- JosMeyer Pinot d'Alsace Les Lutins
- Pierre Sparr Pinot Blanc
- Trimbach Pinot Blanc

RED WINES FROM LANGUEDOC-ROUSSILLON & PROVENCE
- Château de Donjon Cuvée Tradition, Minervois
- Château Gourgazaud, Minervois
- Château La Roque, Pic-Saint-Loup
- Château Routas Traditional, Coteaux Varois
- Commanderie de la Bargemone, Coteaux d'Aix-en-Provence
- Mas Champart, St-Chinian
- Mas de la Dame Reserve du Mas, Les Baux-de-Provence
- Pierre Clavel Mas de Clavel Vieilles Vignes, Méjanelle
- Val d'Orbieu Pierre Fils, Minervois

RED WINES FROM THE RHONE VALLEY
- Chapoutier Belleruche, Côtes-du-Rhône
- Clos de l'Oratoire, Cairanne Côtes-du-Rhône-Villages
- Daniel Brusset, Cairanne Côtes-du-Rhône-Villages
- Domaine André Brunel Cuvée Sommelongue, Côtes-du-Rhône
- Domaine Santa-Duc, Côtes-du-Rhône

Italy

WHITE WINES FROM THE NORTHEAST
- Anselmi Soave Classico, Veneto
- Lageder Pinot Bianco, Alto Adige
- Tiefenbrunner Pinot Bianco, Alto Adige
- Zenato Pinot Grigio, Veneto

WHITE WINES FROM CENTRAL ITALY
- Antinori Castello della Sala Orvieto Classico
- Fontaleoni Vernaccia di San Gimignano
- Gini Soave Classico
- I Campetti Nebbiaie Vino Bianco, Tuscany
- Mazzini Montecarlo Bianco, Tuscany
- Pieropan Soave Classico, Veneto
- Umani Ronchi Verdicchio dei Castelli di Jesi, Marches

WHITE WINES FROM THE SOUTH
- Argiolas Vermentino, Sardinia
- Regaleali Bianco, Sicily

RED WINES FROM THE NORTHWEST

- Chiarlo Barbera d'Asti
- Parusso Dolcetto d'Alba
- Prunotto Fiulot Barbera d'Asti
- Ratti Dolcetto d'Alba

RED WINES FROM THE NORTHEAST

- Acinum Valpolicella Classico Superiore
- Allegrini Valpolicella Classico Superiore
- Cavalchina Bardolino

RED WINES FROM CENTRAL ITALY

- Antinori Santa Cristina Sangiovese, Tuscany
- Capanna Rosso di Montepulciano
- Castello d'Albola Chianti Classico
- Col d'Orcia Rosso di Montalcino
- Dei Rosso di Montepulciano
- Falesco Vitiano, Lazio
- Fattoria le Corti Chianti Classico
- Mazzini Montecarlo Rosso, Tuscany
- Villa Cafaggio Chianti Classico

RED WINES FROM THE SOUTH

- Argiolas Perdera, Sardinia
- Taurino Notarpanaro, Apulia

Spain

CAVA

- Codorníu Blanc de Blancs
- Sumarrocca Extra Brut

RED WINES

- Bodegas Magaña Eventum, Navarra
- Bodegas Ochoa Tempranillo, Navarra
- Bodegas Sierra Cantabria, Rioja
- Cooperativa de la Asunción Ibernoble, Ribera del Duero
- La Rioja Alta Viña Alberdi, Rioja
- Miguel Torres Gran Sangre de Toro Reserva, Penedès
- Vinícola del Priorat Onix, Priorato

Portugal

RED WINES

- Montéz Champalimaud Quinta do Cotto, Douro
- P.V.Q. Quinta de Pancas Cabernet Sauvignon, Estremadura
- P.V.Q. Quinta de Parrotes, Alenquer
- Sogrape Duque de Viseu, Dão

California

WHITE WINES

- Beringer Zinfandel, North Coast
- Ravenswood Vintners Blend Zinfandel, California
- Rosenblum Zinfandel Vintners Cuvée, California
- Shooting Star Zinfandel, Lake County

RED WINES

- Haywood Vintner's Select Cabernet Sauvignon, California
- Haywood Vintner's Select Merlot, California
- Marietta Cellars Old Vine Red, California
- Napa Ridge Pinot Noir, North Coast
- Saintsbury Pinot Noir Garnet, Carneros
- Taft Street Merlot, Sonoma County
- Talus Merlot, California

Oregon

WHITE WINES

- Argyle Chardonnay, Willamette Valley
- Bethel Heights Pinot Blanc, Willamette Valley
- King Estate Pinot Gris, Oregon

RED WINES

- Foris Pinot Noir, Rogue Valley
- Willamette Valley Vineyards Whole Cluster Pinot Noir, Oregon

Washington State

WHITE WINES

- Arbor Crest Sauvignon Blanc, Washington State
- Barnard Griffin Fumé Blanc, Columbia Valley
- Canoe Ridge Chardonnay, Columbia Valley
- Columbia Crest Chardonnay, Columbia Valley

RED WINES

- Columbia Winery Syrah, Yakima Valley
- Washington Hills Cabernet Sauvignon, Columbia Valley
- Washington Hills Merlot, Columbia Valley
- W. B. Bridgman Cabernet Sauvignon, Columbia Valley

Australia

WHITE WINES

- David Wynn Unwooded Chardonnay, South Eastern Australia
- Deakin Estate Chardonnay, Victoria
- Lindeman's Bin 65 Chardonnay
- Penfolds Koonunga Hill Semillon/Chardonnay
- Salisbury Estate Chardonnay, Victoria

RED WINES

- Rosemount Grenache/Shiraz, South Eastern Australia
- Rothbury Estate Shiraz, South Eastern Australia
- Wynns Coonawarra Estate Shiraz

Chile

WHITE WINES

- Casa Lapostolle Sauvignon Blanc, Rapel Valley
- Santa Rita Sauvignon Blanc 120, Lontué Valley
- Viña Los Vascos Sauvignon Blanc

RED WINES

- Caliterra Chardonnay Reserve, Aconcagua Valley
- Caliterra Merlot, Valle Central
- Concha y Toro Cabernet Sauvignon Marqués de Casa Concha, Maipo Valley
- Undurraga Cabernet Sauvignon, Colchagua Valley

Argentina

RED WINES

- Bodegas Norton Malbec, Mendoza

Shortcut to Your Favorite Varietals

Wine-Style Finder

Use this chart when you know what style of wine you want but not what particular type within that style. Say you need a light white but are tired of your usual Pinot Grigio; just look below for a whole list of possibilities. The page numbers are for specific recommendations in this book.

COUNTRY	REGION	WINES
LIGHT, DRY WHITE WINES		
CHILE		Sauvignon Blanc, **194**
FRANCE	Alsace	Muscat and Sylvaner, **14**
	Loire Valley	Savennières, **52**; Muscadet, **54**; Quincy, **55**
GERMANY	Mosel-Saar-Ruwer	Riesling Kabinett, **130**
ITALY	Friuli	Pinot Bianco and Pinot Grigio, **84**
	Marches	Verdicchio, **97**
	Piedmont	Arneis and Gavi, **82**
	Umbria	Orvieto, **97**
	Veneto	Soave, **84**
NEW ZEALAND		Sauvignon Blanc, **189**
OREGON		Riesling, **162**
PORTUGAL	Vinho Verde	Vinho Verde, **121**
SOUTH AFRICA		Sauvignon Blanc, **176**
SPAIN	Galicia	Albariño, **111**
WASHINGTON STATE		Sauvignon Blanc, **165**
MEDIUM-BODIED, DRY WHITE WINES		
ARGENTINA		Chardonnay, **199**
AUSTRALIA		Riesling, **181**
CALIFORNIA		Unoaked Chardonnay, **138**; Sauvignon Blanc, **141**; Viognier, **151**
CHILE		Chardonnay, **194**
FRANCE	Alsace	Pinot Blanc, **11**; Riesling, **13**
	Bordeaux	Graves and other whites, **22**
	Burgundy	Côte d'Or, **29**; Côte Chalonnaise, **33**; Mâconnais, **34**; Chablis **36**

COUNTRY	REGION	WINES
	Loire Valley	Montlouis and Vouvray sec, 52; Pouilly-Fumé and Sancerre, 55
	Rhône Valley	Condrieu, 68
ITALY	Campania	Fiano di Avellino and Greco di Tufo, 100
NEW ZEALAND		Chardonnay, 190
OREGON		Pinot Gris, 160; Chardonnay, 162
SOUTH AFRICA		Chardonnay, 176
SPAIN	Rueda	Rueda, 111
WASHINGTON STATE		Semillon, 165; Chardonnay, 166

FULL-BODIED, DRY WHITE WINES

AUSTRALIA		Chardonnay, 179; Semillon, 181
CALIFORNIA		Oaked Chardonnay, 138
FRANCE	Alsace	Gewürztraminer, 10; Pinot Gris, 12
	Burgundy	*Premier* and *grand cru*, 28

SLIGHTLY SWEET TO MODERATELY SWEET WHITE WINES

FRANCE	Loire Valley	Vouvray demi-sec, 52
GERMANY		Riesling Spätlese and Auslese, 130 and 133
PORTUGAL	Madeira	Bual, 126
SPAIN	Jerez	Palo Cortado, 115

VERY SWEET WHITE WINES

AUSTRALIA		Late-harvest whites, 187
FRANCE	Alsace	Sélection de Grains Nobles, 10
	Bordeaux	Barsac, Sauternes, and Ste-Croix-du-Mont, 24
	Loire Valley	Vouvray *moelleux*, 52
ITALY	Piedmont	Moscato d'Asti, 82
PORTUGAL	Madeira	Malmsey, 126
SPAIN	Jerez	Oloroso and Cream Sherry, 115

LIGHT, FRESH RED WINES

FRANCE	Burgundy	Beaujolais, 37
ITALY	Piedmont	Barbera, 81
	Veneto	Valpolicella, 84

MEDIUM-BODIED RED WINES

ARGENTINA		Cabernet Sauvignon and Malbec, 197
AUSTRALIA		Cabernet Sauvignon, 184
CALIFORNIA		Pinot Noir, 154
CHILE		Cabernet Sauvignon and Merlot, 193

COUNTRY	REGION	WINES
FRANCE	Bordeaux	Bordeaux, **16**
	Burgundy	Côte d'Or, **29**; Côte Chalonnaise, **33**; *Crus* Beaujolais, **37**
	Languedoc-Roussillon	Coteaux du Languedoc, **45**; Corbières and Minervois, **47**
	Loire Valley	Bourgueil and Chinon, **58**
	Rhône Valley	Côte-Rôtie, Crozes-Hermitage, and St-Joseph, **65**; Côtes du Ventoux, **70**
ITALY	Abruzzi	Montepulciano d'Abruzzo, **97**
	Piedmont	Barbaresco, **76**; other Nebbiolos, **79**; Dolcetto, **81**
	Chianti	Chianti, **89**
	Tuscany	Carmignano, Rosso di Montalcino, and Vino Nobile di Montepulciano, **93**
OREGON		Pinot Noir, **159**
PORTUGAL	Alentejo	Alentejo, **119**
	Dão	Dão, **119**
	Douro	Douro, **119**
SOUTH AFRICA		Cabernet Sauvignon and Pinotage, **175**
SPAIN	Navarre	Navarre, **108**
	Rioja	Rioja, **105**
WASHINGTON STATE		Cabernet Sauvignon and Merlot, **169**

FULL-BODIED RED WINES

COUNTRY	REGION	WINES
AUSTRALIA		Shiraz, **182**
CALIFORNIA		Cabernet Sauvignon, **143**; Merlot, **146**; Zinfandel, **148**; Rhône-style, **151**
FRANCE	Provence	Bandol, **60**
	Rhône Valley	Cornas and Hermitage, **65**; Gigondas and Châteauneuf-du-Pape, **69**
ITALY	Piedmont	Barolo, **76**
	Sardinia	Reds, **100**
	Tuscany	Brunello di Montalcino, **93**; super-Tuscans, **95**
	Veneto	Amarone, **84**
SPAIN	Ribera del Duero	Ribera del Duero, **107**

Pairing
Wine with Food

The advice on matching recommended wines with food (from the At the Table sections throughout the book) is indexed here for your convenience.

Ingredients

Courses, Cuisines, Dishes & Cooking Methods

Tips on Starting a Wine Cellar

Many of the world's best wines need aging, anywhere from a few years to several decades, in order to reach their peak of lusciousness. The number of these ageworthy bottles is small, perhaps 5 percent of all that is produced in a given year—truly the crème de la crème. You can enjoy such wines *if* you buy them near the time that they're released for sale. But if you wait until they're ready to drink, they'll have become incredibly scarce and, even when you can find them, sky-high in price.

Where to store your wine

If you have a basement, or an old-fashioned cellar, you're probably all set. You need a dark, humid but not damp place where the temperature is cool and fairly constant, ideally below 60 degrees Fahrenheit, but below 70 will do.

What to buy

As a rule of thumb, buy three reds for every white, even if you drink more white than red. Many more red wines need aging than whites, most of which tend to be best young.

REDS Slow-developing, long-lived Bordeaux remain, deservedly, the backbone of many a cellar. Since Bordeaux take at least a decade to come to mellow maturity and can be decidedly unrewarding until they do, be sure to choose some other reds as well. Unlike Bordeaux, many of the following can be enjoyed along the way toward that perfect peak: Burgundies, of course, though they're tricky to understand due to a complicated and less-than-crystal-clear naming and classification system; Hermitage and Côte-Rôtie from the Rhône Valley; the underappreciated reds of Provence and Languedoc; Italy's Borolo, Barbaresco, and

Brunello; Spain's Rioja Reservas and Gran Reservas, already well aged on release; and Cabernet Sauvignons from California.

WHITES Choose among top Chardonnays, such as those from Burgundy; Rieslings, especially from Germany and Alsace; and Loire Valley Chenin Blancs. Also consider a few outsize bottles of Champagne. A magnum of nutty, mature bubbly is somehow twice as much fun as the same quantity in standard-size bottles.

DESSERT WINES Sauternes is the obvious choice, and a dandy one, too, if you want to spend the necessary cash. Also consider wines made nearby in the same style or late-harvest German, Alsace, and Loire Valley bottlings. Half bottles are often the perfect size since few people will want more than a smallish glass.

PORTS Vintage ports tend to disappear from shops rather early in their lives. And they can take up to 25 years to reach their full, mellow maturity. If you love them, buy them.

VINTAGES As with financial investments, *diversify* is a key word here. There's more out there than the highly touted great years. Follow our What to Buy charts for suggestions.

How much to buy

The quantities of various wines that you buy are a strictly personal matter. What's right for you may be wrong for the next person. You need to be aware of your own drinking and entertaining patterns and then plan accordingly. There's nothing worse than suddenly realizing that a batch of now-valuable bottles is finally ready, ready, ready, and you can't possibly use them all up before they start to fade.

When to drink your wine

Experts often tell you to open a bottle every so often to see how it's coming, and of course, sampling is the only way to know for sure whether or not a wine has aged sufficiently. But most of us don't buy huge quantities, perhaps a case or two of each particular wine, and could, by tasting, go through all the bottles in the case before the wine is ready. Our best advice, if you're not a big buyer, is to use our Ready, Set, Drink graphs to give you an idea of where your stash stands. We have provided one for each category of collectible wine that's in the guide.

Top Wine Shops

Stocking the wines that give the best value requires a special effort, not to mention good connections with quality-conscious importers. These retailers can be relied upon to carry many of the wines recommended in this guide, or to special-order for you.

■Alabama

OVERTON & VINE
3150 Overton Rd.
Birmingham, AL
205-967-1409

■Arizona

SPORTSMAN'S FINE WINES & SPIRITS
3205 E. Camelback Rd.
Phoenix, AZ
602-955-7730

PLAZA LIQUORS
2642 N. Campbell Ave.
Tucson, AZ
520-327-0452

■California

NORTH BERKELEY WINE
1505 Shattuck Ave.
Berkeley, CA
510-848-8910
800-266-6585

THE WINE STOP
1300 Burlingame Ave.
Burlingame, CA
800-283-9463

ENOTECA WINE SHOP
1345 Lincoln Ave., Ste. C
Calistoga, CA
707-942-1117

DUKE OF BOURBON
20908 Roscoe Blvd.
Canoga Park, CA
818-341-1234
800-434-6394

HI-TIME WINE CELLARS
250 Ogle St.
Costa Mesa, CA
714-650-8463
800-331-3005

RED CARPET WINE
400 E. Glen Oaks Blvd.
Glendale, CA
818-247-5544
800-339-0609

WALLY'S FOOD, WINES AND SPIRITS
2107 Westwood Blvd.
Los Angeles, CA
310-475-0606

THE WINE HOUSE
2311 Cotner Ave.
Los Angeles, CA
310-479-3731
800-626-9463

BELTRAMO'S WINE & SPIRITS
1540 El Camino Real
Menlo Park, CA
650-325-2806

DRAEGER'S SUPERMARKET
1010 University Dr.
Menlo Park, CA
650-688-0688

WINE EXCHANGE
2368 N. Orange Mall
Orange, CA
714-974-1454
800-769-4639

CORTI BROTHERS
5810 Folsom Blvd.
Sacramento, CA
916-736-3800

ST. HELENA WINE MERCHANTS
699 St. Helena Hwy. S.
St. Helena, CA
707-963-7888
800-729-9463

SAN DIEGO WINE CO.
5282 Eastgate Mall
San Diego, CA
619-535-1400

PLUMPJACK WINES
3201 Fillmore St.
San Francisco, CA
415-346-9870

THE WINE CLUB
953 Harrison St.
San Francisco, CA
415-346-9870
800-966-7835

THE WINE HOUSE LIMITED
535 Bryant St.
San Francisco, CA
415-495-8486

THE WINE RACK
6136 Bollinger Rd.
San Jose, CA
408-253-3050

THE WINE CASK
813 Anacapa St.
Santa Barbara, CA
805-966-9463

MISSION WINES
1114 Mission St.
South Pasadena, CA
626-403-9463

PRIMA TRATTORIA & NEGOZIO DI VINI
1522 N. Main St.
Walnut Creek, CA
510-935-7780

■ Colorado

LIQUOR MART
1750 15th St.
Boulder, CO
303-449-3374
800-597-4440

ARGONAUT WINES & LIQUOR
700 E. Colfax Ave.
Denver, CO
303-831-7788

THE VINEYARD
261 Fillmore St.
Denver, CO
303-355-8324

APPLEJACK LIQUORS
3320 Youngfield St.
Wheatridge, CO
303-233-3331
800-879-5225

■ Connecticut

HORSENECK WINE & LIQUOR
25 E. Putnam Ave.
Greenwich, CT
203-869-8944

SPIRITUS WINES
367 Main St.
Hartford, CT
860-247-5431

M&R LIQUORS
120 Tolland Turnpike
Manchester, CT
860-643-9014

■ Delaware

KRESTON LIQUOR MART
904 Concord Ave.
Wilmington, DE
302-652-3792

■ Florida

WINE WATCH
901 Progresso Dr.
Ft. Lauderdale, FL
954-523-9463

ABC FINE WINE & SPIRITS
11850 Biscayne Blvd.
Miami, FL
305-895-4711

FOREMOST SUNSET CORNERS
8701 Sunset Dr.
Miami, FL
305-271-8492

ABC FINE WINE & SPIRITS
3015 W. Kennedy Blvd.
Tampa, FL
813-876-5330

B-21 FINE WINE & SPIRITS
43380 U.S. 19 N.
Tarpon Springs, FL
813-937-5049

DEXTER'S OF WINTER PARK
200 W. Fairbanks Ave.
Winter Park, FL
407-629-1150

■ Georgia

ANSLEY WINE MERCHANTS
1544 Piedmont Rd.
Atlanta, GA
404-876-6790

BUCKHEAD FINE WINE
3906 Roswell Dr.
Atlanta, GA
404-231-8566

PEACHTREE WINE MERCHANTS
3891 Peachtree Rd.
Atlanta, GA
404-237-7128

■ Hawaii

R. FIELD WINE COMPANY
1460 S. Beretania St.
Honolulu, HI
808-596-9463

■ Illinois

GOLD STANDARD
3000 N. Clark St.
Chicago, IL
773-935-9400

SAM'S WINES & SPIRITS
1720 N. Marcey St.
Chicago, IL
312-664-4394
800-777-9137

MAINSTREET
5425 S. LaGrange Rd.
Countryside, IL
708-354-0355

FAMOUS LIQUORS
7714 W. Madison St.
Forest Park, IL
708-366-2500

SCHAEFER'S
9965 Gross Point Rd.
Skokie, IL
847-673-5711
800-833-9463

■ Indiana

KAHN'S FINE WINES
5369 N. Keystone Ave.
Indianapolis, IN
317-251-9463

21ST AMENDMENT
5561 N. Illinois St.
Indianapolis, IN
317-475-9463

■ Kentucky

THE PARTY SOURCE
95 Riviera Dr.
Bellevue, KY
606-291-4007

LIQUOR BARN
3040 Richmond Rd.
Lexington, KY
606-269-4170

THE PARTY SOURCE
4301 Towne Center Dr.
Louisville, KY
502-426-4222

■ Louisiana

MARTIN WINE CELLAR
714 Elmeer Ave.
Metairie, LA
504-896-7300

MARTIN WINE CELLAR
3827 Baronne St.
New Orleans, LA
504-899-7411
800-298-4274

■Maryland

MILL'S
87 Main St.
Annapolis, MD
410-263-2888

**NORTH CHARLES
FINE WINE & SPIRITS**
6213 A. N. Charles St.
Baltimore, MD
410-377-4655

**WELLS DISCOUNT
LIQUORS**
6310 York Rd.
Baltimore, MD
410-435-2700

**EDGEWATER
LIQUORS**
58 W. Central Ave.
Edgewater, MD
410-956-5948

JAYCO LIQUORS
1101 E. Pulaski Hwy.
Elkton, MD
410-398-4744
800-528-9463

STATE LINE LIQUORS
1610 Elkton Rd.
Elkton, MD
410-398-3838
800-446-9463

■Massachusetts

**BROOKLINE
LIQUOR MART**
1354 Commonwealth
Ave.
Allston, MA
617-731-66440

**BAUER WINE
& SPIRITS**
330 Newbury St.
Boston, MA
617-262-0083

**FEDERAL
WINE & SPIRITS**
29 State St.
Boston, MA
617-367-8605

MARTIGNETTI'S
64 Cross St.
Boston, MA
617-227-4343

MARTY'S FINE WINES
675 Washington St.
Newtonville, MA
617-332-1230

**BIG Y WINES
& LIQUORS**
150 N. King St.
Northampton, MA
413-584-7775

YANKEE SPIRITS
376 Main St.
Sturbridge, MA
508-347-2231

■Michigan

MERCHANT OF VINO
2789 Plymouth Rd.
Ann Arbor, MI
734-769-0900

VILLAGE CORNER
601 S. Forest Ave.
Ann Arbor, MI
734-995-1818

MERCHANT OF VINO
254 W. Maple St.
Birmingham, MI
248-433-3000

■Minnesota

HASKELL'S
81 S. Ninth St.
Minneapolis, MN
612-333-2434

SURDYK'S LIQUOR
303 E. Hennepin Ave.
Minneapolis, MN
612-379-3232

■Missouri

THE CHEESE PLACE
7435 Forsythe Blvd.
Clayton, MO
314-727-8788

THE WINE MERCHANT
20 S. Hanley St.
Clayton, MO
314-863-6282

**GOMER'S MIDTOWN
FINE WINES & SPIRITS**
3838 Broadway
Kansas City, MO
816-931-4170

MEINERS' SUNFRESH
14 W. 62nd Terr.
Kansas City, MO
816-523-3700

**BROWN DERBY INT'L.
WINE CENTER**
2023 S. Glenstone Ave.
Springfield, MO
417-883-4066

■Nebraska

**THE OMAHA
WINE COMPANY**
701 N. 114th St.
Omaha, NE
402-431-8558
800-594-8558

THE WINERY
741 N. 98th St.
Omaha, NE
402-391-3535
800-884-9463

■Nevada

**LEE'S DISCOUNT
LIQUOR**
9110 Las Vegas Blvd. S.
Las Vegas, NV
702-269-2400

■New Hampshire

THE WINE CELLAR
650 Amherst St.
Nashua, NH
603-883-4114

■New Jersey

TRIANGLE LIQUORS
1200 Broadway
Camden, NJ
609-365-1800

**SPARROW WINE
& LIQUORS**
126 Washington St.
Hoboken, NJ
201-659-1500

**CARLO RUSSO'S
WINE & SPIRIT WORLD**
626 N. Maple Ave.
Ho-Ho-Kus, NJ
201-444-2033

CANALS
10 W. Route 70
Marlton, NJ
609-983-4991

New Mexico

KOKOMAN CIRCUS
301 Garfield St.
Santa Fe, NM
505-983-7770

New York

GATES CIRCLE LIQUOR
1430 Delaware Ave.
Buffalo, NY
716-884-1346

POP'S WINES & SPIRITS
256 Long Beach Rd.
Island Park, NY
516-431-0025

ACKER, MERRALL & CONDIT
160 W. 72nd St.
New York, NY
212-787-1700

ASTOR WINES AND SPIRITS
12 Astor Pl.
New York, NY
212-674-7500

BEST CELLARS
1291 Lexington Ave.
New York, NY
212-426-4200

CORK & BOTTLE
1158 First Ave.
New York, NY
212-838-5300

CROSSROADS WINES & LIQUORS
55 W. 14th St.
New York, NY
212-924-3060

GARNET WINES & LIQUORS
929 Lexington Ave.
New York, NY
212-772-3211

K&D LIQUORS
1366 Madison Ave.
New York, NY
212-289-1818

MORRELL & CO.
535 Madison Ave.
New York, NY
212-688-9370

PARK AVENUE LIQUOR SHOP
292 Madison Ave.
New York, NY
212-685-2442

SHERRY-LEHMANN
679 Madison Ave.
New York, NY
212-838-7500

67 WINE & SPIRITS
179 Columbus Ave.
New York, NY
212-724-6767

HOUSE OF BACCHUS
1050 E. Ridge Rd.
Rochester, NY
716-266-6390

ZACHYS WINE & LIQUOR
16 E. Pkwy.
Scarsdale, NY
914-723-0241

North Carolina

THE WINE VAULT
813 Providence Rd.
Charlotte, NC
704-334-9463

CAROLINA WINE COMPANY
6601 Hillsborough St.
Raleigh, NC
919-852-0236
888-317-4499

Ohio

VILLAGE BOOTLEGGER
8945 Brecksville Rd.
Brecksville, OH
440-526-5885

CHUCK'S CHEESE AND WINE
23 Bell St.
Chagrin Falls, OH
440-247-7534

THE WINE MERCHANT
3972 Edwards Rd.
Cincinnati, OH
513-731-1515

WESTERN RESERVE WINES
34101 Chagrin Blvd.
Cleveland, OH
216-831-2116

HILL'S MARKET
7860 Olentangy River Rd.
Columbus, OH
614-846-3220

DOROTHY LANE MARKETS
6177 Far Hills Ave.
Dayton, OH
937-434-1294

HINMAN'S
19300 Detroit Rd.
Rocky River, OH
440-333-0202

Oklahoma

BYRON'S LIQUOR WAREHOUSE
2322 N. Broadway
Oklahoma City, OK
405-525-2158

PARKHILL'S LIQUORS & WINES
5111 S. Louis Ave.
Tulsa, OK
918-742-4187

RANCH ACRES LIQUOR
3324 A E. 31st St.
Tulsa, OK
918-747-1171

Oregon

LINER & ELSEN
202 N.W. 21st Ave.
Portland, OR
503-241-9463

MT. TABOR FINE WINES
4316 S.E. Hawthorne Blvd.
Portland, OR
503-235-4444

PORTLAND WINE MERCHANTS
1430 S.E. 35th St.
Portland, OR
503-234-4399
888-520-8466

■ Rhode Island

TOWN WINE & SPIRITS
179 Newport Ave.
Providence, RI
401-434-4563

■ Tennessee

ARTHUR'S WINE & LIQUORS
964 June Rd.
Memphis, TN
901-767-9463

BUSTER'S LIQUORS & WINES
191 S. Highland Ave.
Memphis, TN
901-458-0929

NASHVILLE WINE & SPIRITS
4556 Harding Rd.
Nashville, TN
615-292-2676

■ Texas

THE CELLAR
3520 Bee Caves Rd.
Austin, TX
512-328-6464

TWIN LIQUORS
5408 Balcones Dr.
Austin, TX
512-323-2775

WIGGY'S
1130 W. 6th St.
Austin, TX
512-474-9463

MARTY'S MERCHANTS OF FINE FOODS
3316 Oaklawn Ave.
Dallas, TX
214-526-7796
800-627-8971

POGO'S BEVERAGES
5360 W. Lovers Ln.,
Ste. 200
Dallas, TX
214-350-8989

RED COLEMAN'S
7560 Greenville Ave.
Dallas, TX
214-363-0201

SIGEL'S BEVERAGES
2960 Anode Ln.
Dallas, TX
214-350-1271

MAJESTIC LIQUOR
1111 Jacksboro Hwy.
Ft. Worth, TX
817-335-5252

RICHARD'S LIQUORS & FINE WINES
5630 Richmond Ave.
Houston, TX
713-783-3344

SPEC'S LIQUOR STORES
2410 Smith St.
Houston, TX
713-526-8787
888-526-8787

SEAZAR'S FINE WINE & SPIRITS
6422 N. New Braunfels
San Antonio, TX
210-822-6094

■ Virginia

ARROWINE
4508 Lee Hwy.
Arlington, VA
703-525-0990

TOTAL BEVERAGE
13055 C. Lee Jackson
Hwy.
Chantilly, VA
703-817-1177

TASTINGS
502 E. Market St.
Charlottesville, VA
804-293-3663

CORK & KEGS
7110 A Patterson Ave.
Richmond, VA
804-288-0816

TASTE UNLIMITED
638 Hilltop West
Shopping Center
Virginia Beach, VA
757-425-1858

■ Washington, D.C.

ACE BEVERAGE
3301 New Mexico Ave.
NW
Washington, D.C.
202-966-4444

ADDY BASSIN'S MacARTHUR BEVERAGES
4877 MacArthur Blvd. NW
Washington, D.C.
202-338-1433

CALVERT-WOODLEY
4339 Connecticut Ave.
NW
Washington, D.C.
202-966-4400

SCHNEIDER'S OF CAPITAL HILL
300 Massachusetts Ave.
NE
Washington, D.C.
202-543-9300
800-377-1461

■ Washington State

DELAURENTI SPECIALTY FOODS & WINES
1435 First Ave.
Seattle, WA
206-622-0141

LARRY'S MARKETS
10008 Aurora Ave. N.
Seattle, WA
206-527-5333

McCARTHY & SCHIERING WINE MERCHANTS
6500 Ravenna Ave. N.E.
Seattle, WA
206-524-9500

PIKE & WESTERN WINE SHOP
1934 Pike Pl.
Seattle, WA
206-441-1307

■ Wisconsin

STEVE'S LIQUOR & MORE
8302 Middle Point Rd.
Madison, WI
608-833-5995

HEIDEN'S WINE & SPIRITS
8510 W. Lisbon Ave.
Milwaukee, WI
414-462-0440

OTTO'S WINE CASK
4600 W. Brown Deer Rd.
Milwaukee, WI
414-354-5831

Glossary of Terms Used in this Guide

ACIDIFICATION The addition of acid (usually tartaric) before or during fermentation, frequently necessary in hot climates where grapes tend to over-ripen and become deficient in acidity, thereby losing freshness.

ACIDITY The acids in a wine (principally tartaric, malic, citric, and lactic) provide liveliness, longevity, and balance: Too much acidity leaves a sour or sharp taste on the palate; while too little results in a flabby, shapeless wine.

AFTERTASTE The flavor that lingers in your mouth after you swallow the wine. The length of the aftertaste is perhaps the single most reliable indicator of wine quality (see Finish).

ASTRINGENT Having mouthpuckering tannins. Time may soften an astringent wine.

AUSTERE Tough, dry, and unforthcoming, often due to a severe tannic structure or simply to the extreme youth of a wine.

BALANCE In a balanced wine, the key components—fruitiness,

sweetness, acidity, tannin, and alcohol—are in harmony. No single element dominates.

BARREL OR CASK Most of the world's greatest wines are at least partially aged in barrels, usually made from oak.

BARRIQUE The standard barrel in Bordeaux, holding 225 liters, or the equivalent of about 300 bottles of wine.

BODY The weight of a wine on the palate, determined by its alcoholic strength and level of extract (see Extract). Wines are typically described as ranging from light bodied to full bodied.

BOUQUET The richer, more complex fragrances that develop as a wine ages.

BRIGHT Lively; generally the result of fresh fruit flavors and sound acidity.

BROODING Suggesting depth, power, and solid structure, but currently in a dumb phase and difficult to taste.

CRISP Refreshing, thanks to sound acidity.

DENSE Used to describe a rich, tactile, mouth-filling wine that conveys an impression of strong extract and weight.

EARTHY Can be a component of complexity deriving from the wine's distinctive soil character or a pejorative description for a rustic wine.

EXPRESSIVE Revealing, rather than hiding, its aromas and flavors. Similar to open; the opposite of closed or dumb.

EXTRACT Essentially the minerals and other trace elements in a wine; sugar-free dry extract is everything in a wine except water, sugar, acids, and alcohol, and is usually measured in grams per liter. High extract often gives wine the impression of dusty, tactile density. Extract frequently serves to buffer, or mitigate, high alcohol or strong acidity.

FAT Rich to the point of being unctuous, with modest balancing acidity.

FERMENTATION The conversion of grape juice into wine through the action of yeasts present in the juice, which turn sugar into alcohol. This alcoholic fermentation is also known as primary fermentation.

FINISH The final taste left by a sip of wine after you swallow. Wines can be said to have long or short finishes (see Aftertaste).

FIRM Perceptibly tannic and/or acidic, in a positive way.

FLABBY Lacking acidity and therefore lacking shape.

FLAMBOYANT Highly expressive to the point of ostentation.

FLESHY Having good body and conveying a glycerol palate impression or a meaty quality, most often from rather high alcohol and extract.

FRESH Lively and refreshing, usually due to sound acidity.

FRUITY The aromas and flavors that derive from the grape, as opposed to the winemaking process or the barrels in which the wine was aged.

GENEROUS Well-constituted; possessing good texture, thorough ripeness, and a pliant quality.

GREEN Too acidic, raw, or herbal; this may be due to stems or under-ripe grapes, but may simply mean the wine needs time to develop.

GRIP An emphatically firm, tactile finish.

HARD Too tannic or acidic; often a characteristic of a wine that needs more time in bottle.

HIGH-TONED Lively and intensely aromatic, due to a level of volatile acidity that is just short of excessive.

HOT Noticeably alcoholic.

JAMMY Having the slightly cooked flavors of jam rather than fresh fruit, often a characteristic of red wines from hot climates.

JUICY An impression of palate-cleansing freshness, like that found in fruit juice featuring brisk acidity.

LAYERED Describes a wine with an almost three-dimensional texture.

LEAN Lacking flesh (see Fleshy) and body. Not necessarily pejorative, since, for wines that are lean by nature, light body is simply characteristic.

LEES The solid residue (mostly dead yeast cells and grape pulp, pips, and skins) that remains in the cask after the wine has been drawn off. Many white wines and some reds are kept on their lees for a period of time to retard oxidation (see Oxidized), enrich their textures, and add complexity. Wines kept in contact with their lees can often be made with less sulfur, but care is essential to ensure that off aromas don't develop.

MIDDLE PALATE The impact of a wine in the mouth. The part of the tasting experience that occurs between the nose of the wine and its finish.

MOUTH FEEL The physical impression of a wine in the mouth; its texture.

MUST A sort of slush of unfermented crushed grapes including juice, skins, stems, and seeds.

NEW WORLD The newer wine-growing countries: the United States, South Africa, Australia, New Zealand, Chile, and Argentina (see box, page 180).

NOSE The aroma or bouquet of a wine.

NOTE A word for an aroma or flavor found in a wine.

OAKY Smell or taste of the oak cask in which the wine was vinified and/or aged; oak notes can include such elements as vanilla, clove, cinnamon, cedar, smoke, toast, bourbon, and coffee.

OPEN Easy to taste, expressive; opposite of closed.

OXIDIZED Possessing a tired or stale taste due to excessive exposure to air. An oxidized white wine may have a darker than normal or even brown color.

PITCH A musical term that can

be used metaphorically to describe the aromas or flavors of wine. High-pitched notes are vibrant—for example, the notes of framboise and kirsch in the case of red wines, and lemon, lime, and gooseberry in the case of whites. Lower-pitched elements are deeper bass notes like earth and meat in the case of reds; or honey, resin, and dried fruits for whites.

PLIANT Supple or giving in texture; the opposite of unyielding.

PLUMP Similar to fat (see Fat): rich and very ripe, with low acidity; usually rich in alcohol and glycerin.

POWERFUL Generally high in alcohol and/or extract (see Extract).

PURE Used to describe clear aromas and flavors; often used more specifically to describe unadulterated fruit or soil characteristics.

RICH Giving an impression of strong extract (see Extract), concentration, and texture.

RIPE Having the aromas and flavors of thoroughly mature grapes.

SEAMLESS Harmonious; a wine with no rough edges.

SHARP Unpleasantly bitter or hard-edged.

SOFT Low in tannin and/or acidity.

SPINE The structural underpinning (provided by acidity and tannin), or backbone, of a wine.

SPRITZ The faint prickle on the tongue of carbon dioxide, generally found in young, light white wines.

STEELY An almost metallic taste often noted in wines high in acidity and/or made from mineral-rich soil. Found especially in Riesling.

STRUCTURE The framework of a wine, generally provided by acidity and tannins, that holds its various elements together.

STUFFING Fullness on the palate, usually a function of extract (see Extract) and concentration.

SUPPLE Round and smooth, as opposed to noticeably tannic or acidic.

SWEET A term applied not just to wines with significant residual sugar but also to those that show outstanding richness or ripeness.

TANNIN A bitter, mouth-drying substance found in the skins, stems, and seeds of the grapes—as well as in wood barrels. Tannin acts as a preservative and is thus an important component if the wine is to be aged over a long period. Tannins are frequently harsh in a young wine but gradually soften or dissipate as the wine ages in the bottle.

TART Noticeably acidic.

TEXTURE The feel that a wine has on the palate.

THICK Rich in texture, usually due to low acidity.

TONE Like note; a particular aroma or flavor found in a wine.

TOUGH Generally used to describe a red wine that shows excessive tannin (but may, with age, turn out to be a great wine).

VINOUS Literally winelike, in terms of liveliness and acidity, but often used to describe the overall impression conveyed by a wine beyond simple fruitiness. This can include subtle flavors that come from the soil that produced the grapes, as well as from the winemaking and the aging process.

VOLATILE Slightly vinegary due to a high level of acetic acid; referred to as volatile acidity (VA). But a minimum level of VA often helps to project a wine's aromas without hurting the flavor.

YEAST The various microorganisms that cause fermentation.

Wild yeasts are naturally present on grape skins, but cultivated yeasts are generally used for more controlled fermentation.

ZONE A synonym for a defined wine area or region.

Index

Specific wine listings are in regular type: Argyle 1996 Riesling.
Producers are in bold black type: **BASSERMAN-JORDAN**.
General categories are in bold colored type: **AMONTILLADO**.
Countries are in italic colored type: *Argentina*.

B